The
Philosophy
of
DESCARTES

*Twenty-two of the most important
publications on Descartes philosophy
reprinted in twenty-five volumes.*

Edited by
WILLIS DONEY
Dartmouth College

A GARLAND SERIES

TWENTY-FIVE YEARS OF DESCARTES SCHOLARSHIP, 1960–1984

A Bibliography

Vere Chappell and Willis Doney, editors

Garland Publishing, Inc.
New York & London
1987

For a complete list of the titles in this
series, see the final pages of this volume.

Library of Congress Cataloging-in-Publication Data

Chappell. V. C. (Vere Claiborne), 1930–
  Twenty-five years of Descartes scholarship,
1960–1984.

  (The Philosophy of Descartes)
  Includes index.
  1. Descartes, René, 1596–1650—Bibliography.
I. Doney, Willis. II. Title. III. Title: 25 years of
Descartes scholarship, 1960–1984. IV. Series.
Z8227.7C48 1987   [B1873]   016.194   87-7604
ISBN 0-8240-4650-1

All volumes in this series are printed on
acid-free, 250-year-life paper.

Printed in the United States of America

Contents

Introduction

Scholarly interest in the work of René Descartes has burgeoned in the last twenty-five years. Much of the resulting literature has been produced by philosophers, who have approached Descartes not only as historians concerned to understand and interpret the Cartesian texts, but also as metaphysicians and epistemologists preoccupied with the same problems that confronted Descartes. But Descartes was not just a philosopher in the restricted twentieth-century sense of the word. He also made important contributions to the sciences—mathematics, physics, and biology. And his writings have influenced dramatists, poets, and novelists. Thus Cartesian studies have been pursued by recent historians of science and literary scholars as well as by philosophers.

Our aim in this bibliography has been to document the entire scholarly literature on Descartes, from 1960 through 1984, in most of the languages in which it has been produced and in all of the fields in which Descartes is currently a subject of interest. We took 1960 as our starting point because that is the last year covered by Gregor Sebba in his monumental *Bibliographia Cartesiana*. Our reason for stopping with 1984 is simply that we had collected enough items by then to fill a sizeable volume.

The items we have included are written in Danish, Dutch, English, French, German, Italian, Norwegian, Portuguese, Spanish, and Swedish. We have listed a few items in other languages in cases where a published translation into one of the above-mentioned languages exists. In the course of our investigations, we found references to a number of works on Descartes in Polish, Russian, and Japanese; to a few in other Slavic languages; and to one or two each in Hungarian, Romanian, Greek, Hebrew, and Arabic. We have also been told of some recent studies in Chinese. Since we lacked the resources to verify these references, however, we have left them out of our list. (Information about recent Polish and Japanese scholarship is provided by three items that we do include, nos. 1695 [Polish] and 1618 and 2276 [Japanese].)

It is interesting to note that, during our period, more items of Cartesian scholarship were published in English than in any other language. Of the 2,502 entries in our main list, 1,141 or 46% are in English. The next most prevalent language is French, with 747 entries (29%). Then come German, Italian, and Spanish, with 215, 214, and 116 (9%, 9%, and 4%), respectively.

The work of Descartes had a strong impact on the philosophers, scientists, and writers who succeeded him. A good deal of Cartesian scholarship deals with these later "Cartesians" as well as, or instead of, with Descartes himself. It is impossible to draw a clear line between studies which are primarily devoted to Descartes himself and those in which the primary emphasis is on some other Cartesian thinker or thinkers. But we have sought to include everything that might reasonably be thought to belong in the former category; and we have deliberately excluded some items that we judged to fall in the latter. We have not in any case made a systematic survey of works in which Cartesian writers other than Descartes himself are the main object of concern.

The present volume is of course not the first bibliography of Cartesian scholarship to have been produced in recent years. We have already mentioned the work of Gregor Sebba, whose coverage stops just at the point at which ours begins. One of us (Doney) is himself the compiler of two previous Descartes bibliographies (nos. 0658 and 0662 below); these indeed provided the seed from which the present project has grown. Others whose work in this genre has preceded ours are H.P. Caton (0375), Alan Gabbey and Jean-Luc Marion (0836), and the Équipe Descartes. A special word needs to be said about the Équipe Descartes. This group of primarily French scholars has, since 1972, been producing an annual "Bulletin cartésien," in which the previous-but-one year's Descartes literature is listed and, in many cases, commented on in reviews ranging from a paragraph to several pages in length. Each "Bulletin" also includes one or more "Liminaires" dealing with a topic of current interest to Descartes scholars. (Each year's "Bulletin cartésien" is given a separate entry in our bibliography, with Équipe Descartes as author; each "Liminaire" is listed by itself, under its individual author's name.) The Équipe Descartes is providing an enormously valuable service to Descartes scholars and its work is cited many times in the following pages.

Apart from published bibliographies, the 14 "Bulletins cartésiens" that have come out to date, and our own browsing in journals and libraries, we have collected information in a systematic way from a dozen or so bibliographical periodicals. A complete list of these—and of other works we have consulted—is given at the end of this introduction. It may be of use to our colleagues to know that, in our opinion at least, the most comprehensive and reliable of these periodicals for the Descartes scholar are the *Répertoire bibliographique de la philosophie*, the *Bulletin signalétique*, the *Philosopher's Index*, *Isis*, *French 17*, and the *Bibliographie de la littérature française* (now defunct but being continued in the *Revue d'histoire littéraire de la France*).

With respect to our sources, we make the following claim: our list of recent Descartes studies is both more nearly complete and more accurate than any that could be extracted from any of them. It is inevitable that we will have missed some items, and that there will be mistakes in our work—mistaken information as well as typographical errors. But we have taken pains to do better in these two ways than scholarly bibliographers, at least in the field of Descartes studies, are wont to do.

We must acknowledge, however, that not every item we have listed has been personally verified, either by us or by one of the people who have assisted us (whose names are given below). We simply have not been able to locate certain journals and books and in these cases we have had to rely on one or more references supplied by our sources. There are 244 such cases in our bibliography; we have marked each of them with an asterisk.

On the matter of completeness, we have indeed aimed at it; but we have not sought to list every type of work on Descartes that has been published. Our emphasis is on scholarship produced in the last 25 years; and so we have deliberately excluded both popular works and school (and some college) textbooks, on the one hand, and reprints and unrevised new editions of works first published before 1960, on the other. (We have listed post-1960 editions of pre-1960 books, however, in cases in which a substantial amount of new material has been added to the new edition.) We have also not included dissertations (unless published as independent works), or published abstracts of papers read at conferences. As for book reviews, we have included all the substantial reviews (and review articles) that we have found of the books on Descartes that we have listed, and many shorter reviews as well. But we have deliberately omitted some short reviews and we have not made a systematic effort to find all the reviews of all the books that were published in our period. There is doubtless a measure of arbitrariness in our decisions regarding what to include. But the bibliographer's task is potentially infinite; some arbitrariness is hardly avoidable in making it actually manageable.

Our paramount concern has been to produce a research tool that would be of use to scholars and students in their work on Descartes. The 2,502 distinct items that fill the main body of our work are of several different bibliographical types: whole books (monographs and collections), parts of books (chapters and collection-components), articles in periodicals (including journals and annual reports) and in conference proceedings, and reviews. But we have put all of these items together into one single list, sequentially numbered and alphabetically ordered by author's last name. Items by the same author are arranged chronologically by date of publication. We have tried to present the essential information concerning each item perspicuously and economically. This has led us to eliminate gratuitous punctuation, to use initials in place of authors' first names, to abbreviate journal titles (those mentioned four times or more), and to omit publishers' names and the titles of most publication series. On the other hand, we have provided some kinds of information that are not normally found in scholars' bibliographies. Journal articles which comment on earlier articles are identified as "discussions of" the latter, and the entries for the latter indicate that they, in turn, are "discussed by" the former. In the case of books which themselves are not mainly about Descartes, but have one or two chapters that are, the titles of these chapters are given. Reprints of articles and some translations of books—namely those into languages likely to be more accessible to most of our readers than the original—are noted. Finally, an extensive subject-index has been provided. This index is neither as finely grained nor as comprehensive as we would have liked it to be. But we hope that students of Descartes will nonetheless be able to get some guidance from it.

The items listed in the main body of our bibliography are all "secondary" works—publications about Descartes. A number of "primary" Cartesian works were published during the 1960–1984 period as well—new editions or translations of Descartes's own writings. We have listed many of these—30 editions and 107 translations—in an Appendix. In this case we have included items in every language in which we have found them, which is to say, in Latin and French for the editions, and in Dutch, English, French, German, Hebrew, Hungarian, Italian, Japanese, Polish, Portuguese, Romanian, Spanish, and Turkish for the translations. (We have also included publishers' names and series titles for these items.) We have not seen actual copies of any of the translations into Hebrew, Hungarian, Japanese, Polish, or Romanian (nor of all those into the other languages, for that matter). So our information is not guaranteed in all cases. We have not followed the practice in this Appendix, however, of marking items not seen with an asterisk.

The present work is a "computerized" bibliography. We have relied on computers at every stage, initially to store and manipulate bibliographical data, and eventually to produce the final printed text. We started with the University of Massachusetts's mainframe and then switched to a personal computer—a Morrow MD-11, running *New Word* and *Notebook*. There is no doubt that our task was much facilitated by the use of these machines.

Computers set their own tasks, however, and it is not clear to us that the whole project took less time than it would have taken had we done everything "by hand."

We also had human assistance. Blake Barley and Tom Ryckman helped enter data early on. Jon Shanfield helped with verification at the end. The bulk of the final checking was done by Beth Dixon in Massachusetts and Marilynn Philipps in Paris: we owe a special debt to these two young scholars for the dedication and care with which they carried out their assignments.

It is a pleasure for us to acknowledge the support and cooperation of several institutions as well. Our respective employers, the University of Massachusetts and Dartmouth College, both provided grants that enabled us to travel to libraries, hire assistants, and buy supplies. A number of libraries gave us access to their collections. Besides those of our own institutions, we (or our assistants) made use of the following: the Biblioteca Nazionale in Rome, the Bibliothèque Nationale in Paris, the Bibliothéque Sainte-Geneviève, the Bibliothèque de la Sorbonne, the British Library, the Newberry Library, the New York Public Library, and the libraries of Amherst College, Boston College, Boston University, Columbia University, the École Normale Supérieure, Harvard University, the Institute for Advanced Study, Princeton University, Smith College, and Yale University. The Interlibrary Loan staffs at the University of Massachusetts and Dartmouth College were helpful on several occasions; and we wish to give special thanks to M. Cavallonne at the Bibliothèque Sainte-Geneviève, to Mme. Bercière at the Sorbonne, and to librarians at the Bibliothèque Nationale and the École Normale Supérieure, who provided special assistance to Marilynn Phillips.

Bibliographies Restricted to Works on Descartes

Bibliographia Cartesiana, by G. Sebba (The Hague: Nijhoff, 1964).

"Bibliography," in **Descartes: A Collection of Critical Essays,** ed. by W. Doney (Garden City NY: Doubleday, 1967) 369-86.

"Bibliography of Descartes Literature, 1960-1970," in **The Origin of Subjectivity,** by H.P. Caton (New Haven CT: Yale University Press, 1973) 223-43.

"Some Recent Work on Descartes: A Bibliography," by W. Doney. **PRA** 2 (1976) 299-312.

"Descartes," by A. Gabbey, J.-L. Marion et al., in **The Seventeenth Century: Supplement,** ed. by H.G. Hall. Vol. 3A of **A Critical Bibliography of French Literature,** ed. by D.C. Cabeen et al. (Syracuse NY: Syracuse University Press, 1983) 377-419.

Bibliographies Including Works on Descartes

Bibliografía filosófica argentina (1900-1975), by C.A. Lértora Mendoza (Buenos Aires: Fundación para la Educación, la Ciencia y la Cultura, 1983).

Bibliografia filosófica brasileira: Período contemporâneo (1931/1977), by A. Paim (São Paulo: GRD, 1979).

Bibliografía filosófica hispanica (1901-1970), by G. Díaz Díaz and C. Santos Escudero (Madrid: CSIC, 1982).

Bibliography of the International Congresses of Philosophy: Proceedings 1900-1978, by L. Geldsetzer (München: Saur, 1981).

Frühe Neuzeit: 17. Jahrhundert. Vol. 4 of **Handbuch der Geschichte der Philosophie,** by W. Totok (Frankfurt am Main: Klostermann, 1981).

ISIS Cumulative Bibliography...1913-65, ed. by M. Whitrow (London: Mansell, 1971).

ISIS Cumulative Bibliography 1966-1975, ed. by J. Neu (London: Mansell, 1980).

The Philosopher's Index: A Retrosepctive Index to U.S. Publications from 1940. 3 vols. (Bowling Green OH: Philosophy Documentation Center, 1978).

The Philosopher's Index: A Retrospective Index to Non-U.S. English Language Publications from 1940. 3 vols. (Bowling Green OH: Philosophy Documentation Center, 1980).

Periodicals

Bibliographia Filosofica Italiana.

Bibliographie der Französischen Literaturwissenschaft.

Bibliographie de la Litterature Française.

Bibliography of Philosophy.

Bulletin Cartésien (in Archives de Philosophie).

Bulletin Signalétique 519 Philosophie.

French 17.

Internationale Bibliographie der Zeitschriftenliteratur.

Modern Language Association International Bibliography.

Philosopher's Index.

Répertoire Bibliographique de la Philosophie.

Revue d'Histoire Littéraire de la France.

Romanische Bibliographie.

Bibliographies of Bibliographies

A Bibliography of Philosophical Bibliographies, ed. by H. Guerry (Westport CT: Greenwood, 1977).

French Literature: An Annotated Guide to Selected Bibliographies, by R. Kempton (New York: MLA, 1981).

Handbuch der bibliographischen Nachschlagewerke, ed. by W. Totok, K.-H. Weimann and R. Weitzel. 4th ed. (Frankfurt am Main: Klostermann, 1972).

Style Manuals

The Chicago Manual of Style. 13th ed. (Chicago: University of Chicago Press, 1982).

The MLA Style Manual, by W.S. Achert and J. Gibaldi (New York: MLA, 1985).

ABBREVIATIONS

A   = Analysis
ACPA = Proceedings of the American Catholic Philosophical Association
AGP = Archiv für Geschichte der Philosophie
AHES = Archive for History of Exact Sciences
AIHS = Archives Internationales d'Histoire des Sciences
AJP = Australasian Journal of Philosophy
ANTW = Algemeen Nederlands Tijdschrift voor Wijsbegeerte
AP   = Archives de Philosophie
APQ = American Philosophical Quarterly
Arb = Arbor
AS   = Proceedings of the Aristotelian Society
ASc = Annals of Science
ASM = Anales del Seminario de Metafísica
BC   = Bulletin Cartésien
BJHS = British Journal for the History of Science
BJPS = British Journal for the Philosophy of Science
BSFP = Bulletin de la Société Française de Philosophie
CE   = Cartesian Essays, ed. by B. Magnus and J.B. Wilbur
CJP = Canadian Journal of Philosophy
CNSM = Atti del XXII Congresso Nazionale di Storia della Medicina
Crit = Critique
CS   = Cartesian Studies, ed. by R.J. Butler
D   = Dialogue [Canada]
DCCE = Descartes: A Collection of Critical Essays, ed. by W. Doney
DCIE = Descartes: Critical and Interpretive Essays, ed. by M. Hooker
Di   = Dialogue [USA]
Dia = Dialogos
Dian = Diánoia
DODS = Démarches originales de Descartes savant, by P. Costabel
DPMP = Descartes: Philosophy, Mathematics and Physics, ed. by S. Gaukroger
DsS = Dix-septième Siècle
EDSM = Etudes sur Descartes, Spinoza, Malebranche et Leibniz, by M. Gueroult
EL   = Ecole des Lettres
EP   = Etudes Philosophiques
EPHE = Annuaire de l'Ecole Pratique des Hautes Etudes
Eras = Erasmus
Eur = Europe
F   = Filosofia
FE   = Fact and Existence, ed. by J. Margolis
FR   = French Review
FS   = French Studies
FZPT = Freiburger Zeitschrift für Philosophie und Theologie
GCFI = Giornale Critico della Filosofia Italiana
GM   = Giornale di Metafisica
HPQ = History of Philosophy Quarterly
HSc = History of Science
I   = Isis
IJP = Independent Journal of Philosophy
ILR = International Logic Review
IPQ = International Philosophical Quarterly

```
ISP  = International Studies in Philosophy
JHI  = Journal of the History of Ideas
JHP  = Journal of the History of Philosophy
JP   = Journal of Philosophy
JT   = Journal of Thought
KS   = Kant-Studien
LS   = Language Sciences
M    = Mind
MA   = Modern Age
MAK  = Mélanges Alexandre Koyré, ed. by F. Braudel et al.
Met  = Metaphilosophy
MLN  = Modern Language Notes
Mon  = Monist
MS   = Modern Schoolman
MSP  = Midwest Studies in Philosophy
MW   = Man and World
N    = Nous
NM   = Nature Mathematized, ed. by W.R. Shea
NRF  = Nouvelle Revue Française
NS   = New Scholasticism
P    = Philosophy
PaRa = La passion de la raison, ed. by J.-L. Marion and J. Deprun
PB   = Philosophical Books
PBS  = Philosophy of Baruch Spinoza, ed. by R. Kennington
PC   = Problems of Cartesianism, ed. by T.M. Lennon et al.
PCa  = Pensée Catholique
Pens = Pensée
Per  = Personalist
PF   = Philosophical Forum
PFo  = Philosophy Forum
PFSL = Papers on French Seventeenth-century Literature
Phi  = Philosophia [Israel]
Phil = Philosophia [Argentina]
PJ   = Philosophisches Jahrbuch
PL   = Philosophy and Literature
PLa  = Philosophischer Literaturanzeiger
PPC  = Proceedings of the Pakistan Philosophical Congress
PPJ  = Pakistan Philosophical Journal
PPQ  = Pacific Philosophical Quarterly
PPR  = Philosophy and Phenomenological Research
PQ   = Philosophical Quarterly [Scotland]
PR   = Philosophical Review
PRA  = Philosophy Research Archives
PRef = Philosophia Reformata
PRu  = Philosophische Rundschau
PS   = Philosophical Studies [USA]
PSM  = Pagine di Storia della Medicina
PSt  = Philosophical Studies [Ireland]
PTod = Philosophy Today
R    = Ratio
RCSF = Rivista Critica di Storia della Filosofia
RDS  = Recherches sur le XVIIe Siècle
RF   = Rivista di Filosofia
RFN  = Rivista di Filosofia Neo-scolastica
```

RFP = Revue Française de Psychanalyse
RHS = Revue d'Histoire des Sciences
RIP = Revue Internationale de Philosophie
RLF = Revista Latinoamericana de Filosofía
RM   = Review of Metaphysics
RMM = Revue de Métaphysique et de Morale
RP   = Revue Philosophique
RPL = Revue Philosophique de Louvain
RS   = Revue de Synthèse
RSH = Revue des Sciences Humaines
RT   = Revue Thomiste
SA   = Sudhoffs Archiv für Geschichte der Medizin und der Wissenschaften
SbJP = Salzburger Jahrbuch für Philosophie
SC   = Studia Cartesiana
SCop = Studia Copernicana
SFr = Studi Francesi
SHPS = Studies in History and Philosophy of Science
SJP = Southern Journal of Philosophy
SL   = Studia Leibnitiana
Sop = Sophia [Italia]
Soph = Sophia [Australia]
SV   = Sinnlichkeit und Verstand, ed. by H. Wagner
SwJP = Southwestern Journal of Philosophy
TF   = Tijdschrift voor Filosofie
TKR = Truth, Knowledge, and Reality, ed. by G.H.R. Parkinson
TLL = Travaux de Linguistique et de Littérature
YFS = Yale French Studies
ZAW = Zeitschrift für Allgemeine Wissenschaftstheorie
ZPF = Zeitschrift für Philosophische Forschung
#CIL = Atti del #o Colloquio Internazionale del Lessico Intellettuale Europeo
##CI = Actes du ##e Congrès International d'Histoire des Sciences
##CM = Actes du ##e Colloque de Marseille
##CS = Actes du ##e Congrès des Sociétés de Philosophie de Langue Française
##IC = Proceedings of the ##th International Congress of Philosophy

0001   Aarnes, A.   **Fransk tanke og idéliv. Cartesianske perspektiver** (Oslo 1981).

0002* Aarnes, A.   **Debatten om Descartes. Innvendinger og svar** (Oslo 1982).

0003   Aarsleff, H.   "The History of Linguistics and Professor Chomsky" **Language** 46 (1970) 570-85.
       Dis. of: Chomsky, N.   **Cartesian Linguistics** (New York 1966).
       Dis. by: Verhaar, J.W.M.   **LS** 14 (1971).
                  Bracken, H.M.   **LS** 22 (1972).

0004   Aarsleff, H.   "'Cartesian Linguistics': History or Fantasy?" **LS** 17 (1971) 1-12.
       Dis. of: Chomsky, N.   **Cartesian Linguistics** (New York 1966).
                  Verhaar, J.W.M.   **LS** 14 (1971).
       Dis. by: Bracken, H.M.   **LS** 22 (1972).

0005* Abadi, M.N.   "A propósito del argumento ontológico en Descartes" **Revista de la Universidad de Buenos Aires** (1960).

0006   Abraham, W.E.   "Disentangling the 'Cogito'" **M** 83 (1974) 75-94.

0007   Adams, R.M.   "Where Do Our Ideas Come From?--Descartes vs. Locke" **Innate Ideas,** ed. by S.P. Stich (Berkeley CA 1975) 71-87.

0008   Adler, M.J.   "Little Errors in the Beginning" **Thomist** 38 (1974) 27-48.

0009   Afnan, R.M.   **Descartes' Theory of Knowledge. The Revelation of Baha'u'llah and the Bab** 1 (New York 1970).

0010   Aiton, E.J.   **The Vortex Theory of Planetary Motions** (London 1972).
       Rev. by: Gabbey, A.   **Centaurus** 18 (1973) 86-87.
                  C[ostabel], P.   **BC** 3 (1974) 480-82.

0011* Akagi, S.   "Rohault, Descartes et le Fragment de Physique de Cyrano de Bergerac" **Gallia** 23 (1983) 1-9.

0012   Alanen, L.   "On the So-called 'Naive Interpretation' of Cogito, ergo sum" **Acta Philosophica Fennica** 32 (1981) 9-29.

0013   Alanen, L.   **Studies in Cartesian Epistemology and Philosophy of Mind. Acta Philosophica Fennica** 33 (Helsinki 1982).
       Rev. by: Beyssade, J.-M.   **RP** 108 (1983) 465-67.

0014   Albanese, R., Jr.   **Initiation aux problèmes socioculturels de la France au XVIIe siècle** (Montpellier 1977).

1

0015* Albert, K. "Descartes und die französische Philosophie der Gegenwart" **Begegnung** 23 (1968) 61-66.

0016 Alberti, A.M. "Lo scetticismo apologetico di Pierre Daniel Huet" **GCFI** 57 (1978) 210-37.
Dis. by: Tognon, G.   **BC** 9 (1981) 46-48.

0017 Alcover, M. "Cartésianisme et anti-scolastique" Chap. iv of **Poullain de la Barre: une aventure philosophique. PFSL** Supp. 1 (1981) 47-78.

0018 Aldrich, V.C. "The Pineal Gland Up-Dated" **JP** 67 (1970) 700-10.

0019 Alexander, R.E. "The Problem of Metaphysical Doubt and its Removal" **CS** (Oxford 1972) 106-22.

0020 Allaire, E.B. "The Attack on Substance: Descartes to Hume" **D** 3 (1964-65) 284-87.

0021 Allaire, E.B. "The Circle of Ideas and the Circularity of the Meditations" **D** 5 (1966-67) 131-53.

0022 Allard, J.-L. **Le mathématisme de Descartes** (Ottawa 1963); new ed. (1975).
Rev. by: McRae, R.   **D** 3 (1964-65) 92-93.
         Perini, G.   **Divus Thomas** 69 (1966) 479-82.

0023 Alleau, R. "L'Ange de Novembre ou Descartes en Bohème" **Quinzaine Littéraire** 355 (1981) 17-20.

0024 Allen, H.J. "Doubt, Common Sense and Affirmation in Descartes and Hume" **CE** (The Hague 1969) 36-54.

0025 Alquié, F. **La découverte métaphysique de l'homme chez Descartes** (Paris 1950); 2nd ed. (1966).

0026 Alquié, F. **Descartes. L'homme et l'oeuvre** (Paris 1956); new ed. (1960); new ed. (1969).
Trans. as **Descartes,** by C. Schwarze, with an essay by I. Fetscher (Stuttgart 1962).

0027 Alquié, F. "Conscience et signes dans la philosophie moderne et le cartésianisme" **Polarité du symbole. Etudes Carmélitaines** 39 (Bruges 1960) 221-26.

0028 Alquié, F. "Les philosophes du XVIIe siècle devant l'homme" **DsS** 54-55 (1962) 43-53.
Repr. in **Etudes cartésiennes** (Paris 1982) 79-89.

0029 Alquié, F. <Introductions and Notes> **Oeuvres philosophiques,** by René Descartes; ed. by F. Alquié. 3 vols. (Paris 1963-73) passim.

0030 Alquié, F. "L'idée de causalité de Descartes à Kant" Chap. vii of **Les lumières,** ed. by F. Chatelet. **Histoire de la philosophie** 4 (Paris 1972) 203-19.

0031 Alquié, F. **Le cartésianisme de Malebranche** (Paris 1974).
Rev. by: Brun, J.   **EP** (1974) 527-29.
          [Marion, J.-L.]   **RPL** 72 (1974) 772-76.
          Robinet, A.   **RIP** 28 (1974) 532-39.
          Philonenko, A.   **RMM** 80 (1975) 209-39.
          Deprun, J.   **BC** 5 (1976) 457-62.
          Gori, G.   **RCSF** 34 (1979) 211-21.
          Spallanzani, M.F.   **RF** 72 (1981) 321-27.

0032 Alquié, F. "Sources cartésiennes de Malebranche. De l'influence, sur
Malebranche, de la conception substantialiste du sujet pensant" **EP** 29
(1974) 437-48.

0033 Alquié, F. "Une lecture cartésienne de la 'Critique de la raison pure'
est-elle possible?" **RMM** 80 (1975) 145-55.
Repr. in **Etudes cartésiennes** (Paris 1982) 107-17.

0034 Alquié, F. **Malebranche et le rationalisme chrétien** (Paris 1977).

0035 Alquié, F. **Le rationalisme de Spinoza** (Paris 1981).

0036 Alquié, F. **Etudes cartésiennes** (Paris 1982).

0037 Alquié, F. "Le rapport de la science et de la religion selon Descartes,
Malebranche et Spinoza" **Le statut de la littérature. Mélanges offerts
à Paul Bénichou**, ed. by M. Fumaroli (Genève 1982) 187-202.
Repr. in **Etudes cartésiennes** (Paris 1982) 91-106.

0038 Alquié, F. "Liminaire I. Descartes et la chaleur cardiaque" **BC** 13
(1984) 1-2.

0039 Alston, W.P. "The Ontological Argument Revisited" **PR** 69 (1960) 452-74.
Repr. in **DCCE** (Garden City NY 1967) 278-302.
Dis. by: Plantinga, A.   **DCCE** (Garden City NY 1967).

0040 Alvarez Gómez, A. "El sentido del 'cogito' cartesiano según Heidegger"
Revista de Filosofía [España] 27 (1968) 91-115.
Dis. of: Heidegger, M.   **Nietzsche** 2 (Pfullingen 1961).

0041* Alvarez Gómez, A. "Lógica de la verdad y lógica de la apariencia. El
Discurso preliminaire de la conformite de la Foy avec la Raison de
Leibniz, y los Principia Philosophiae de Descartes" **Cuadernos
Salmantinos de Filosofía** 6 (1979) 47-59.

0042 Alvarez Gómez, A. "De la tradición a la razón" Review of **Discurso del
método, la dióptrica, los meteoros y la geometría,** by René Descartes;
tr. by G. Quintás Alonso [Madrid 1981]. **Contextos** 1 (1983) 155-62.

0043 Alvarez, J.R. "Un contexto de análisis para las ciencias humanas"
Dian 30 (1984) 173-209.

0044 Ambacher, M. "Les philosophies naturelles dans les temps modernes. Les
physiciens, les naturalistes, les positivistes" Chap. ii of **Les
philosophies de la nature** (Paris 1974) 46-68.

0045   Amerio, A.   "L'influsso in medicina di Cartesio sui sistemisti del
Settecento"   **PSM** 15 (1971) No. 2, 38-44.

0046   Anderson, D.E.   "Descartes and Atheism"   **Tulane Studies in Philosophy**
29 (1980) 11-24.

0047   Anderson, D.R.   "Three Views of the Cogito"   **Kinesis** 13 (1983-84) 11-20.

0048   Anderson, W.E.   "Cartesian Motion"   **Motion and Time, Space and Matter,**
ed. by P.K. Machamer and R.G. Turnbull (Columbus OH 1976) 200-23.

0049   Angelelli, I.   "En torno al principio 'Nihili nulla sunt attributa'"
Anuario Filosófico [Navarra] 10 (1977) No. 2, 9-17.

0050   Angelet, B.   "Une logique de l'ignorance: la dialectique du pouvoir dans
la lignée de Bacon, Descartes et Hobbes"   **Philosophica** 24 (1979) 55-145.

0051   Anscombe, G.E.M.   "The First Person"   **Mind and Language,** ed. by S.
Guttenplan (Oxford 1975) 45-65.
Dis. by: Kenny, A.   **Intention and Intentionality**
                                     (Ithaca NY 1979).

0052   Ansmann, L.   "Descartes"   Pt. II, chap. iii of **Die 'Maximen' von La
Rochefoucauld** (München 1972) 58-74.

0053* Antonietta, E.   "El método en la filosofía de Descartes"   **Nordeste** 1
(1960) 15-49.

0054   Antonietta, E.   "La sexta meditación cartesiana"   **Humanitas**
[Argentina] 25 (1977) 11-29.

0055   Apostolidès, J.-M.   "Les méthodologies du voyage - Commentaire"
Voyages. Récits et imaginaire. Actes de Montréal, ed. by B. Beugnot.
PFSL Supp. 11 (1984) 33-40.
Dis. of: Van den Abbeele, G.Y.   **PFSL** Supp. 11 (1984) 3-14.

0056   Aquila, R.E.   "Brentano, Descartes, and Hume on Awareness"   **PPR** 35
(1974-75) 223-39.

0057   Aquila, R.E.   "Brentano and the Problem of Awareness"   Chap. i of
Intentionality: A Study of Mental Acts (University Park PA 1977) 1-25.

0058   Arata, C.   **Discorso sull'essere e ragione rivelante** (Milano 1967).

0059   Arbini, R.   "Did Descartes Have a Philosophical Theory of Sense
Perception?"   **JHP** 21 (1983) 317-37.

0060* Arce Carrascoso, J.L.   "Metodología cartesiana y lógica de Port-Royal"
ASM 7 (1972) 65-84.

0061* Arce Carrascoso, J.L.   "Dios y la gnoseología del error en Descartes"
ASM 14 (1979) 25-46.

0062 Arcuno, O. "Blondel interprete di Descartes, Malebranche, Spinoza, Pascal" **Attualità del pensiero di M. Blondel. Atti del 1. Convegno di Studio sul Pensiero di Maurice Blondel** (Milano 1976) 119-33.

0063 Ardao, A. "De Descartes a Feijóo: La idea del proyectil cósmico" **Cuadernos Americanos** 21 (1962) 109-14.

0064 Arias Arcos, E. "Descartes y el humanismo de su época" **Atenea** 447 (1983) 131-40.

0065* Arieti, S. "R. Descartes, la ghiandola pineale e le riflessioni di Niels Stensen" **Biennali Studi di Storia dell'Arte della Medicina** 2 (1975) 1-4.

0066 Ariew, R. Review of **Descartes' Conversation with Burman,** tr. by J.G. Cottingham [Oxford 1976]. **SC** 1 (1979) 183-87.
       Dis. by: Cottingham, J.G.   **SC** 1 (1979).

0067 Ariew, R. "Mind-Body Interaction in Cartesian Philosophy: A Reply to Garber" **SJP** 21 Supp. (1983) 33-37.
       Dis. of: Garber, D.   **SJP** 21 Supp. (1983).

0068 Armogathe, J.-R. "Saisie et maniement de l'information dans le Discours de la méthode" **Les applications de l'informatique à la philosophie,** ed. by A. Robinet (Paris 1971) 70-75.

0069 Armogathe, J.-R. "Les théologies eucharistiques de Dom Desgabets" **RS** 95 (1974) 19-29.

0070 Armogathe, J.-R. **Theologia Cartesiana. L'explication physique de l'Eucharistie chez Descartes et Dom Desgabets** (The Hague 1977).
       Rev. by: Lennon, T.M.   **SC** 1 (1979) 189-92.
                 Beaude, J.   **SC** 1 (1979) 192-94.
                 Rodis-Lewis, G.   **BC** 8 (1979) 52-55.
                 Watson, R.A.   **JHP** 17 (1979) 468-69.
                 Reix, A.   **RP** 105 (1980) 102-03.

0071 Armogathe, J.-R. "Histoire du Catholicisme - Le temps et l'éternité en Europe au XVIIe siècle (La mesure du temps. Les sources scolastiques du temps cartésien)" **EPHE. Ve Section: Sciences Religieuses** 87 (1978-79) 415-18.

0072 Armogathe, J.-R. "Vers un autre Descartes: état présent des recherches sur la formation et la reception de la pensée cartésienne" **08CM** (Marseille 1979) 189-98.

0073 Armogathe, J.-R. "Les sources scolastiques du temps cartésien: Eléments d'un débat" **RIP** 37 (1983) 326-36.

0074 Armogathe, J.-R., and Marion, J.-L. **Index des Regulae ad directionem ingenii de René Descartes** (Roma 1976).
       Rev. by: Gabaude, J.-M.   **RP** 101 (1976) 482-83.
                 Beyssade, J.-M.,
                 and Beyssade, M.   **RMM** 82 (1977) 571-72.

0075   Arndt, H.W.   "Descartes' Begriff der Methode im Verhältnis zu seiner
       Konzeption einer 'Mathesis Universalis'"   Chap. ii of **Methodo
       scientifica pertractatum. Mos geometricus und Kalkülbegriff in der
       philosophischen Theorienbildung des 17. und 18. Jahrhunderts** (Berlin
       1971) 29-67.
       Rev. by: Auroux, S.   **AP** 37 (1974) 510-15.

0076   Arnheim, R.   "A Plea for Visual Thinking"   **Critical Inquiry** 6 (1979-
       80) 489-97.

0077   Arnold, P.   "Descartes et les Rose-Croix"   **Mercure de France** 340
       (1960) 266-84.

0078   Aron, R.   **Discours contre la méthode** (Paris 1974).

0079   Artur, J.   "Descartes, Voltaire et l'Encyclopédie"   **PCa** 31 (1977) 83-89.

0080   Ashworth, E.J.   "Descartes' Theory of Clear and Distinct Ideas"   **CS**
       (Oxford 1972) 89-105.

0081   Ashworth, E.J.   "Descartes' Theory of Objective Reality"   **NS** 49 (1975)
       331-40.

0082   Ashworth, E.J.   "Descartes and Human Reason"   Review of **Descartes: The
       Project of Pure Enquiry,** by B. Williams [Harmondsworth 1978].   **Queen's
       Quarterly** 86 (1979-80) 653-56.

0083   Astrada, C.   "Vico y Descartes"   **Ensayos filosóficos,** by C. Astrada
       (Bahia Blanca 1963) 125-34.

0084   Attig, T.   "Descartes and Circularity: The Precipitous Rush to Defence"
       MS 54 (1976-77) 368-78.

0085   Attig, T.   "Husserl's Interpretation and Critique of Descartes in His
       Cartesian Meditations"   **MS** 55 (1977-78) 271-81.

0086   Attig, T.   "Husserl and Descartes on the Foundations of Philosophy"
       Met 11 (1980) 17-35.

0087   Auger, L.   **Un savant méconnu: Gilles Personne de Roberval (1602-1675).
       Son activité intellectuelle dans les domaines mathématique, physique,
       mécanique et philosophique** (Paris 1962).

0088   Augst, B.   "Descartes's Compendium on Music"   **JHI** 26 (1965) 119-37.

0089   Augustyn, W.   "Le rôle du scepticisme dans la méthode de Descartes"
       12CI 3B (Paris 1971) 5-8.

0090* Aulizio, F.   "Cartesio e la psicologia moderna"   **PSM** 11 (1967) No. 1,
       113-19.

0091   Auroux, S.   "Le rationalisme empiriste"   **D** 13 (1974) 475-503.

0092 Averill, J.R. "An Analysis of Psychophysiological Symbolism and its Influence on Theories of Emotions" **Journal for the Theory of Social Behavior** 4 (1974) 147-90.

0093 Ayers, M. "Locke's Logical Atomism" **Proceedings of the British Academy** 67 (1981) 209-25.

0094 Aziza-Shuster, E. "Descartes" Pt. I of **Le médecin de soi-même** (Paris 1972) 9-30.
Rev. by: Schuhl, P.-M.   **RP** 100 (1975) 147-52.

0095 Azouvi, F. "Le rôle du corps chez Descartes" **RMM** 83 (1978) 1-23.

0096 Baccini, D., ed. **Renato Descartes. Il discorso sul metodo. Interpretazione ed esposizione essenziale** (Roma 1970).

0097 Bachelard, S. "L'inscription de la cosmologie de Copernic dans la mécanique de Descartes" **Colloquia Copernicana IV**, ed. by M.H. Malewicz. **SCop** 14 (1975) 207-17.

0098* Backhouse, M. "Het rationalisme van Descartes en het Protestantisme" **Dialoog** 10 (1969-70) 240-67.

0099 Bader, F. **Genese und Systematik der Methodenreflexion. Die Ursprünge der Transzendentalphilosophie bei Descartes** 1 (Bonn 1979).
Rev. by: B[uzon], F. de.   **BC** 10 (1981) 15-17.

0100 Bader, F. **Descartes' erste Philosophie. Die Systematik des methodischen Zweifels. Die Ursprünge der Transzendentalphilosophie bei Descartes** 2 (Bonn 1983).

0101 Bader, F. "Die Einheit des transzendentalen Wissens in Descartes' Methodenlehre" **Franziskanische Studien** 65 (1983) 297-333.

0102 Baier, A.C. "Cartesian Persons" **Phi** 10 (1981) 169-88.
Dis. by: Strawson, P.F.   **Phi** 10 (1981).

0103 Baillot, A.-F. "Descartes à la recherche de la vérité" **Bulletin de l'Association de Guillaume Budé** 22 (1963) 209-15.

0104 Bakalar, H.N. "The Cartesian Legacy to the Eighteenth-Century Grammarians" **MLN** 91 (1976) 698-721.

0105 Bannan, J.F. "Contemporary French Readings of Descartes" **RM** 13 (1959-60) 412-38.

0106 Bannan, J.F. "Theories of Truth and Methodic Doubt" **MS** 58 (1980-81) 105-12.

0107 Bar-Hillel, Y. "On Lalic Implication and the <u>Cogito</u>" **PS** 11 (1960) 23-25.
Dis. by: Peltz, R.W.   **PPR** 23 (1962-63).

0108   Barchilon, J. "Les songes de Descartes du 10 novembre 1619, et leur interprétation" **PFSL** 11 (1984) 99-113.

0109   Barchilon, J. "Le désert, l'engagement et la retraite à travers Descartes, Pascal, Racine, La Fontaine et les dictionnaires" **Actes de Tucson**, ed. by J.-J. Demorest and L. Leibacher-Ouvrard. **PFSL** Supp. 21 (1984) 193-205.

0110   Barjonet-Huraux, M. **Descartes** (Paris 1963).
        Rev. by: Rochot, B.   **RS** 85 (1964) 78-83.

0111   Barker, J.A. "The Fallacy of Begging the Question" **D** 15 (1976) 241-55.

0112   Barnes, J. **The Ontological Argument** (London 1972).

0113   Barnett, R.L. "Descartes' 'Les passions de l'âme': The Stylistics of Cartesian Rhetoric" **USF Language Quarterly** 16 (1977-78) No. 1-2, 41-46; No. 3-4, 49-55.

0114   Barrett, R. "Education and Imperfect Rationality: Thoughts on Pascal and Descartes" **Philosophy of Education** 39 (1983) 119-27.

0115   Bartley, W.W., III. "Approaches to Science and Scepticism" **PF** 1 (1968-69) 318-31.

0116   Baruzzi, A. "Schaustellung und Notwendigkeit im Denken" Chap. i of **Mensch und Maschine. Das Denken sub specie machinae** (München 1973) 20-45.

0117   Basset, G. "Notoriété d'une fille de Basse-Bretagne à travers l'Europe savante au XVIIe siècle" **Cahiers de l'Iroise** 26 (1979) 167-69.

0118   Batalha, W. de Souza Campos "O Cartesianismo: o pensamento universal" Chap. i of **A filosofia e a crise do homen. Panorama da Filosofia Moderna de Descartes a Sartre** (São Paulo 1968) 4-18.

0119   Battail, J.-F. **L'avocat philosophe Géraud de Cordemoy (1626-1684)** (The Hague 1973).

0120   Battail, J.-F. "Commentaire" **Actes de New Orleans**, ed. by F.L. Lawrence. **PFSL** Supp. 5 (1982) 363-68.
        Dis. of: Judovitz, D.   **PFSL** Supp. 5 (1982) 343-62.

0121*   Battail, J.-F. "Essai sur le cartésianisme suédois" **Nouvelles de la République des Lettres** 2 (1982) 25-71.

0122   Battisti, G. "L'occasionalismo in Descartes" **GCFI** 50 (1971) 262-98.

0123   Bauer, J. "Der Zweifel und seine Uberwindung. Bemerkungen zur Noetik Descartes'" **SbJP** 12-13 (1968-69) 49-61.

0124*   Baum, R. "Tradition und Geschichte im Leben der französischen Sprachgemeinschaft" **Archiv** 216 (1979) 291-313.

0125 Bayer, O. "Descartes und die Freiheit" **Zeitschrift für Theologie und Kirche** 75 (1978) 56-81.

0126 Beaude, J. "Lettre inédite de Picot à Carcavi relative à l'expérience barométrique (5 août 1649)" **RHS** 24 (1971) 233-46. Repr. in **Correspondance V**, ed. by C. Adam and P. Tannery; new ed., ed. by P. Costabel, J. Beaude and A. Gabbey. Vol. 5 of **Oeuvres de Descartes** (Paris 1903); new ed. (1974) 601-07.

0127 Beaude, J. "Une page inédite de Descartes" **AP** 34 (1971) 47-49.

0128* Beaude, J. "Laberthonnière et Descartes" **Oratoriana** 17-18 (1971-72) 113-29.

0129 Beaude, J. "Desgabets et son oeuvre. Esquisse d'un portrait de Desgabets par lui-même" **RS** 95 (1974) 7-17.

0130 Beaude, J. "Eclaircissements sur les relations entre Descartes et Picot" **13CI** 1 (Moscow 1974) 156-61.

0131 Beaude, J. "Sur le cartésianisme d'Ignace-Gaston Pardies. A propos de l'ouvrage du Père A. Ziggelaar" **RHS** 29 (1976) 261-67.
   Dis. of: Ziggelaar, A. **Le physicien Ignace-Gaston Pardies, S.J. (1636-1673)** (Odense 1971).

0132 Beaude, J. "Cartésianisme et anticartésianisme de Desgabets" **SC** 1 (1979) 1-24.

0133 Beaude, J. "Le guide de la raison naturelle dans l'oeuvre de Desgabets" **RDS** 4 (1980) 53-60.

0134 Beaude, J. "Deux exemples de théologie post-cartésienne" **RDS** 7 (1984) 7-17.

0135 Beaufret, J. **Evidence et vérité** (Paris 1964).

0136 Beaufret, J. "Remarques sur Descartes" Chap. ii of **Philosophie moderne. Dialogue avec Heidegger** 2 (Paris 1973) 28-53.
   Rev. by: Ca[hné], P.   **BC** 4 (1975) 274-76.
            M[arion], J.-L.   **BC** 4 (1975) 276-78.

0137 Beaujour, M. "Le corps, lieu de l'énonciation" Pt. IV, chap. i of **Miroirs d'encre. Rhétorique de l'autoportrait** (Paris 1980) 307-13.

0138 Beaulieu, A. "La correspondance du P. Marin Mersenne" **RS** 97 (1976) 71-76.

0139 Beaulieu, A. "Voyage de Mersenne en Italie" **RDS** 2 (1978) 72-80.

0140 Beaulieu, A. "Secret ou mystification? Aristarchi de mundi systemate. Avec notes de Roberval" **RDS** 4 (1980) 37-46.

0141 Beaulieu, A. "Lumière et matière chez Mersenne" **DsS** 34 (1982) 311-16.

0142* Beaulieu, A. "Voies ardues pour l'édition d'une correspondance (Mersenne)" **Nouvelles de la République des Lettres** 1 (1981) 41-64.

0143 Becco, A. "Première apparition du terme Substance dans la Méditation troisième de Descartes" **Annales de l'Institut de Philosophie** [Bruxelles] (1976) 45-66.
Dis. by: M[arion], J.-L.   **BC** 7 (1978) 31-35.

0144 Becco, A. "Remarques sur le 'Traité de la substance' de Descartes" **RDS** 2 (1978) 45-56.

0145 Becco, A. "Remarques sur ordo/ordre dans les Méditations de Descartes" **Ordo**, ed. by M. Fattori and M. Bianchi. **2CIL** (Roma 1979) 329-45.

0146 Beck, L.J. **The Metaphysics of Descartes: A Study of the Meditations** (Oxford 1965).
Rev. by: Halbfass, W.   **Eras** 18 (1966) 456-58.
           Sebba, G.   **FR** 40 (1966-67) 836-37.
           Frankfurt, H.G.   **JP** 64 (1967) 133-36.
           Ritchie, A.   **AJP** 45 (1967) 125-29.
           Miller, L.   **PR** 77 (1968) 366-69.
           Röd, W.   **PRu** 16 (1969) 28-39.

0147 Beck, R.N. "Some Remarks on Logic and the Cogito" **CE** (The Hague 1969) 57-64.

0148 Behrens, R. "Die Logik vor Port Royal" Chap. ii of **Problematische Rhetorik. Studien zur französischen Theoriebildung der Affektrhetorik zwischen Cartesianismus und Frühaufklärung** (München 1982) 33-86.

0149 Beijer, A. "La naissance de la paix. Ballet de cour de René Descartes" **Le lieu théâtral à la Renaissance**, ed. by J. Jacquot et al. (Paris 1964) 409-22.

0150 Belaval, Y. **Leibniz critique de Descartes** (Paris 1960); repr. (1978).
Rev. by: Deguy, M.   **NRF** 16 (1960) 1094-1101.
           Brun, J.   **RMM** 66 (1961) 184-90.
           Hofmann, J.E.   **Deutsche Literaturanzeiger** 82
                                  (1961) 1078-81.
           Prenant, L.   **Pens** 97 (1961) 57-82.
           Robinet, A.   **RS** 82 (1961) 73-89.
           Serres, M.   **Crit** 17 (1961) 50-75.
           Itard, J.   **RHS** 16 (1963) 187-92.

0151 Belaval, Y. "Les philosophes du XVIIe siècle devant la nature" **DsS** 54-55 (1962) 29-42.

0152 Belaval, Y., ed. and tr. "Premières Animadversiones sur les Principes de Descartes" **MAK** 2 (Paris 1964) 29-56.
Repr. in **Etudes leibniziennes. De Leibniz à Hegel**, by Y. Belaval (Paris 1976) pp. 57-85.

0153* Belaval, Y. "Leibniz face à Descartes" **Leibniz 1646-1716: Aspects de l'homme et de l'oeuvre,** ed. by M. Gueroult. **Journées Leibniz organisées au Centre International de Synthèse** (Paris 1968) 189-200.

0154   Belaval, Y. "Vico et l'anticartésianisme" **EP** 23 (1968) 311-25. Trans. as "Vico and Anti-Cartesianism" in **Giambattista Vico: An International Symposium,** ed. by G. Tagliacozzo and H.V. White (Baltimore MD 1969) 77-91.

0155   Belaval, Y. "Leibniz und der philosophische Ansatz bei Descartes" **Systemprinzip und Vielheit der Wissenschaften,** ed. by U.W. Bargenda and J. Blühdorn. **SL** Sonderh. 1 (1969) 1-11.

0156   Belaval, Y. "La Naissance de la Rationalité Moderne au XVIIe Siècle" **TKR** (1981) 107-14.

0157   Belaval, Y. "Intuitionnisme cartésien et psychologisme" **RIP** 37 (1983) 319-25.

0158   Belaval, Y. "Liminaire II. Comenius critique de Descartes" **BC** 13 (1984) 2-25.

0159   Bell, P. "Poesy and Argument in Descartes's 'Meditations'" **Newsletter of the Society for Seventeenth-Century French Studies** 3 (1981) 71-78.

0160   Benardete, J. "Mechanism and the Good" **PF** 7 (1975-76) 294-315.

0161   Benardete, J. "Spinozistic Anomalies" **PBS** (Washington DC 1980) 53-72.

0162   Bénassy, M. "Deux poètes, un philosophe: rêves et rêveries" **RFP** 40 (1976) 65-91.

0163   Bencivenga, E. "Descartes, Dreaming, and Professor Wilson" **JHP** 21 (1983) 75-85.
       Dis. of: Wilson, M.D. **Descartes** (London 1978).

0164   Benedikt, M. "Kritische und traditionelle Theorie. Praktische Lebensformen und die zwei Welten des Descartes" **Wissenschaft und Weltbild** 28 (1975) 45-59.

0165   Benhaïm, D. "L'adulte chez Descartes et Spinoza" **Critère** 9 (1973) 145-62.

0166   Benítez, L. "Fundamentos metafísicos de la cosmología cartesiana" **Dian** 30 (1984) 89-101.

0167   Bennett, J. "A Note on Descartes and Spinoza" **PR** 74 (1965) 379-80.

0168   Bennett, J. "The Simplicity of the Soul" **JP** 64 (1967) 648-60.

0169   B[ennington], G.P. "Cogito Incognito: Foucault's 'My Body, This Paper, This Fire'" **Oxford Literary Review** 4 (1979) No. 1, 5-8.

0170   Bergoffen, D.B.   "Cartesian Doubt as Methodology: Reflective Imagination and Philosophical Freedom"   **ACPA** 50 (1976) 186-95.

0171   Bergoffen, D.B.   "Cartesian Dialectics and the Autonomy of Reason" **ISP** 13 (1981) 1-8.

0172   Berkel, K. van.   **Isaac Beeckman (1588-1637) en de mechanisering van het wereldbeeld** (Amsterdam 1983).

0173   Berkel, K. van.   "Beeckman, Descartes et 'La philosophie physico-mathématique'"   AP 46 (1983) 620-26.

0174   Berkel, K. van.   "Descartes in debat met Voetius. De mislukte introductie van het cartesianisme aan de Utrechtse universiteit (1639-1645)"   **Tijdschrift voor de Geschiedenis der Geneeskunde, Natuurwetenschappen, Wiskunde en Techniek** 7 (1984) 4-18.

0175   Berleant, A.   "On the Circularity of the Cogito"   **PPR** 26 (1965-66) 431-33.

0176*   Bernardi, W.   **Filosofia e scienze della vita. La generazione animale da Cartesio a Spallanzani** (Torino 1980).

0177   Bernardini, L.   "Antonio Arnauld: natura e soprannaturale nella questione della 'res extensa' cartesiana" [Translation of Arnauld's Examen d'un écrit qui a pour titre Traité de l'essence du corps et de l'union de l'âme avec le corps, contre la philosophie de Descartes] **Miscellanea Seicento** 1 (Firenze 1971) 235-369.

0178   Bernhardt, J.   "La polémique de Hobbes contre la Dioptrique de Descartes dans le Tractatus Opticus II (1644)"   **RIP** 33 (1979) 432-42.

0179   Bernhardt, J.   "Note sur le mécanisme ordonné chez Descartes"   **RP** 109 (1984) 219-20.

0180   Bernier, R.   "Expérimentation et spéculation dans la genèse de la conception de la vie chez Descartes"   **11CI** 2 (Wroclaw 1967) 259-64.

0181   Bernoulli, R.   "Descartes' Grundgedanken in medizinhistorischer Sicht" **Gesnerus** 35 (1978) 44-53.

0182   Bernoulli, R.   "Uberlegungen zu Descartes' 'Ego cogito, ergo sum'" **Gesnerus** 36 (1979) 266-76.

0183   Berquist, D.H.   "Descartes and Dialectics"   **Laval Théologique et Philosophique** 20 (1964) 176-204.

0184   Berti, E.   "Le origini del matematismo moderno"   **GCFI** 51 (1972) 337-65.

0185   Berti, G.   **Introduzione al pensiero religioso di René Descartes** (Padova 1964).

0186   Bertocci, P.A.   "Descartes and Marcel on the Person and His Body: A Critique"   **AS** 68 (1967-68) 207-26.

0187 Bertocci, P.A. "The Person and His Body: Critique of Existentialist Responses to Descartes" **CE** (The Hague 1969) 116-44.

0188 Besse, G. "Libre arbitre et vertu. La Nouvelle Héloïse et l'héritage cartésien" **Roman et lumières au XVIIIe siècle,** ed. by W. Krauss et al. (Paris 1970) 284-96.

0189* Bestor, T.W. "There are no Certain Indications by Which We May Clearly Distinguish Wakefulness from Sleep" **JT** 13 (1978) 216-25.

0190 Bestor, T.W. "Gilbert Ryle and the Adverbial Theory of Mind" **Per** 60 (1979) 233-42.

0191 Beyssade, J.-M. "Descartes" Chap. iv of **La philosophie du monde nouveau,** ed. by F. Chatelet. **Histoire de la philosophie** 3 (Paris 1972) 89-126.

0192 Beyssade, J.-M. "Commentaires" **Discours de la méthode,** by René Descartes; ed. by J.-M. Beyssade (Paris 1973) 183-220.

0193 Beyssade, J.-M. "'Mais quoi ce sont des fous'. Sur un passage controverse de la 'Première Méditation'" **RMM** 78 (1973) 273-94.
   Dis. of: Foucault, M.   **Folie et déraison** (Paris 1961).
             Derrida, J.   **RMM** 68 (1963); 69 (1964).
             Foucault, M.   **Folie et déraison** 2nd ed. (Paris 1972).
   Dis. by: B[uzon], C. de   **BC** 4 (1975) 279-80.

0194 Beyssade, J.-M. "L'analyse du morceau de cire. Contribution à l'étude des 'degrés du sens' dans la Seconde Méditation de Descartes" **SV** (Bonn 1976) 9-25.

0195 Beyssade, J.-M. "L'ordre dans les Principia" **EP** (1976) 387-403.

0196 Beyssade, J.-M. **La philosophie première de Descartes. Le temps et la cohérence de la métaphysique** (Paris 1979).
   Rev. by: Gabaude, J.-M.   **RP** 105 (1980) 103-05.
             C[ostabel], P.   **BC** 10 (1981) 17-20.
             Marion, J.-L.   **EP** (1981) 87-88.

0197 Beyssade, J.-M. "Création des vérités éternelles et doute métaphysique" **SC** 2 (1981) 86-105.

0198 Beyssade, J.-M. "Note sur la théorie cartésienne de l'attribut" Review of **La structure du cartésianisme,** by R. Lefèvre [Lille 1978]. **SC** 2 (1981) 189-92.

0199 Beyssade, J.-M. "RSP ou Le monogramme de Descartes" **L'entretien avec Burman,** by René Descartes; tr. by J.-M. Beyssade (Paris 1981) 153-207.

0200 Beyssade, J.-M. "Réflexe ou admiration. Sur les mécanismes sensori-moteurs selon Descartes" **PaRa** (Paris 1983) 113-30.

0201 Beyssade, J.-M. "La classification cartésienne des passions" **RIP** 37 (1983) 278-87.
Dis. by: Taylor, C.   **RIP** 37 (1983).

0202 Beyssade, M. **Descartes** (Paris 1972).
Rev. by: Marion, J.-L.   **EP** (1975) 215.

0203* Biarnais, M.-F. "Les Principia de Newton. Genèse et structure des chapitres fondamentaux avec traduction nouvelle" **Cahiers d'Histoire et de Philosophie des Sciences** 2 (1982) 1-287.

0204 Biasiol, P. "Christophe de Villiers: un savant di provincia nella corrispondenza di M. Mersenne" **RCSF** 36 (1981) 379-400.

0205 Bidney, D. "Introduction" **Earlier Philosophical Writings,** by Baruch Spinoza; tr. by F.A. Hayes (Indianapolis IN 1963) ix-xxxvi.

0206 Bieńkowska, B. "From Negation to Acceptance. The Reception of the Heliocentric Theory in Polish Schools in the 17th and 18th Centuries" **Colloquia Copernicana** I, ed. by J. Dobrzycki. **SCop** 5 (1972) 79-116.

0207 Birault, H. "Science et métaphysique chez Descartes et chez Pascal" **AP** 27 (1964) 483-526.

0208 Bjelke, J.F. "Descartes" Chap. ii of **Intuisjon og natur. To avsnitt av erkjennelsesteoriens historie** (Oslo 1971) 13-34.

0209 Blackwell, R.J. "Descartes' Laws of Motion" **I** 57 (1966) 220-34.

0210 Blackwell, R.J. "Descartes' Concept of Matter" **The Concept of Matter in Modern Philosophy,** ed. by E. McMullin (Notre Dame IN 1978) 59-75.

0211 Blackwell, R.J. "Reflections on Descartes' Methods of Analysis and Synthesis" **History of Philosophy in the Making: A Symposium of Essays to Honor Professor James D. Collins on his 65th Birthday,** ed. by L.J. Thro (Washington DC 1982) 119-32.

0212 Blake, R.M. "The Role of Experience in Descartes' Theory of Method" Chap. iv of **Theories of Scientific Method: The Renaissance through the Nineteenth Century,** by R.M. Blake, C.J. Ducasse and E.H. Madden (Seattle WA 1960) 75-103.

0213* Blasucci, S. **La sapienza di Socrate. La saggezza di Cartesio** (Bari 1974).

0214 Blasucci, S. **Il problema dell'intuizione in Cartesio, Kant e Bergson** (Bari 1979).

0215 Blay, M. "Le rejet au XVIIe siècle de la classification traditionnelle des couleurs: les réelles et les apparentes" **DsS** 34 (1982) 317-30.

0216* Blay, M. Chap. iii of **La conceptualisation newtonienne des phénomènes de la couleur** (Paris 1983).
Rev. by: Acloque, P.   **RDS** 105 (1984) 200-02.

0217* Blázquez Ruiz, F.J. "La liberdad en Descartes" **Dokos** 1 (1983) 11-47.

0218* Blázquez Ruiz, F.J. **Moral y la voluntad en Descartes** (Cordoba 1984).

0219 Blizman, J. "Models, Analogies, and Degrees of Certainty in Descartes" **MS** 50 (1972-73) 1-32, 183-208.

0220 Bloch, O.R. "Gassendi critique de Descartes" **RP** 91 (1966) 217-36.

0221 Bloch, O.R. **La philosophie de Gassendi. Nominalisme, matérialisme et métaphysique** (The Hague 1971).
Rev. by: Rodis-Lewis, G.   **RP** 97 (1972) 203-05.
         Duchesneau, F.   **LTP** 29 (1973) 84-90.
         Schmitt, C.   **BJHS** 7 (1974) 188-89.

0222 Bloch, O.R. "Descartes et Gassendi" **Eur** 56 (1978) 15-27.

0223 Bloch, O.R. "Sur les premières apparitions du mot 'matérialiste'" **Raison Présente** 47 (1978) 3-16.

0224 Bluhm, W.T. **Force or Freedom? The Paradox in Modern Political Thought** (New Haven CT 1984).

0225 Blumenfeld, D., and Blumenfeld, J.B. "Can I Know That I Am Not Dreaming?" **DCIE** (Baltimore MD 1978) 234-55.

0226 Boardman, W.S. "Dreams, Dramas, and Scepticism" **PQ** 29 (1979) 220-28.
Dis. by: Mosley, J.   **PQ** 31 (1981).

0227 Bobeldijk, H. "Volgt Klever Spinoza? Een reaktie op 'Spinoza's methodebegrip' van W.N.A. Klever" **ANTW** 74 (1982) 195-97.
Dis. of: Klever, W.N.A.   **ANTW** 74 (1982).
Dis. by: Klever, W.N.A.   **ANTW** 74 (1982).

0228 Boeder, H. "Leibniz und das Prinzip der neueren Philosophie" **PJ** 81 (1974) 1-29.

0229 Boer, R.R. de. "Cartesian Categories in Mind-Body Identity Theories" **PF** 7 (1975-76) 139-58.

0230 Bogen, J., and Beckner, M. "An Empirical Refutation of Cartesian Scepticism" **M** 88 (1979) 351-69.

0231 Böhm, W. "John Mayow und Descartes" **SA** 46 (1962) 45-68.

0232 Boitel, F. "Cartésianisme et spiritualité à travers l'analyse de Louis Lavelle" **Revue de l'Agenais** 110 (1984) 411-19.

0233 Bolle, L. "La Méthode existe-t-elle?" **Lettres Romanes** 26 (1972) 315-31; 28 (1974) 134-55.

0234 Bolton, D. "Tradition and Originality in the <u>Tractatus</u>" Chap. ii of **An Approach to Wittgenstein's Philosophy** (London 1979) 46-92.

0235   Bonansea, B.M.   "The Ontological Argument: Proponents and Opponents"
       Studies in Philosophy and the History of Philosophy 6 (1973) 135-92.

0236   Bonnot, G.   **Ils ont tué Descartes. Einstein. Freud. Pavlov** (Paris
       1969).

0237   Bonzon, N.   "Quand la fiction déjoue la maîtrise"   **Revue de Théologie
       et de Philosophie** 115 (1983) 355-72.

0238   Boos, W.   "A Self-Referential Cogito"   **PS** 44 (1983) 269-90.

0239   Booth, C.S.   "Cogito: Performance or Existential Inconsistency?"
       Journal of Critical Analysis 4 (1972-73) 1-8.
       Dis. of: Hintikka, J.   **PR** 71 (1962).

0240   Booth, E.   "An Epistemological Variation in Descartes and its Probable
       Neo-Stoic Origin"   **Angelicum** 60 (1983) 580-606.

0241* Borghero, C.   **La certezza e la storia. Cartesianismo, pirronismo e
       cognoscenza storica** (Milano 1983).
       Rev. by: Alberti, A.   **JHP** 23 (1985) 589-91.

0242   Borgmann, A.   "Language and the Rise of the Modern Era"   Pt. I, chap. iv
       of **The Philosophy of Language: Historical Foundations and Contemporary
       Issues** (The Hague 1974) 68-88.

0243   Bormann, C.V.   "Das wissenschaftliche Denken in der Theologie"   **PJ** 79
       (1972) 19-38.

0244   Borne, E.   "Faut-il tuer Descartes?"   **Croix** (3 Feb. 1977) 16.

0245   Bortolotti, A.   "Sulla datazione della 'Recherche de la vérité' di
       Descartes"   **RCSF** 36 (1981) 343-78.

0246* Bortolotti, A.   **Saggi sulla formazione del pensiero di Descartes**
       (Firenze 1983).

0247   Bos, H.J.M.   "On the Representation of Curves in Descartes' Géométrie"
       AHES 24 (1981) 295-338.

0248   Bossong, G.   "Uber die zweifache Unendlichkeit der Sprache. Descartes,
       Humboldt, Chomsky und das Problem der sprachlichen Kreativität"
       Zeitschrift für Romanische Philologie 95 (1979) 1-20.

0249   Botkin, R.   "Descartes First Meditation: A Point of Contact for
       Contemporary Philosophical Methods"   **SJP** 10 (1972) 353-58.
       Dis. by: Davis, R.   **SJP** 10 (1972).

0250   Botkin, R.   "What Can We Do When Dreaming: A Reply to Professor Davis"
       SJP 10 (1972) 367-72.
       Dis. of: Davis, R.   **SJP** 10 (1972).
       Dis. by: Davis, R.   **SJP** 10 (1972).

0251 Bots, H. "Descartes 'le bon Français'. Une lettre inédite de Jean van Foreest à René Descartes" **DsS** 92 (1971) 133-41. Repr. in **Correspondance V**, ed. by C. Adam and P. Tannery; new ed., ed. by P. Costabel, J. Beaude and A. Gabbey. Vol. 5 of **Oeuvres de Descartes** (Paris 1903); new ed. (1974) 658.

0252 Bots, J. **Tussen Descartes en Darwin. Geloof en natuurwetenschap in de achttiende eeuw in Nederland** (Assen 1972).

0253 Botson, C. "Descartes et l'art de vivre" **Synthéses** 17 (1962) No. 196-97, 229-39.

0254* Bottin, F., Longo, M., and Piaia, G. **Dall'età cartesiana a Brucker.** Vol. 2 of **Storia delle storie generali della filosofia**, ed. by G. Santinello (Brescia 1979). Rev. by: Masi, S.   **RF** 72 (1981) 165-69.

0255* Boulad Ayoub, J. "Descartes face à Leibniz sur la question de la substance" **Philosophiques** 11 (1984) 225-50.

0256 Bouligand, G. "Descartes, Leibniz, Euler et les débuts de l'heuristique moderne" **Comptes Rendus des Séances de l'Académie des Sciences** [Paris] 256 (1963) 4138-42.

0257 Bouligand, G. "Sur une affinité dans les textes de Descartes" **RP** 88 (1963) 363-64.

0258 Bourassa, A. "Descartes et la connaissance intuitive" **D** 6 (1967-68) 539-54.

0259 Bourdil, P.-Y. "La parole occidentale" **Liberté de l'Esprit** 7 (1984) 5-39.

0260* Bouttes, B., and Granel, G. **Cartesiana** (Mauvezin 1983).

0261 Bouveresse, J. "La linguistique cartésienne: Grandeur et décadence d'un mythe" **Crit** 35 (1979) 420-28.

0262 Bouveresse, J. "La théorie du possible chez Descartes" **RIP** 37 (1983) 293-310. Dis. by: Ishiguro, H.   **RIP** 37 (1983).

0263 Bouveresse, J. "Réponse à Anthony Kenny" **RIP** 37 (1983) 257-64. Dis. of: Kenny, A.   **RIP** 37 (1983).

0264 Bouvier-Ajam, M. "Quelques retouches proposées à un portrait conventionnel" **Eur** 56 (1978) 49-58.

0265 Bouwsma, O.K. "I think I am" **The Nature of Philosophical Inquiry**, ed. by J. Bobik (Notre Dame IN 1970) 237-51.

0266 Bouwsma, O.K. "Failure I: Are Dreams Illusions?" **Toward a New Sensibility: Essays of O.K. Bouwsma**, ed. by J.L. Craft and R.E. Hustwit (Lincoln NE 1982) 61-88.

17

0267   Bouwsma, O.K. "Remarks on the Cogito" **Toward a New Sensibility: Essays of O.K. Bouwsma,** ed. by J.L. Craft and R.E. Hustwit (Lincoln NE 1982) 137-69.

0268*   Bovet, D. "L'uomo e l'animale. La formazione del pensiero meccanicistico in biologia dopo Cartesio" **Rivista di Antropologia** 61 (1980-81) 5-20.

0269   Bowen, M. "Science and Geography: The Seventeenth-Century Encounter" Chap. ii of **Empiricism and Geographical Thought: From Francis Bacon to Alexander von Humboldt** (Cambridge 1981) 58-90.

0270   Bracken, H.M. "Some Problems of Substance Among the Cartesians" **APQ** 1 (1964) 129-37.

0271   Bracken, H.M. "Chomsky's Variations on a Theme by Descartes" **JHP** 8 (1970) 181-92.
        Dis. of: Chomsky, N.   **Cartesian Linguistics** (New York 1966).

0272   Bracken, H.M. "Chomsky's Cartesianism" **LS** 22 (1972) 11-17.
        Repr. in **Mind and Language: Essays on Descartes and Chomsky,** by H.M. Bracken (Dordrecht 1984) 113-23.
        Dis. of: Chomsky, N.   **Cartesian Linguistics** (New York 1966).
                 Aarsleff, H.   **Language** 46 (1970).
                 Aarsleff, H.   **LS** 17 (1971).

0273   Bracken, H.M. "Descartes-Orwell-Chomsky: Three Philosophers of the Demonic" **Human Context** 4 (1972) 523-36.
        Repr. in **Mind and Language: Essays on Descartes and Chomsky,** by H.M. Bracken (Dordrecht 1984) 97-112.

0274   Bracken, H.M. **Berkeley** (London 1974).

0275   Bracken, H.M. "Berkeley: Irish Cartesian" **PSt** 24 (1976) 39-51.

0276   Bracken, H.M. **Mind and Language: Essays on Descartes and Chomsky** (Dordrecht 1984).

0277   Bracken, H.M. "Rationalism and Dualism in Descartes" **Mind and Language: Essays on Descartes and Chomsky,** by H.M. Bracken (Dordrecht 1984) 1-38.

0278   Brands, H. **'Cogito ergo sum'. Interpretationen von Kant bis Nietzsche** (Freiburg 1982).

0279   Braudel, F., Cohen, I.B., and Taton, R., edd. **Mélanges Alexandre Koyré.** 2 vols. (Paris 1964).

0280   Brecher, R. "Pure Objects and the Ontological Argument" **Soph** 14 (1975) No. 3, 10-18.
        Dis. of: Kenny, A.   **FE** (Oxford 1969).

0281   Brecher, R. "Descartes' Causal Argument for the Existence of God" **International Journal for Philosophy of Religion** 7 (1976) 418-32.

0282 Breger, H. "Uber die Hannoversche Handschrift der Descartesschen Regulae" **SL** 15 (1983) 108-14.

0283 Breton, S. "Origine et principe de raison" **Revue des Sciences Philosophiques et Théologiques** 58 (1974) 41-57.

0284 Brett, N. "Doubt and Descartes' Will" **D** 19 (1980) 183-95.

0285 Brewer, D. "The Philosophical Dialogue and the Forcing of Truth" **MLN** 98 (1983) 1234-47.

0286 Brewster, L.E. "How to Know Enough About the Unknown Faculty" **JHP** 12 (1974) 366-71.
Dis. of: Norton, D.F.   **JHP** 6 (1968).
Dis. by: Norton, D.F.   **JHP** 12 (1974).
         Stevens, J.C.   **JHP** 16 (1978).

0287 Brissoni, A. "Descartes e Wittgenstein: epistemologia e linguaggio" **Rivista d'Europa** 10-11 (1981) 46-52.

0288 Brix, A. "Der Einfluss des hl. Franz von Sales von Descartes und Pascal bis in die Gegenwart" **Jahrbuch für Salesianische Studien** (1970) 123-34.

0289 Broadie, F. **An Approach to Descartes' 'Meditations'** (London 1970).
Rev. by: Keefe, T.   **PB** 12 (1971) 6-10.
         Cress, D.   **NS** 46 (1972) 532-36.

0290 Brockhaus, R. "On Descartes' 'Real Distinction' and the Indivisibility of the Mind" **SJP** 21 (1983) 325-42.

0291 Brockliss, L.W.B. "Aristotle, Descartes and the New Science: Natural Philosophy at the University of Paris, 1600-1740" **ASc** 38 (1981) 33-69.

0292 Brockliss, L.W.B. "Philosophy Teaching in France, 1600-1740" **History of Universities** 1 (1981) 131-68.

0293 Brodbeck, M. "Descartes and the Notion of a Criterion of External Reality" **Royal Institute of Philosophy Lectures** 5 (London 1972) 1-14.

0294 Brodeur, J.-P. "Thèse et performance dans les 'Méditations' de Descartes" **D** 14 (1975) 51-79.

0295 Brons, K.J. "Heidegger en Descartes. Enige aantekeningen bij Heideggers interpretatie van Descartes" **De Geest in het Geding. Opstellen aangeboden aan J.A. Oosterbaan**, ed. by I.B. Horst, A.F. de Jong and D. Visser (Alphen aan den Rijn 1978) 29-46.
Dis. of: Heidegger, M.   **Nietzsche** 2 (Pfullingen 1961).

0296 Brooks, H.F. "Guez de Balzac, Eloquence, and the Life of the Spirit" **Esprit Créateur** 15 (1975) 59-78.

0297 Broome, J.H. "The Foundations of Pascal's Thought: 2. Philosophy and Theology" Chap. iv of **Pascal** (London 1965) 75-106.

0298   Broughton, J.   "Skepticism and the Cartesian Circle"   **CJP** 14 (1984)
593-616.

0299   Broughton, J., and Mattern, R.   "Reinterpreting Descartes on the Notion
of the Union of Mind and Body"   **JHP** 16 (1978) 23-32.

0300   Brown, G.   "Vera Entia: The Nature of Mathematical Objects in Descartes"
JHP 18 (1980) 23-37.

0301   Brown, T.M.   "Descartes: Physiology"   **Dictionary of Scientific
Biography,** ed. by C.C. Gillispie.   4 (New York 1971) 61-65.

0302   Browne, A.   "Descartes's Dreams"   **Journal of the Warburg and Courtauld
Institutes** 40 (1977) 256-73.

0303   Brun, J.   "Leibniz critique de Descartes"   Review of **Leibniz critique
de Descartes,** by Y. Belalval [Paris 1960].   **RMM** 66 (1961) 184-90.

0304   Brun, J.   "Le Zen et le cogito cartésien"   Chap. viii of **Les vagabonds
de l'Occident. L'expérience du voyage et la prison du moi** (Paris 1976)
151-61.

0305   Brüning, W.   "Möglichkeiten und Grenzen des methodischen Zweifels bei
Descartes"   **ZPF** 14 (1960) 536-52.

0306   Brüning, W.   "Posibilidades y límites de la duda metódica en Descartes"
Revista de Humanidades 6 (1963) 39-63.

0307*   Bruno, A.   **Etica moderno. Contributo ad una storia delle dottrine
etiche** (Milano 1983).

0308   Bruns, G.L.   "A Literary Man's Guide to the Discourse on Method (1637)"
Boundary 2 8 (1980) 141-64.

0309   Bruns, G.L.   "A Grammarian's Guide to the Discourse on Method"   Chap.
iii of **Inventions: Writing, Textuality, and Understanding in Literary
History** (New Haven CT 1982) 63-87.

0310   Brunschwig, J.   "La preuve ontologique interpretée par M. Gueroult"
RP 85 (1960) 251-65.
        Dis. of: Gueroult, M.   **Nouvelles réflexions sur la preuve
                                        ontologique de Descartes** (Paris
                                        1955).
        Dis. by: Rochot, B.   **RP** 86 (1961).

0311   Brunschwig, J.   "Réponse aux objections de M. Rochot"   **RP** 87 (1962)
365-70.
        Dis. of: Rochot, B.   **RP** 86 (1961).

0312   Brykman, G.   "Le cartésianisme dans le De Motu"   **RIP** 33 (1979) 552-69.

0313   Brykman, G.   "Le modèle visuel de la connaissance chez Berkeley"   **RP**
108 (1983) 427-41.

0314* Buchdahl, G. **The Image of Newton and Locke in the Age of Reason** (London 1961).

0315 Buchdahl, G. "The Relevance of Descartes's Philosophy for Modern Philosophy of Science" **BJHS** 1 (1962-63) 227-49.

0316 Buchdahl, G. "Descartes's Anticipation of a 'Logic of Scientific Discovery'" **Scientific Change,** ed. by A.C. Crombie (New York 1963) 399-417.
Dis. by: Leibowitz, F. **Nature and System** 3 (1981).

0317 Buchdahl, G. "Descartes: Method and Metaphysics" Chap. iii of **Metaphysics and the Philosophy of Science: The Classical Origins Descartes to Kant** (Oxford 1969) 79-180.
Rev. by: Gianformaggio, L.   **RF** 62 (1971) 286-91.
Kopper, J.   **KS** 62 (1971) 126-36.
Leyden, W. von   P 46 (1971) 38-42.
Röd, W.   **AGP** 53 (1971) 100-05.
Röd, W.   **PRu** 18 (1971) 87-89.
Toulmin, S.   **Encounter** 36 (1971) 53-64.
Yolton, J.   **HS** 10 (1971) 102-13.
McRae, R.   **SHPS** 3 (1972) 89-99.

0318 Bucher, T.G. "Das Verhältnis der Deduktion zur Intuition in den 'Regulae' von Descartes" **PJ** 87 (1980) 16-40.

0319 Buczyńska-Garewicz, H. "Peirce's Idea of Sign and the Cartesian Cogito" **Sign, System and Function,** ed. by J. Pelc et al. (Berlin 1984) 37-47.

0320* Buonadonna, G. "Gilson interprete di Cartesio" **Studi Filosofici Pedagogici** 1 (1977) 137-62.

0321 Buonajuto, M. "A proposito delle cartesiane 'nature semplici'" **Pensiero** 6 (1961) 357-70.

0322 Buonajuto, M. "Libertà e storia" **GCFI** 48 (1969) 400-45.

0323 Burke, J.G. "Descartes on the Refraction and the Velocity of Light" **American Journal of Physics** 34 (1966) 390-400.

0324 Burkill, T.A. "Une critique de la tendance subjectiviste de Descartes à Sartre" **D** 6 (1967-68) 347-54.

0325 Burnyeat, M.F. "Idealism and Greek Philosophy: What Descartes Saw and Berkeley Missed" **PR** 91 (1982) 3-40.
Repr. in **Royal Institute of Philosophy Lectures** 13 (1982) 19-50.

0326 Burnyeat, M.F. "The Sceptic in his Place and Time" **Philosophy in History: Essays on the Historiography of Philosophy,** ed. by R. Rorty, J.B. Schneewind and Q. Skinner (Cambridge 1984) 225-54.

0327* Busacchi, V. "La chiamata di Cartesio alla Cattedra Eminente di Teorica della Medicina nello Studio di Bologna nel 1633" **CNSM** (Roma 1967) 287-91.
Repr. in **PSM** 11 (1967) No. 2, 9-13.

0328 Busacchi, V., and Gallassi, A. "Descartes e Newton nel pensiero di Claude Bernard" **PSM** 11 (1967) No. 1, 78-81.

0329 Butler, R.J., ed. **Cartesian Studies** (Oxford 1972).
Rev. by: Rodis-Lewis, G.   **RP** 99 (1974) 315-16.

0330 Buzon, F. de. "Le Compendium musicae de Descartes" **08CM** (Marseille 1979) 185-88.

0331 Buzon, F. de. "Liminaire. Descartes, Beeckman et l'acoustique" **BC** 10 (1981) 1-8.

0332 Buzon, F. de. "Sympathie et antipathie dans le Compendium Musicae" **AP** 46 (1983) 647-53.

0333 Cabanis, J. "Descartes" **Plaisir et lectures,** by J. Cabanis. 1 (Paris 1964) 7-17.

0334 Cabrera, M. "Cartesianismo, fenomenología y solipsismo" **Dian** 30 (1984) 103-110.

0335* Cacciavillani, G. "Descartes e la repressione del corpo" **Vel** 8 (1978).
Repr. in **Il corpo testuale. Saggi e ricerche sulla letteratura francese,** by G. Cacciavillani (Albano-Terme 1982) 16-54.

0336 Cahné, P.-A. **Index du Discours de la méthode de René Descartes** (Roma 1977).

0337 Cahné, P.-A. "Autour de la phrase de Descartes" **Eur** 56 (1978) 59-72.

0338 Cahné, P.-A. "René Descartes 1596-1650" **Les grands siècles.** Vol. 3 of **Les grands écrivains du monde,** ed. by P. Brunel and R. Jouanny (Paris 1978) 61-70.

0339 Cahné, P.-A. "Descartes et l'analogie" **08CM** (Marseille 1979) 199-203.

0340 Cahné, P.-A. **Un autre Descartes: Le philosophe et son langage** (Paris 1980).
Rev. by: Dethier, L.   **RPL** 80 (1982) 517-19.
          Larthomas, P.   **BC** 11 (1982) 49-51.
          Relyea, S.L.   **PFSL** 9 (1982) 740-45.
          Beyssade, J.-M.   **RP** 108 (1983) 107-10.
          Specht, R.   **ZPF** 37 (1983) 599-605.

0341 Cahné, P.-A. "Saint Augustin et les philosophes au XVIIe siècle: Ontologie et autobiographie" **DsS** 34 (1982) 121-32.

0342 Cahné, P.-A. "Ordre et désordre dans les Olympica" **AP** 46 (1983) 627-36.

0343 Calvert, B. "Descartes and the Problem of Evil" **CJP** 2 (1972-73) 117-26.

0344 Campailla, S. "Metodo cartesiano e metodo baconiano nel De nostri temporis studiorum ratione del Vico" **Belfagor** 26 (1971) 253-72.

0345 Cane, E. "Jean d'Alembert Between Descartes and Newton: A Critique of Thomas L. Hankins' Position" I 67 (1976) 274-76.
      Dis. of: Hankins, T.L.   **Jean d'Alembert: Science and Enlightenment** (Oxford 1970).
      Dis. by: Hankins, T.L.   I 67 (1976).

0346 Canguilhem, G. "Descartes e a técnica" **Trans/Form/Ação** 5 (1982) 111-22.

0347 Canziani, G. **Filosofia e scienza nella morale di Descartes** (Firenze 1980).
      Rev. by: Rodis-Lewis, G.   **DsS** 34 (1982) 341.

0348 Canziani, G. "Ermeneutica cartesiana. In margine ad un recente libro di J.-L. Marion" Review of **Sur la théologie blanche de Descartes,** by J.-L. Marion [Paris 1981]. **Rivista di Storia della Filosofia** 39 (1984) 91-106.

0349 Caponigri, A.R. "René Descartes" Pt. II, chap. ii of **Philosophy from the Renaissance to the Romantic Age. A History of Western Philosophy** 3 (Notre Dame IN 1963) 157-95.

0350 Capossela, E. **Il cartesianesimo in Vico e Pascal** (Campobasso 1966).

0351 Caramella, S. "Lo stoicismo di Seneca e il neo-stoicismo di Cartesio" **Crisis** 12 (1965) 253-59.
      Repr. in **Actas del Congreso Internacional de Filosofía en Conmemoración de Séneca** 2 (Madrid 1966) 121-27.

0352 Caramella, S. "Renato Descartes. Introduzione" **Il pensiero moderno (Secoli XVII-XVIII),** ed. by M.F. Sciacca and M. Schiavone. **Grande antologia filosofica** 12 (Milano 1968) 329-97.
      Rev. by: Di Girolamo, N.   **Culture Française** 16 (1969) 69-71.

0353 Caramella, S. "Gli studi cartesiani in Italia nell'ultimo venticinquennio (1945-1969)" **Cultura e Scuola** 8 (1969) 75-84.

0354 Carbonara, C. **Renato Cartesio** (Napoli 1965).

0355 Cardona, C. **René Descartes. Discurso de método** (Madrid 1975).

0356 Cardona, G. "Ammonio Sacca, Erennio e il 'cogito'" **De Homine** 22-23 (1967) 176-90.

0357 Carnes, R.D. "Descartes and the Ontological Argument" **PPR** 24 (1963-64) 502-11.

0358   Carney, J.D.   "Cogito, Ergo Sum and Sum Res Cogitans"   **PR** 71 (1962)
       492-96.
       Dis. of: Hintikka, J.   **PR** 71 (1962).
       Dis. by: Hintikka, J.   **PR** 72 (1963).

0359   Caroti, S.   "Nicole Oresme precursore di Galileo e di Descartes?"
       RCSF 32 (1977) 11-23, 413-35.
       Dis. by: Tognon, G.   **BC** 8 (1979) 43-46.

0360   Carr, D.   "The 'Fifth Meditation' and Husserl's Cartesianism"   **PPR** 34
       (1973-74) 14-35.

0361* Carraud, V.   "Laberthonnière et Descartes"   **Revue de l'Institut
       Catholique de Paris** 8 (1983) 13-31.

0362   Carré, M.-R.   "Le Moi du philosophe et le Je de Descartes"   **PFSL** 9
       (1982) 283-303.

0363   Carter, R.B.   "Volitional Anticipation and Popular Wisdom in Descartes"
       Interpretation 7 (1978) 75-98.

0364   Carter, R.B.   "Gilbert and Descartes: The Science of Conserving the
       Compound Body"   **ZAW** 13 (1982) 224-33.

0365   Carter, R.B.   **Descartes' Medical Philosophy: The Organic Solution to
       the Mind-Body Problem** (Baltimore MD 1983).

0366   Carter, R.B.   "Descartes' Methodological Transformation of Homo Sapiens
       into Homo Faber"   **SA** 68 (1984) 225-29.

0367   Carter, W.R.   "Plantinga on Disembodied Existence"   **PR** 81 (1972) 360-63.
       Dis. of: Plantinga, A.   **PR** 79 (1970).

0368   Carvin, W.P.   "Leibniz on Motion and Creation"   **JHI** 33 (1972) 425-38.

0369   Cathala, J.   "Des bribes arrachées aux actuels introducteurs auprès de
       M. Descartes et son temps"   **Presse Médicale** 70 (1962) 847-48, 903-07.

0370   Caton, H.P.   "On the Interpretation of the Meditations"   **MW** 3 (1970)
       224-45.
       Dis. by: Dascal, M.   **MW** 4 (1971).

0371   Caton, H.P.   "The Theological Import of Cartesian Doubt"   **International
       Journal for Philosophy of Religion** 1 (1970) 220-32.

0372   Caton, H.P.   "The Problem of Descartes' Sincerity"   **PF** 2 (1970-71)
       355-70.

0373   Caton, H.P.   "The Status of Metaphysics in the Discourse on Method"
       MW 5 (1972) 468-474.
       Dis. of: Dascal, M.   **MW** 4 (1971).

0374 Caton, H.P. **The Origin of Subjectivity: An Essay on Descartes** (New Haven CT 1973).
Rev. by: Cooke, V.M.   **Thought** 49 (1974) 336-37.
          Curtler, H.M.   **MA** 18 (1974) 213-16.
          Crittenden, P.   **AJP** 53 (1975) 70-75.
          Dorter, K.   **D** 14 (1975) 530-32
          Marks, C.   **PR** 84 (1975) 457-60.
          Rogers, G.A.J.   **PB** 16 (1975) 10-13.
          Watson, R.A.   **JHP** 13 (1975) 251-56.
          Gabaude, J.-M.   **RP** 101 (1976) 257-58.

0375 Caton, H.P. "Bibliography of Descartes Literature, 1960-1970" **The Origin of Subjectivity**, by H.P. Caton (New Haven CT 1973) 223-43.

0376 Caton, H.P. "Kennington on Descartes' Evil Genius" **JHI** 34 (1973) 639-41.
Dis. of: Kennington, R.   **JHI** 32 (1971).
Dis. by: Kennington, R.   **JHI** 34 (1973).

0377 Caton, H.P. "Rejoinder: The Cunning of the Evil Demon" **JHI** 34 (1973) 643-44.
Dis. of: Kennington, R.   **JHI** 34 (1973).

0378 Caton, H.P. "Will and Reason in Descartes's Theory of Error" **JP** 72 (1975) 87-104.
Dis. of: Kenny, A.   **CS** (Oxford 1972).

0379 Caton, H.P. "Les écrits anonymes de Descartes" **EP** (1976) 405-14.

0380 Caton, H.P. "Analytic History of Philosophy: The Case of Descartes" Review of **Descartes Against the Skeptics,** by E.M. Curley [Cambridge MA 1978]; of **Descartes: The Project of Pure Enquiry,** by B. Williams [Harmondsworth 1978]; and of **Descartes,** by M.D. Wilson [London 1978]. **PF** 12 (1980-81) 273-94.

0381 Caton, H.P. "Descartes' Anonymous Writings: A Recapitulation" **SJP** 20 (1982) 299-311.

0382 Cavallo, G. "Studi recenti su Cartesio" Review of **Descartes: Critical and Interpretive Essays,** ed. by M. Hooker [Baltimore MD 1978]; and of **Le beau roman de la physique cartésienne et la science exacte de Galilée,** by E. Namer [Paris 1979]. **F** 30 (1979) 585-92.

0383 Caveing, M. "Recherches récentes: la publication des 'Cahiers Spinoza' de K. Marx; la physique cartésienne dans Spinoza" **Raison Présente** 43 (1977) 111-23.
Dis. of: Lecrivain, A.   **Cahiers Spinoza** 1 (1977).

0384 Cazabon, G. "Deux approches antithétiques du problème du comportement" **RPL** 67 (1969) 546-81.

0385 Celeyrette[-Pietri], N. "Les avatars du cogito" **RSH** 160 (1975) 621-32.

0386 Celeyrette-Pietri, N. "Une méthode à la Descartes: Le 'langage absolu'" **Revue des Lettres Modernes** 554-59 (1979) 157-76.

0387 Celsa, V. **Da Cartesio a Lamennais e Ventura** (Palermo 1975).

0388 Centore, F.F. "The Mechanics of Terrestrial Local Motions" Chap. iv of **Robert Hooke's Contributions to Mechanics: A Study in Seventeenth Century Natural Philosophy** (The Hague 1970) 63-91.

0389 Cerezo, M. del C. "Del 'Discurso' al 'Recurso del Método': Descartes y Carpentier" **Sin Nombre** 12 (1981) No. 2, 96-106.

0390* Cesareo, R. "L'evoluzione del problema morale nel pensiero di Cartesio" **Contributo** 7 (1983) 15-50.

0391 Chaix-Ruy, J. "Vico et Descartes" **AP** 31 (1968) 628-39.

0392 Chambers, C.J. "The Progressive Norm of Cartesian Morality" **NS** 42 (1968) 374-400.

0393* Chamizo Domínguez, P.J. "El Discurso del método de Descartes como ensayo" **Aporia** 4 (1981-82) 69-83.

0394 Chandra, S. "Wittgensteinian Technique and the Cartesian Doubt" **Philosophical Quarterly** [India] 33 (1960-61) 181-89.

0395 Chapman, H.M. "Descartes's Direct Argument for Sensations" Chap. iii of **Sensations and Phenomenology** (Bloomington IN 1966) 31-44.

0396 Chapman, H.M. "The Indirect Arguments for Sensations" Chap. iv of **Sensations and Phenomenology** (Bloomington IN 1966) 45-71.

0397 Charlton, W. "La certitude cartésienne" **AP** 38 (1975) 595-601.

0398 Château, J., et al. "Descartes" Pt. I, chap. ii of **Les grandes psychologies modernes. Du temps des philosophes au temps des scientifiques** (Bruxelles 1977) 49-78.

0399 Chauvois, L. **Descartes. Sa méthode et ses erreurs en physiologie** (Paris 1966).
     Rev. by: D[...], T.   **Bulletin des Lettres** (15 March 1966) 111.
              Huard, P.   **RHS** 20 (1967) 90-91.
              Rat, M.   **Revue des Deux Mondes** 19 (1967) 387-90.

0400 Chauvois, L. "A propos d'un récent débat sur Descartes et la physiologie animale et humaine" **Revue Générale des Sciences Pures et Appliquées** 73 (1966) 151-55.

0401* Chauvois, L. <Response> **PCa** 20 (1966) 91-94.
     Dis. of: Rostand, J.   **PCa** 19 (1965).

0402 Chavagne, A. **Descartes** (Bruxelles 1965).

0403 Chaves de Almeida, L.H. "Em torno de uma exigência humanística no ponto de partida da filosofia cartesiana" **Actas da Assembleia Internacional de Estudios Filosóficos. Revista Portuguesa de Filosofia** 25 (1969) No. 3-4, 277-81.

0404* Chaves de Almeida, L.H. "A idea cartesiana de melhor" **Revista da Faculdade de Letras. Série de Filosofia** [Porto] 1 (1971) 179-204.

0405 Chevalier, J. "Deux initiateurs: Descartes et Pascal" Chap. ii of **La pensée moderne. De Descartes à Kant. Histoire de la pensée** 3 (Paris 1961) 106-93.

0406 [Chevalley] de Buzon, C. "La métaphore optique dans la théorie cartésienne de la connaissance" **O8CM** (Marseille 1979) 181-84.

0407 Chevalley de Buzon, C. "Rationalité de l'anamorphose" **DsS** 31 (1979) 289-96.

0408 Chevalley [de Buzon], C. "Sur le statut d'une question apparemment denuée de sens: la nature immatérielle de la lumière" **DsS** 34 (1982) 257-66.

0409 Chevroton, D. "L'instinct, objet d'une controverse, a l'époque de Descartes: Pierre Chanet et Marin Cureau de la Chambre" **Histoire et Nature** 8 (1976) 3-20.

0410 Chinn, E.Y. "A Journey Around the Cartesian Circle" **PRA** 9 (1983) 279-92.

0411 Chomsky, N. **Cartesian Linguistics: A Chapter in the History of Rationalist Thought** (New York 1966).
Trans. as **La linguistique Cartésienne**, by N. Delanoë and D. Sperber (Paris 1969).

Rev. by:	Harman, G.	**PR** 77 (1968) 229-35.
	Zimmer, K.E.	**International Journal of American Linguistics** 34 (1968) 290-303.
	Salmon, V.	**Journal of Linguistics** 5 (1969) 165-87.
	Uitti, K.D.	**Romance Philology** 23 (1969-70) 75-85.
	Xirau, R.	**Dian** 18 (1972) 138-52.
Dis. by:	Miel, J.	**JHI** 30 (1969).
	Aarsleff, H.	**Language** 46 (1970).
	Bracken, H.M.	**JHP** 8 (1970).
	Verhaar, J.W.M.	**LS** 14 (1971).
	Aarsleff, H.	**LS** 17 (1971).
	Bracken, H.M.	**LS** 22 (1972).
	Percival, W.K.	**CS** (Oxford 1972).
	Joly, A.	**Beiträge zur Romanischen Philologie** 1 (1972-73).
	Land, S.K.	**Linguistics** 122 (1974).

Meisel, J.M.   **Linguistics** 122 (1974).
Clarke, D.M.   **PSt** 24 (1976).
Pochtar, R.   **RLF** 2 (1976).
Sullivan, J.L.   **Psychology of Language and Thought,**
                     ed. by R.W. Rieber (New York 1980).

0412   Chopra, Y.N. "The Cogito and the Certainty of One's Own Existence"
       JHP 12 (1974) 171-79.

0413   Chouillet, J. "Descartes et le problème de l'origine des langues au 18e
       siècle" **Dix-huitième Siècle** 4 (1972) 39-60.

0414   Christensen, B.J. "The Apple in the Vortex: Newton, Blake, and
       Descartes" **PL** 6 (1982) 147-61.

0415* Christiansen, L. "Cogito hos Augustin og Descartes" **Studier i Antik
       og Middelalderlig Filosofi og Idéhistorie,** ed. by B. Alkjaer et al.
       (København 1980) 465-79.

0416   Chung, A.C. "The Meditations of Descartes" **Chinese Culture** 7 (1966)
       61-76.

0417   Ciger, J. "Descartes - philosophe inconnu" **Zborník Filozofickej
       Fakulty Univerzity Komenského. Philosophica** 10 (1969) 79-110.

0418* Ciger, J. "Von Descartes zur wissenschaftlichen Revolution des XX.
       Jahrhunderts" **Zborník Filozofickej Fakulty Univerzity Komenského.
       Philosophica** 16 (1975) 139-72.

0419   Ciuffreda, K.J., and Stark, L. "Descartes' Law of Reciprocal
       Innervation" **American Journal of Optometry and Physiological Optics**
       52 (1975) 663-73.

0420   Clair, P. "Biographie" **Jacques Rohault (1618-1672). Bio-bibliographie
       avec l'édition critique des Entretiens sur la philosophie,** by P.
       Clair. **RDS** 3 (1978) 17-99.
       Rev. by: McClaughlin, T.   **SC** 2 (1981) 173-77.

0421   Clair, P. "De Gueudreville, interlocuteur de Rohault" **RDS** 4 (1980)
       47-52.

0422   Clarke, D.M. "Innate Ideas: Descartes and Chomsky" **PSt** 24 (1976) 52-63.
       Dis. of: Chomsky, N.   **Cartesian Linguistics** (New York 1966).

0423   Clarke, D.M. "The Ambiguous Role of Experience in Cartesian Science"
       **PSA 1976. Proceedings of the 1976 Biennial Meeting of the Philosophy
       of Science Association** 1 (1976) 151-64.

0424   Clarke, D.M. "The Concept of Experience in Descartes' Theory of
       Knowledge" **SL** 8 (1976) 18-39.
       Dis. by: Garber, D.   **SC** 1 (1979).

0425   Clarke, D.M. "Descartes' Use of 'Demonstration' and 'Deduction'" **MS**
       54 (1976-77) 333-44.

0426 Clarke, D.M. "The Impact Rules of Descartes' Physics" I 68 (1977) 55-66.

0427 Clarke, D.M. "Physics and Metaphysics in Descartes' Principles" SHPS 10 (1979) 89-112.

0428 Clarke, D.M. "Physique et métaphysique chez Descartes" AP 43 (1980) 465-86.

0429 Clarke, D.M. "Pierre-Sylvain Régis: A Paradigm of Cartesian Methodology" AGP 62 (1980) 289-310.

0430 Clarke, D.M. "Descartes' Critique of Logic" TKR (1981) 27-35.

0431 Clarke, D.M. Descartes' Philosophy of Science (Manchester 1982).
Rev. by: Gaukroger, S.   I 74 (1983) 445-46.
         C[ostabel], P.   BC 13 (1984) 40-42.
         Schankula, H.A.S.   PB 25 (1984) 197-200.
         Schouls, P.A.   Canadian Philosophical Reviews 4
                               (1984) 16-18.
         Milton, J.R.   FS 39 (1985) 198-99.

0432* Clarke, E. "The Early History of the Cerebral Ventricles"
Transactions and Studies of the College of Physicians of Philadelphia
30 (1962) 85-89.

0433 Clarke, E. "Brain Anatomy before Steno" Steno and Brain Research,
ed. by G. Scherz (Oxford 1968) 27-34.

0434 Clarke, E., and O'Malley, C.D. The Human Brain and Spinal Cord: A
Historical Study Illustrated by Writings from Antiquity to the
Twentieth Cenutry (Berkeley CA 1968).

0435 Clarke, W.N. "A Curious Blindspot in the Anglo-American Tradition of
Antitheistic Argument" Mon 54 (1970) 181-200.

0436 Clarkson, E.N.K., et al. "Trilobite Eyes and the Optics of Des Cartes
and Huygens" Nature 254 (1975) 663-67.

0437 Clatterbaugh, K.C. "Descartes's Causal Likeness Principle" PR 89
(1980) 379-402.

0438 Closset, F. "Kende René Descartes de Nederlandse taal?" Revue des
Langues Vivantes 26 (1960) 466-69.
Dis. of: Oegema van der Wal, T. De mens Descartes (Brussel 1960).

0439 Clouser, R.A. "A Critique of Descartes and Heisenberg" PRef 45
(1980) 157-77.

0440 Coady, C.A.J. "Descartes' Other Myth" AS 83 (1982-83) 121-41.

0441   Cobb-Stevens, V. "Descartes' Cogito: A Reply to Orenstein and Ratzsch"
        ILR 11 (1980) 146.
        Dis. of: Orenstein, A.   **ILR** 6 (1975).
                  Ratzsch, D.   **ILR** 8 (1977).

0442   Cohen, A. "Certainty, Doubt and Anxiety: Towards a Theory of the
        Psychology of Metaphysics" **Met** 12 (1981) 113-44.

0443   Cohen, A. "Descartes, Consciousness and Depersonalization: Viewing the
        History of Philosophy from a Strausian Perspective" **Journal of
        Medicine and Philosophy** 9 (1984) 7-27.

0444   Cohen, E. "Decomposing Dualism" **PF** 14 (1982-83) 131-34.
        Dis. of: Sommers, F.   **DCIE** (Baltimore MD 1978).

0445   Cohen, I.B. "'Quantum in se est': Newton, Kepler, Galileo, Descartes
        and Lucretius" **ACPA** 38 (1964) 36-46.

0446   Cohen, I.B. "'Quantum in se est': Newton's Concept of Inertia in
        Relation to Descartes and Lucretius" **Notes and Records of the Royal
        Society of London** 19 (1964) 131-55.

0447   Cohen, I.B. "Scientific Revolution and Creativity in the Enlightenment"
        Eighteenth-Century Life 7 (1982) no. 2, 41-54.

0448   Colin, P. "Le pouvoir de la philosophie" **Le pouvoir,** by J. Châtillon
        et al. (Paris 1978) 135-73.

0449*   Collins, A.W. "The Scientific Background of Descartes' Dualism" **St.
        John's Review** 31 (1979-80) 30-59.
        Repr. in **Thought and Nature: Studies in Rationalist Philosophy,** by
        A.W. Collins (Notre Dame IN 1985) 26-60.

0450   Collins, J.D. "The Cartesian Theory of Wisdom" Sect. 2 of **The Lure of
        Wisdom** (Milwaukee WI 1962) 40-122.

0451   Collins, J.D. **Descartes' Philosophy of Nature.** **APQ** Mon. 5 (Oxford
        1971).
        Rev. by: Allard, J.-L.   **D** 13 (1974) 179-80.
                  Watson, R.A.   **JHP** 13 (1975) 525-28.

0452   Combès, J. **Le dessein de la sagesse cartésienne** (Lyon 1960).
        Rev. by: Rescher, N.   **Eras** 14 (1961) 642-43.
                  Deregibus, A.   **GM** 17 (1962) 176-79.

0453*   Conca, N. "Il significato pedagogico del Discorso sul metodo"
        Pedagogia e Vita 17 (1964) 145-56.

0454   Conche, M. "Le 'cogito' axiologique" **12IC** 12 (Firenze 1961) 101-08.

0455   Connell, D. "Malebranche's Critique of Descartes" Chap. ii of **The
        Vision in God: Malebranche's Scholastic Sources** (Paris 1967) 23-57.

0456   Connelly, R.J.   "The Ontological Argument: Descartes' Advice to
       Hartshorne"   **NS** 43 (1969) 530-54.

0457   Connors, P.   "Samuel Beckett's Whoroscope as a Dramatic Monologue"
       Ball State University Forum 19 (1978) No. 2, 26-32.

0458   Conry, Y.   "Robert Boyle et la doctrine cartésienne des animaux-
       machines"   **RHS** 33 (1980) 69-74.

0459   Cook, M.L.   "The Alleged Ambiguity of 'Idea' in Descartes' Philosophy"
       SwJP 6 (1975) No. 1, 87-94.

0460   Cooney, B.   "Descartes and the Eternal Darkness"   **NS** 49 (1975) 251-79.

0461   Cooney, B.   "Arnold Geulincx: A Cartesian Idealist"   **JHP** 16 (1978)
       167-80.

0462   Cooper, D.E.   "Innateness: Old and New"   **PR** 81 (1972) 465-83.

0463   Corcoran, P.E.   "Descartes' Method of Humour"   **Dalhousie Review** 52
       (1972-73) 280-87.

0464   Cornelissen, R.   "Molière et Descartes"   **Romanische Forschungen** 90
       (1978) 48-59.

0465   Corsano, A.   "Vico, Plauto e Cartesio"   **Bollettino del Centro di Studi
       Vichiani** 4 (1974) 140-42.

0466   Corsano, A.   "Cicerone tra Cartesio e Vico"   **F** 26 (1975) 67-70.

0467   Corsano, A.   "La morte di Cartesio"   **GCFI** 58 (1979) 234-38.

0468   Corsano, A.   "Studi sull'atomismo del seicento" Review of **Ricerche
       sull'atomismo del seicento,** ed. by M. Pra and R. Crippa [Firenze 1977].
       GCFI 58 (1979) 239-49.

0469* Corsi, M.   "Il problema della 'natura umana' nelle Meditazioni di
       Cartesio"   **Atti dell'Accademia Pontaniana** 18 (1968-69) 25-38.

0470   Corsi, M., ed.   "Due lettere di Luigi Scaravelli"   **F** 30 (1979) 33-44.

0471   Corte, M. de.   "Descartes et la morale"   **Ordre Français** 185 (1974) 26-
       36.

0472   Cortese, R.   "Pierre Bayle. La ragione alla ricerca di nuove certezze"
       F 29 (1978) 559-76.

0473   Cosenza, P.   "Descartes e la logica stoica"   **Studi Filosofici** 4 (1981)
       127-55.

0474   Cosenza, P.   "La 'consequentia' nelle Regulae di Descartes"   **RFN** 75
       (1983) 200-22.

0475* Cosenza, P. **Sillogismo e concatenazione nelle Regulae di Descartes** (Napoli 1984).

0476   Costa, M.J. "What Cartesian Ideas Are Not" **JHP** 21 (1983) 537-49.

0477   Costabel, P. "La roue d'Aristote et les critiques françaises à l'argument de Galilée" **RHS** 17 (1964) 385-96. Repr. in **DODS** (Paris 1982) 109-20.

0478   Costabel, P. "Contribution à l'étude de l'offensive de Leibniz contre la philosophie cartésienne en 1691-1692" **RIP** 20 (1966) 264-87.

0479* Costabel, P. "Matière et lumière au XVIIe siècle" **Acta Historiae Rerum Naturalium nec non Technicarum** 3 (1967) 115-30.

0480   Costabel, P. "Essai critique sur quelques concepts de la mécanique cartésienne" **AIHS** 20 (1967) 235-52. Repr. in **DODS** (Paris 1982) 141-58.

0481   Costabel, P. "Descartes et la racine cubique des nombres binômes. Propos sur un document retrouvé concernant le dernier acte de la controverse Stampioen-Waessenaer" **RHS** 22 (1969) 97-116. Repr. [in part] in **Correspondance V**, ed. by C. Adam and P. Tannery; new ed., ed. by P.Costabel, J. Beaude and A. Gabbey. Vol. 5 of **Oeuvres de Descartes** (Paris 1903); new ed. (1974) 611-15. Repr. in **DODS** (Paris 1982) 121-40.

0482   Costabel, P. "La mathématique de Descartes antérieure à la 'Géométrie'" **Medunarodni Simpozij "Geometrija i Algebra Pocetkom XVII Stoljeca** [Symposium en l'honneur du 4e centenaire de Marinus Ghetaldus] (Zagreb 1969) 127-37. Repr. in **DODS** (Paris 1982) 27-37.

0483   Costabel, P. "Florimond de Beaune, érudit et savant de Blois" **RHS** 27 (1974) 73-75.

0484   Costabel, P. "René Descartes, 1596-1650" **Scienziati e tecnologi della origini al 1875** 1 (Milano 1975) 406-09. Repr. in **DODS** (Paris 1982) 1-8.

0485   Costabel, P. "A propos de la correspondance de Descartes" **RS** 97 (1976) 77-80. Repr. in **DODS** (Paris 1982) 194-97.

0486   Costabel, P. "Ignace-Gaston Pardies et la physique cartésienne" **RDS** 1 (1976) 87-91.

0487   Costabel, P. "Les Regulae et l'actualité scientifique de leur temps" **EP** (1976) 415-23. Repr. in **DODS** (Paris 1982) 39-47.

0488   C[ostabel], P. "Propos de bibliographie matérielle. Editions et émissions des oeuvres de Descartes de 1657 à 1673" **BC** 5 (1976) 445-54.

0489 Costabel, P. "Annexes III, IV, V (Problèmes scientifiques dans les Regulae)" **Règles utiles et claires pour la direction de l'esprit en la recherche de la vérité,** by René Descartes; tr. by J.-L. Marion (The Hague 1977) 310-22.
Repr. in **DODS** (Paris 1982) 49-62.

0490 Costabel, P. "La propagation de la lumière sans transport de matière de Descartes à Huygens" **Roemer et la vitesse de la lumière,** ed. by R. Taton (Paris 1978) 83-91.
Repr. in **DODS** (Paris 1982) 77-85.

0491 Costabel, P. "Physique et métaphysique chez Descartes" **Human Implications of Scientific Advance,** ed. by E.G. Forbes. **15CI** (Edinburgh 1978) 268-77.
Repr. in **DODS** (Paris 1982) 181-93.

0492 Costabel, P. "Descartes savant" **08CM** (Marseille 1979) 167-71.
Repr. in **DODS** (Paris 1982) 9-13.

0493 Costabel, P. "La courbure et son apparition chez Descartes" **Mélanges en l'honneur de Charles Moraze. Culture, science et développement. Contribution à une histoire de l'homme** (Toulouse 1979) 337-44.
Repr. in **DODS** (Paris 1982) 159-66.

0494 Costabel, P. "Le théorème de Descartes-Euler" **SC** 1 (1979) 25-35.
Repr. in **DODS** (Paris 1982) 15-25.

0495 Costabel, P. **Démarches originales de Descartes savant** (Paris 1982).

0496 Costabel, P. "La refraction de la lumière et la Dioptrique de Descartes" **DODS** (Paris 1982) 63-76.

0497 Costabel, P. "Matière et lumière au XVIIe siècle. Introduction" **DsS** 34 (1982) 247-55.

0498 Costabel, P. "L'initiation mathématique de Descartes" **AP** 46 (1983) 637-46.

0499 Costabel, P. "Découverte d'un nouveau manuscrit de l''Introduction a la Géométrie'" **BC** 13 (1984) 74.

0500 C[ostabel], P., and A[rmogathe], J.-R. "L'analyse textuelle automatique appliqué aux oeuvres de Descartes. Un état présent des travaux" **BC** 3 (1974) 453-58.

0501 Costabel, P., and Armogathe, J.-R. "Premiers résultats de l''Equipe Descartes'" **1CIL** (Roma 1976) 113-21.

0502 Costabel, P., and Marion, J.-L. "Quelques résultats de l'indexation des textes de Descartes" **RDS** 2 (1978) 3-6.

0503 Cottingham, J.G. "Introduction" **Descartes' Conversation with Burman,** by René Descartes; tr. by J.G. Cottingham (Oxford 1976) ix-xl.
Rev. by: Ariew, R. **SC** 1 (1979) 183-87.

0504 Cottingham, J.G. "Commentary" **Descartes' Conversation with Burman,**
by René Descartes; tr. by J.G. Cottingham (Oxford 1976) 53-120.
Rev. by: Ariew, R.   **SC** 1 (1979) 183-87.

0505 Cottingham, J.G. "The Role of the Malignant Demon" **SL** 8 (1976) 257-64.
Dis. by: O'Briant, W.H.   **SL** 10 (1978).

0506 Cottingham, J.G. "'A Brute to the Brutes?': Descartes' Treatment of
Animals" **P** 53 (1978) 551-59.

0507 Cottingham, J.G. "Descartes on 'Thought'" **PQ** 28 (1978) 208-14.

0508 Cottingham, J.G. "Mathematics in the First Meditation: A Reply to
Professor O'Briant" **SL** 10 (1978) 113-15.
Dis. of: O'Briant, W.   **SL** 10 (1978).

0509 Cottingham, J.G. ‹Response to R. Ariew› **SC** 1 (1979) 187-89.
Dis. of: Ariew, R.   **SC** 1 (1979).

0510* Coturri, E., and Zoli, P. "La posizione critica assunta da M. Stenone
nel suo <u>Discorso</u> <u>sull'anatomia</u> <u>del</u> <u>cervello</u> nei confronti dell'anima
pineale di Cartesio" **CNSM** (Roma 1967) 3-11.

0511 Coulet, H. "La métaphore de l'architecture dans la critique littéraire
au XVIIe siècle" **Critique et création littéraires en France au XVIIe
siècle,** ed. by M. Fumaroli (Paris 1977) 291-309.

0512 Coulomb, J., et al. "Discussion III: les mathématiques et Descartes, la
science moderne, le dualisme, le matérialisme, la liberté, la necessité"
Alain philosophe de la culture et théoricien de la démocratie, ed. by
G. Kahn. **Actes du Colloque "Vigueur d'Alain, Rigueur de Simone Weil"**
(Paris 1976) 77-84.
Dis. of: Lamizet, G.   **Alain philosophe de la culture et
théoricien de la démocratie** (Paris
1976).

0513 Coumet, E. "Mersenne: 'Dictions' nouvelles à l'infini" **DsS** 109
(1975) 3-32.

0514 Courtine, J.-F. "Schelling et l'achèvement de la Métaphysique de la
Subjecti(vi)té" **EP** 29 (1974) 147-70.

0515* Coxeter, H.S.M. "The Problem of Apollonius" **Mathematical Monthly** 75
(1968) 5-15.
0516 Crapulli, G. "Note all'edizione critica di Adam-Tannery delle <u>Regulae
ad directionem ingenij</u> di Descartes" **RCSF** 19 (1964) 54-61.

0517 Crapulli, G. **Mathesis universalis. Genesi di un'idea nel XVI secolo**
(Roma 1969).
Rev. by: Mercier, A.   **Eras** 24 (1972) 129-31.
           Parkinson, G.H.R.   **SL** 4 (1972) 74-76.
           Schmitt, C.   **I** 63 (1972) 277-78.

0518   Crapulli, G. "Le note marginali latine nelle versioni olandesi di opere
        di Descartes di J.H. Glazemaker" **Ricerche lessicali su opere di
        Descartes e Spinoza,** by G. Crapulli and E. Giancotti Boscherini (Roma
        1969) 7-117.
        Rev. by: Namer, E.   **RP** 97 (1972) 196-97.
                  Marion, J.-L.   **EP** (1976) 497-98.

0519   Crapulli, G. "La rédaction et les projets d'édition des Meditationes de
        Prima Philosophia de Descartes" **EP** (1976) 425-41.
        Dis. by: Crapulli, G.   **EP** (1976).

0520   Crapulli, G. "Erratum" **EP** (1977) 369-70.
        Dis. of: Crapulli, G.   **EP** (1976).

0521*   Crapulli, G. "Corpus cartesianum" **Micromegas** [Italia] 4 (1977) 245-49.

0522   Crapulli, G. "La prima edizione delle Meditationes de prima philosophia
        di Descartes e il suo 'esemplare ideale'" **SC** 1 (1979) 37-90.

0523   Crease, R. "Vico and the 'Cogito'" **Vico: Past and Present,** ed. by G.
        Tagliacozzo. 1 (Atlantic Highlands NJ 1981) 171-81.

0524   Crem, T.M. "A Moderate Dualist Alternative to Cartesian Dualism"
        Laval Théologique et Philosophique 35 (1979) 153-75.

0525   Cress, D. "Does Descartes' 'Ontological Argument' Really Stand On Its
        Own?" **SIF** 5 (1973) 127-40.
        Dis. of: Gueroult, M.   **Cahiers de Royaumont** 2 (Paris 1957);
                                        repr. in **EDSM** (Hildesheim 1970).

0526   Cress, D. "Does Descartes Have Two 'Ontological Arguments'?" **ISP** 7
        (1975) 155-66.

0527   Cress, D.A. "Echoes of Bonaventure in Descartes" **San Bonaventura
        maestro di vita francescana e di sapienza cristiana,** ed. by A. Pompei.
        **Atti del Congresso Internazionale per il VII Centenario di San
        Bonaventura da Bagnoregio** 2 (Roma 1976) 127-36.

0528   Crippa, M.L. "Filosofia e storia della filosofia in Etienne Gilson.
        Ragione e antropologia" **Acme** 33 (1980) 149-78.

0529   Crippa, R. "Ontologia e libertà in Cartesio" Chap. i of **Studi sulla
        coscienza etica e religiosa del seicento** [1] (Brescia 1960).

0530   Crippa, R. "Le 'obiezioni' alle 'meditazioni' cartesiane" Chap. ii of
        Studi sulla coscienza etica e religiosa del seicento [1] (Brescia 1960).

0531*   Crippa, R. "Potere e passione in Cartesio" **Potere e responsabilità.
        Atti del XVII Convegno del Centro di Studi Filosofici tra Professori
        Universitari** (Brescia 1963) 123-24.

0532   Crippa, R. "Etica e ontologia nella dottrina cartesiana delle passioni"
        GM 19 (1964) 532-45.

0533   Cristofolini, P.   "Sul problema cartesiano della memoria intellettuale" **Pensiero** 7 (1962) 378-402.

0534   Cristofolini, P.   "Una lettera-trattato inedita di Henry More"   **RCSF** 24 (1969) 73-80.

0535   Cristofolini, P.   **Cartesiani e sociniani. Studio su Henry More** (Urbino 1974).
Rev. by: G[abbey], A.   **BC** 6 (1977) 2-14.

0536   Crocker, S.F.   "Descartes' Ontological Argument and the Existing Thinker"   **MS** 53 (1975-76) 347-77.

0537* Croissant, J.   "Bibliographie cartésienne"   **Morale et Enseignement** 9 (1960) 44-50.

0538   Crombie, A.C.   "Descartes"   **Scientific American** 201 (1959) 160-73.

0539* Crombie, A.C.   "Some Aspects of Descartes' Attitude to Hypothesis and Experiment"   **Actes du Symposium International des Sciences Physiques et Mathématiques dans la Première Moitié du XVIIe Siècle** (Firenze 1960) 192-201.

0540   Crombie, A.C.   "The Mechanistic Hypothesis and the Scientific Study of Vision: Some Optical Ideas as a Background to the Invention of the Microscope"   **Historical Aspects of Microscopy,** ed. by S. Bradbury and G.L'E. Turner (Cambridge 1967) 3-112.

0541   Crombie, A.C.   "Descartes, René du Perron"   **Dictionary of Scientific Biography,** ed. by C.C. Gillispie. 4 (New York 1971) 51-55.

0542* Crombie, A.C.   "Marin Mersenne (1588-1648) and the Seventeenth-century Problem of Scientific Acceptability"   **Physis** 17 (1975) 186-204.

0543   Cromphout, G. van.   "Manductio ad Ministerium: Cotton Mather as Neoclassicist"   **American Literature** 53 (1981-82) 361-79.

0544   Cronin, T.J.   "Eternal Truths in the Thought of Descartes and of His Adversary"   **JHI** 21 (1960) 553-59.

0545   Cronin, T.J.   "Eternal Truths in the Thought of Suarez and of Descartes" **MS** 38 (1960-61) 269-88; 39 (1961-62) 23-38.

0546   Cronin, T.J.   **Objective Being in Descartes and in Suarez** (Roma 1966).

0547   Cronin, T.J.   "Objective Reality of Ideas in Human Thought: Descartes and Suarez"   **Wisdom in Depth: Essays in Honor of Henri Renard, S.J.,** ed. by V.F. Daues, M.R. Holloway and L. Sweeney (Milwaukee WI 1966) 68-79.

0548   Cropsey, J.   "On Descartes' Discourse on Method"   **Interpretation** 1 (1970) 130-43.
Repr. in **Political Philosophy and the Issues of Politics,** by J. Cropsey (Chicago IL 1977) 274-90.

0549 Cruz Cruz, J. "Sobre la posibilidad de la Antropología filosófica"
 Estudios Filosoficos 18 (1969) 375-422.

0550* Cubeddu, I. "L'io penso di Cartesio e di Kant" **Quaderni dell'Istituto
 Galvano della Volpe** 1 (1978) 7-53.

0551 Cummins, P.D. "Vernon on Descartes' Three Substances" **SJP** 5 (1967)
 126-28.
 Dis. of: Vernon, T.S.   **SJP** 3 (1965).

0552 Cummins, R. "Epistemology and the Cartesian Circle" **Theoria** 41
 (1975) 112-24.

0553 Curley, E.M. "Locke, Boyle, and the Distinction Between Primary and
 Secondary Qualities" **PR** 81 (1972) 438-64.

0554 Curley, E.M. "Recent Work on 17th Century Continental Philosophy"
 APQ 11 (1974) 235-55.

0555 Curley, E.M. "Descartes, Spinoza and the Ethics of Belief" **Spinoza:
 Essays in Interpretation,** ed. by M. Mandelbaum and E. Freeman (La Salle
 IL 1975) 159-189.

0556 Curley, E.M. "Dreaming and Conceptual Revision" **AJP** 53 (1975) 119-141.
 Dis. of: Malcolm, N.   **Dreaming** (London 1959).

0557 Curley, E.M. "Spinoza - as an Expositor of Descartes" **Speculum
 Spinozanum, 1677-1977,** ed. by S. Hessing (London 1977) 133-42.

0558 Curley, E.M. **Descartes Against the Skeptics** (Cambridge MA 1978).
 Rev. by: Charlton, W.   **PQ** 29 (1979) 264-65.
           Jolley, N.   **SL** 11 (1979) 150-54.
           Morris, J.M.   **SC** 1 (1979) 195-97.
           Schouls, P.A.   **PB** 20 (1979) 61-66.
           Gabaude, J.-M.   **EP** (1980) 485-86.
           Rubin, R.   **BJPS** 31 (1980) 104-08.
           Watson, R.A.   **JHP** 18 (1980) 228-29.
           Caton, H.P.   **PF** 12 (1980-81) 273-94.
 Dis. by: Doney, W.   **PRA** 6 (1980) No. 1376.

0559 Curley, E.M. "Descartes on the Creation of the Eternal Truths" **PR** 93
 (1984) 569-97.

0560 Curtis, D.E. "Pierre Bayle and the Range of Cartesian Reason" **YFS** 49
 (1973) 71-81.

0561 Curtler, H.M. Review of **The Origin of Subjectivity,** by H.P. Caton
 [New Haven 1973]. **MA** 18 (1974) 213-16.
 Dis. by: Molnar, T.   **MA** 18 (1974).

0562 Cysarz, H. "Descartes und Bergson. Französischer Rationalismus und
 Irrationalismus in Deutschland" **Schopenhauer Jahrbuch** 50 (1969) 38-55.

0563 D'Amico, R. "Text and Context: Derrida and Foucault on Descartes" **The Structural Allegory: Reconstructive Encounters with the New French Thought**, ed. by J. Fekete (Minneapolis MN 1984) 164-82.
Dis. of: Foucault, M.   **Folie et déraison** (Paris 1961).
         Derrida, J.   **RMM** 68 (1963); 69 (1964).
         Foucault, M.   **Folie et déraison** 2nd ed. (Paris 1972).

0564 D'Orsi, D. "Il tramonto della filosofia moderna, ossia verso la 'quarta età'. Prima puntata: Renato Cartesio" **Sop** 28 (1960) 167-85.

0565 Dagognet, F. "Un oubli certain, un probable retour" **EP** (1977) 31-39.

0566 Dalsgard-Hansen, P. "Descartes' Cogito-Argument and his Doctrine of Simple Natures" **Danish Yearbook of Philosophy** 2 (1965) 7-40.

0567 Daniel, S.H. "The Nature of Light in Descartes' Physics" **PF** 7 (1975-76) 323-44.

0568 Daniel, S.H. "Descartes' Treatment of 'lumen naturale'" **SL** 10 (1978) 92-100.

0569 Daniel, S.H. "Doubts and Doubting in Descartes" **MS** 56 (1978-79) 57-65.

0570 Danto, A. "Being Mistaken" Chap. iii of **Analytical Philosophy of Knowledge** (Cambridge 1968) 50-72.

0571 Danto, A. "The Representational Character of Ideas and the Problem of the External World" **DCIE** (Baltimore MD 1978) 287-98.

0572 Darós, W.R. "'Pienso, luego soy': trascendencia metafísica e inmanencia de la razón humana" **Rivista Rosminiana di Filosofia e di Cultura** 77 (1983) 328-42.

0573 Darricau, R. "La spiritualité du prince" **DsS** 62-63 (1964) 78-111.

0574 Dascal, M. "On the Role of Metaphysics in Descartes' Thought" **MW** 4 (1971) 460-70.
Dis. of: Caton, H.P.   **MW** 3 (1970).
Dis. by: Caton, H.P.   **MW** 5 (1972).

0575* Dascal, M. "Signos e pensamento segundo Leibniz, Hobbes, Locke e Descartes" **Revista Discurso** 6 (1975) 133-50.

0576 Dauxerre, G. "René Descartes et son pays natal" **Amis du Pays Civraisien** 22 (1975) 20-23.

0577 David, A. "Sur une antinomie de la subjectivité" **Exercices de la Patience** 5 (1983) 43-58.

0578 Davidson, H.M. "Descartes and the Utility of the Passions" **Romanic Review** 51 (1960) 15-26.

0579 Davies, K. "The Impersonal Formulation of the Cogito" **A** 41 (1980-81) 134-37.

0580 Davies, K. "Empiricism and the Private Language Argument" **PQ** 31 (1981) 343-47.
Dis. of: Kenny, A. **Wittgenstein: The Philosophical In-
vestigations** (Garden City NY 1966).

0581 Davis, R. "I Have on Rare Occasions While Half Asleep Been Deceived" **SJP** 10 (1972) 359-65.
Dis. of: Botkin, R. **SJP** 10 (1972).
Dis. by: Botkin, R. **SJP** 10 (1972).

0582 Davis, R. "Dreams and Dreaming: A Reply to Professor Botkin" **SJP** 10 (1972) 373-78.
Dis. of: Botkin, R. **SJP** 10 (1972).

0583* Davis, W. "The Pineal Gland" **JT** 11 (1976) 159-62.

0584 De Angelis, E. **Il metodo geometrico nella filosofia del Seicento** (Pisa 1964).

0585 De Angelis, E. "Il metodo geometrico da Cartesio a Spinoza" **GCFI** 43 (1964) 393-427.

0586 De Angelis, E. **La critica del finalismo nella cultura cartesiana** (Firenze 1967).

0587 De Dijn, H. "Spinozas geometrische methode van denken" **TF** 35 (1973) 707-65.

0588 De Dijn, H. "Inleiding tot de affectleer van Spinoza" **TF** 39 (1977) 399-408.

0589 De Dijn, H. "Adriaan Heereboord en het Nederlands Cartesianisme" **ANTW** 75 (1983) 56-69.

0590* De Giovanni, B. "'Politica' dopo Cartesio" **Centauro** 7 (1981) 30-52.

0591* De Giovanni, B., Esposito, R., and Zarone, G. **Divenire della ragione moderna. Cartesio, Spinoza, Vico** (Napoli 1981).

0592 DeHaven, S. "Descartes, Frankfurt and Madmen" **A** 38 (1977-78) 107-09.
Dis. of: Frankfurt, H.G. **Demons, Dreamers, and Madmen** (Indianapolis IN 1970).
Dis. by: Fahrnkopf, R. **A** 39 (1978-79).
   Welbourne, M. **A** 40 (1979-80).

0593 Debout-Oleszkiewicz, S. "Fourier et la philosophie cartésienne" **RDS** 1 (1976) 128-39.

0594 Deghaye, P. "La notion théosophique de médiation et le dualisme philosophique au XVIIe et au XVIIIe siècles" **Histoire et littérature. Les écrivains et la politique,** ed. by F. Joukovsky and A. Niderst (Paris 1977) 323-81.

0595 Deguy, M. Review of **Leibniz, critique de Descartes,** by Y. Belaval [Paris 1960]. **NRF** 8 (1960) 1094-1101.

0596 Del Noce, A. **Cartesio. Riforma cattolica e filosofia moderna** 1 (Bologna 1965).
　　Rev. by: Giannini, G.　　**Humanitas** 22 (1967) 480-87.
　　　　　　Olivetti, M.　　**Archivio di Filosofia** 38 (1969) 153-87.

0597 Del Torre, M.A. "Descartes et l'histoire de la philosophie au XVIIe siècle" **O8CM** (Marseille 1979) 205-06.

0598 Delahunty, R. "Descartes' Cosmological Argument" **PQ** 30 (1980) 34-46.

0599 Delamarre, A.J.-L. "Du consentement. Remarques sur Les passions de l'âme, #40" **PaRa** (Paris 1983) 131-43.

0600* Delesalle, J., and Tran Van Toàn. **Quand l'amour éclipse Dieu: rapport à autrui et transcendance** (Paris 1984).

0601 Delft, L. van. "Clarté et Cartésianisme de La Bruyère" **FR** 44 (1970-71) 281-90.

0602 Delhez, J. "Descartes lecteur de Sénèque" **Hommages à Marie Delcourt. Collection Latomus** 114 (Bruxelles 1970) 392-401.

0603 Delhougne, H. "L'argument ontologique est-il philosophique ou théologique? Examen critique de la position de Karl Barth" **Revue des Sciences Religieuses** 53 (1979) 43-63.

0604 Delon, J. "Les conférences de Retz sur le cartésianisme" **DsS** 31 (1979) 265-76.

0605 Delon, M. "Cartésianisme(s) et féminisme(s)" **Eur** 56 (1978) 73-86.

0606 Delorme, S. "Un cartésien ami de Gassendi: Henri-Louis Habert de Montmor" **RHS** 27 (1974) 68-72.

0607 Dematteis, P.B. "The Ontological Argument as Wishful Thinking" **Kinesis** 1 (1968-69) 1-14.

0608 Denissoff, E. "L'énigme de la science cartésienne: La physique de Descartes est-elle positive ou déductive? Essai d'interprétation de deux extraits du 'Discours de la méthode'" **RPL** 59 (1961) 31-75.

0609 Denissoff, E. "La nature du savoir scientifique selon Descartes, et l''Histoire de mon esprit', autobiographie intellectuelle" **RPL** 66 (1968) 5-35.

0610 Denissoff, E. **Descartes, premier théoricien de la physique mathématique. Trois essais sur le 'Discours de la méthode'** (Louvain 1970).
Rev. by: Cavailles, R.   **Homo** 10 (1971) 218-20.
          Lefèvre, R.   **DsS** 92 (1971) 163-64.
          Rochot, B.   **RS** 92 (1971) 85-92.
          Röd, W.   **PRu** 18 (1971) 78-92.
          Bernhardt, J.   **RP** 97 (1972) 191-96.
          A[rmogathe], J.-R.   **BC** 1 (1972) 296-300.

0611 Dennert, J. "Die neue Philosophie" Chap. viii of **Die ontologisch-
aristotelische Politikwissenschaft und der Rationalismus. Eine
Untersuchung des politischen Denkens Aristoteles', Descartes', Hobbes',
Rousseaus und Kants** (Berlin 1970) 142-66.

0612 Dennett, D. "Wondering Where the Yellow Went" **Mon** 64 (1981) 102-08.
Dis. of: Sellars, W.   **Mon** 64 (1981).

0613 Deprun, J. "L'interprète de Descartes" **Sud** 9 (1973) 39-49.

0614 Deprun, J. "Mme de Sévigné et les controverses post-cartésiennes: des
'Animaux-Machines' aux 'Ames Vertes'" **Marseille** 95 (1973) 43-52.

0615 Deprun, J. "Chercher la vérité: notes sur le statut de l''homo
quaerens' chez Descartes et Malebranche" **Le XVIIe siècle et la
recherche. A la mémoire de Raymond Picard,** ed. by R. Duchêne. **06CM**
(Marseille 1976) 29-40.

0616 Deprun, J. "Perspectives métaphysiques" Chap. xii of **La philosophie
de l'inquiétude en France au XVIIIe siècle** (Paris 1979) 185-210.

0617 Deprun, J. "Cartésianisme et mythologie" **La mythologie au XVIIe
siècle,** ed. by L.G. de Donville. **11CM** (Marseille 1982) 17-24.

0618 Deprun, J. "Descartes et le 'génie' de Socrate (Note sur un traité
perdu et sur une lettre énigmatique)" **PaRa** (Paris 1983) 145-58.

0619 Deregibus, A. "Cartesio" **Dall'umanesimo a Rousseau,** ed. by V. Mathieu.
Pt. I, Vol. 2 of **Questioni di storiografia filosofica. La storia della
filosofia attraverso i suoi interpreti** (Brescia 1974) 207-71.

0620* Deregibus, A. "Spinoza e Descartes" **GM** 32 (1977) 507-54.

0621 Deregibus, A. "La dottrina filosofica di Cartesio nell'interpretazione
'critica' di Gallo Galli" **Filosofia Oggi** 7 (1984) 585-606.

0622 Derrida, J. "Cogito et histoire de la folie" **RMM** 68 (1963) 460-94;
69 (1964) 116-19.
Repr. in **L'écriture et la différence,** by J. Derrida (Paris 1967) 51-97.
Dis. of: Foucault, M.   **Folie et déraison** (Paris 1961).
Dis. by: Foucault, M.   **Folie et déraison** 2nd ed. (Paris
                                1972).

          Beyssade, J.-M.   **RMM** 78 (1973).
          Felman, S.   **YFS** 52 (1975).

Giovannangeli, D.   **Cahiers Internationaux de Symbolisme**
40-41 (1980).
D'Amico, R.   **The Structural Allegory** (Minneapolis
MN 1984).

0623* Derrida, J. "Languages and Institutions of Philosophy" **Semiotic
Inquiry/Recherches Sémiotiques** 4 (1984) 91-154.

0624 Deutscher, M. "René Descartes 1596-1650" Chap. vii of **Early
Seventeenth Century Scientists**, ed. by R. Harré (Oxford 1965) 159-88.

0625 Deutscher, M. "I Exist" **M** 76 (1967) 583-86.
Dis. of: Margolis, J.   **M** 73 (1964).

0626* Di Giovanni, A. "Il mondo, il corpo e l'anima nel pensiero cartesiano"
CNSM (Roma 1967) 143-48.
Repr. in **PSM** 11 (1967) No. 1, 28-34.

0627 Di Maio, A. **La condizione umana e le passioni in Cartesio** (Napoli
1966).

0628 Di Maio, A. "Il progetto della morale cartesiana" **Scritti in onore di
Cleto Carbonara** (Napoli 1976) 247-65.

0629 Di Marco, M. "Spiriti animali e meccanicismo fisiologico in Descartes"
Phys 13 (1971) 21-70.

0630* Díaz Estrada, J. "El método y la verdad en Descartes" **Revista de
Filosofía** [México] 4 (1971) 180-209.

0631 Dibon, P. "Histoire des idées au XVIIe siècle (Les rapports de
Descartes et de Rivet. Samuel Desmarets. Samuel Desmarets et la
philosophie de Descartes)" **EPHE. IVe Section: Sciences Historiques et
Philologiques** 103 (1970-71) 585-600.

0632 Dibon, P. **Inventaire de la correspondance d'André Rivet (1595-1650)**
(The Hague 1971).

0633 Dibon, P. "Note critique sur deux lettres de la correspondance de
Descartes" **JHP** 9 (1971) 63-67.

0634 Dibon, P. "Histoire des idées au XVIIe siècle (La diffusion européenne
du cartésianisme. La Respublica litteraria dans la première moitié du
XVIIe siècle)" **EPHE. IVe Section: Sciences Historiques et
Philologiques** 104 (1971-72) 515-28.

0635 Dibon, P. "Histoire des idées au XVIIe siècle (La diffusion du
cartésianisme dans les Provinces-Unies, 1668-1676. Les relations anglo-
néerlandais au sein de la Respublica litteraria et christiana)" **EPHE.
IVe Section: Sciences Historiques et Philologiques** 105 (1972-73) 539-47.

0636 Dibon, P. "Histoire des idées au XVIIe siècle (Lambert van Velthuysen (1622-1685). Les relations anglo-néerlandais au sein de la Respublica litteraria et christiana)" **EPHE. IVe Section: Sciences Historiques et Philologiques** 106 (1973-74) 595-605.

0637 Dibon, P. "L'Université du Leyde et la République des Lettres au 17e siècle" **Quaerendo** 5 (1975) 5-38.

0638 Dibon, P. "Histoire des idées au XVIIe siècle (Descartes en Hollande, étude critique des sources bio-bibliographiques)" **EPHE. IVe Section: Sciences Historiques et Philologiques** 108 (1975-76) 749-54.

0639 Dibon, P. "Le séjour de Descartes en Hollande" **Septentrion** [Nederland] 5 (1976) 83-93.

0640 Dibon, P. "Histoire des idées au XVIIe siècle (Descartes dans les Provinces-Unies)" **EPHE. IVe Section: Sciences Historiques et Philologiques** 109 (1976-77) 787-92.

0641 Dibon, P. "En marge de la Préface à la traduction latine des Passions de l'âme de Descartes" **SC** 1 (1979) 91-110.

0642 Dibon, P. "A propos de la mort de Descartes" **Nouvelles de la République des Lettres** 1 (1981) 185-91.

0643 Dick, S.J. "Cartesian Vortices, the Infinite Universe, and the Plurality of Solar Systems" Chap. v of **Plurality of Worlds: The Origins of the Extraterrestrial Life Debate from Democritus to Kant** (Cambridge 1982) 106-41.
     Rev. by: Crowe, M.J.   **I** 74 (1983) 268-70.

0644 Dickopp, K.-H. "Zum Wandel von Nietzsches Seinsverständnis--African Spir und Gustav Teichmüller" **ZPF** 24 (1970) 50-71.

0645 Dierckes, C.E. "Descartes and the Unlimited Freedom of the Will" **Di** 23 (1980-81) 1-13.

0646 Dietl, P.J. "The Feasibility of Hyperbolical Doubt" **PS** 20 (1969) 70-73.

0647 Dijksterhuis, E.J. "Descartes" Pt. IV, chap. iii of **The Mechanization of the World Picture** (Oxford 1961) 403-18.
     Rev. by: Yolton, J.W.   **HSc** 10 (1972).

0648 Dilley, F.B. "Descartes' Cosmological Argument" **Mon** 54 (1970) 427-40.

0649 Dobrzanski, L. "On the Concept of 'Cartesianism'" **Danish Yearbook of Philosophy** 20 (1983) 7-42.

0650 Dobzhansky, T. "On Cartesian and Darwinian Aspects of Biology" **Graduate Journal** 8 (1968) 99-117.

0651 Doig, J.C. "Denial of Hierarchy: Consequences for Scotus and Descartes" **Studies in Medieval Culture** 11 (1977) 109-17.

0652 Doig, J.C. "Suarez, Descartes, and the Objective Reality of Ideas"
      NS 51 (1977) 350-71.
      Dis. by: Wells, N.J.   **NS** 53 (1979).

0653 Donagan, A. "A Note on Spinoza, Ethics, I. 10" **PR** 75 (1966) 380-82.
      Dis. of: Bennett, J.   **PR** 74 (1965).

0654 Donagan, A. "Spinoza and Descartes on Extension: A Comment" **MSP** 1
      (1976) 31-33.

0655 Donagan, A. "Descartes's 'Synthetic' Treatment of the Real Distinction
      between Mind and Body" **DCIE** (Baltimore MD 1978) 186-96.

0656 Donagan, A. "Spinoza's Dualism" **PBS** (Washington DC 1980) 89-102.

0657 Doney, W., ed. **Descartes: A Collection of Critical Essays** (Garden
      City NY 1967).

0658 Doney, W. "Bibliography" **DCCE** (Garden City NY 1967) 369-86.

0659 Doney, W. "Descartes' Conception of Perfect Knowledge" **JHP** 8 (1970)
      387-403.

0660 Doney, W. "Spinoza on Philosophical Skepticism" **Mon** 55 (1971) 617-35.

0661 Doney, W. "The Geometrical Presentation of Descartes's A Priori Proof"
      DCIE (Baltimore MD 1978) 1-25.

0662 Doney, W. "Some Recent Work on Descartes: A Bibliography" **PRA** 2
      (1976).
      Repr. in **DCIE** (Baltimore MD 1978) 299-312.

0663 Doney, W. <Discussion of 'Leibniz's Completion of Descartes's Proof'>
      SC 1 (1979) 221-23.
      Dis. of: Götterbarn, D.   **SL** 8 (1976).

0664 Doney, W. "Curley and Wilson on Descartes" **PRA** 6 (1980) No. 1376.
      Dis. of: Curley, E.M.   **Descartes Against the Skeptics**
                                      (Cambridge MA 1978).
                Wilson, M.D.   **Descartes** (London 1978).

0665 Doney, W. "Is Berkeley's a Cartesian Mind?" **Berkeley: Critical and
      Interpretive Essays,** ed. by C.M. Turbayne (Minneapolis MN 1982) 273-82.

0666 Doney, W. "Rationalism" **SJP** 21 Supp. (1983) 1-14.

0667 Doney, W. "L'argument de Descartes à partir de la toute-puissance"
      RDS 7 (1984) 59-68.

0668 Dore, C. "Descartes's Meditation V Proof of God's Existence" **The
      Existence and Nature of God,** ed. by A.J. Freddoso (Notre Dame IN 1983)
      143-60.
      Repr. in **Theism,** by C. Dore (Dordrecht 1984).

0669* Dörr, H. "Genealogisches zum Cogito. Uber ein Motiv des cartesischen Denkens" **Conceptus** 18 (1984) 104-15.

0670 Dorter, K. "First Philosophy: Metaphysics or Epistemology?" **D** 11 (1972) 1-22.

0671 Dorter, K. "Science and Religion in Descartes' Meditations" **Thomist** 37 (1973) 313-40.

0672 Dostert, L. "Descartes on Language" **Studies in Linguistics in Honor of George L. Trager,** ed. by M.E. Smith (The Hague 1972) 44-49.

0673* Doucet, L. "Descartes et la longevité des Patriarches" **Bulletin des Facultés Catholiques de Lyon** 66 (1982) 35-42.

0674 Doz, A. "Sur le passage du concept à l'être chez Descartes et Hegel" **RMM** 72 (1967) 216-30.

0675 Doz, A. "Sur la signification de 'instar archetypi', Descartes, 'Troisième Méditation'" **RP** 93 (1968) 380-87.

0676 Doz, A. "Quatre études brèves sur Descartes" **EP** (1984) 321-35.

0677 Draaisma, D. "Descartes en de Turingtest" **De Gids** 146 (1983) 368-73.

0678 Dreisbach, D.F. "Circularity and Consistency in Descartes" **CJP** 8 (1978) 59-78.

0679 Dreyfus, G. "La réfutation kantienne de l'idéalisme cartésien" **14IC** 5 (Wien 1968) 505-09.

0680 Dreyfus, G. "Descartes, les Cartésiens" **AGP** 59 (1977) 293-301.

0681 Drury, S. "The Relationship of Substance and Simple Natures in the Philosophy of Descartes" **CJP** Supp. 4 (1978) 37-58.

0682 Duarte, P.G. "Testimonio di presencia" **Homenaje a Xavier Zubiri** 2 (Madrid 1970) 109-12.

0683 Dubarle, D. "Sur la notion cartésienne de quantité de mouvement" **MAK** 2 (Paris 1964) 118-28.

0684 Duchesneau, F. "Du modèle cartésien au modèle spinoziste de l'être vivant" **CJP** 3 (1973-74) 539-62.

0685 Duchesneau, F. "La méthode cartésienne et l'interprétation de P.A. Schouls" **CJP** 4 (1974-75) 603-609.
Dis. of: Schouls, P.A.   **CJP** 4 (1974-75).
Dis. by: Schouls, P.A.   **CJP** 4 (1974-75).

0686 Duchesneau, F. "Malpighi, Descartes, and the Epistemological Problems of Iatromechanism" **Reason, Experiment, and Mysticism in the Scientific Revolution,** ed. by M.L. Righini Bonelli and W.R. Shea (New York 1975) 111-30.

0687 Duchesneau, F. "Modèle cartésien et modèle spinoziste de l'être vivant" **Cahiers Spinoza** 2 (1978) 241-85.

0688 Duchesneau, F. "The Role of Hypotheses in Descartes's and Buffon's Theories of the Earth" **PC** (Kingston and Montreal 1982) 113-25.

0689 Duchesneau, F. "The 'More Geometrico' Pattern in Hypotheses from Descartes to Leibniz" **NM** (Dordrecht 1983) 197-214.

0690 Dufourt, H. "L'oeuvre de Descartes" **RP** 97 (1972) 437-45.

0691 Dulmet, F. "A propos d'un centenaire. Voyage autour de Descartes" **Ecrits de Paris** 249 (1975) 88-102.

0692 Dunlap, J.T., and Hawkins, B.S. "Cogito, Ergo Sum: Neither Inference nor Performance" **Per** 57 (1976) 386-90.
Dis. of: Hintikka, J.   **PR** 71 (1962).

0693 Dunlop, C.E.M. "Introduction" **Philosophical Essays on Dreaming**, ed. by C.E.M. Dunlop (Ithaca NY 1977) 13-51.

0694 Dunoyer de Ségonzac, J.-M. "Deux hommes de sciences dans les pays de la Loire aux XVIe et XVIIe siècles: Francois Viete et René Descartes" **Comptes Rendus du 97e Congrès National des Sociétés Savantes. Section des Sciences** 1 (1976) 123-38.

0695 Durant, W., and Durant, A. "Philosophy Reborn: 1564-1648" Chap. xxiii of **The Age of Reason Begins. The Story of Civilization** 7 (New York 1961) 613-47.

0696 Dussel, E.D. "Supuestos modernos europeos de la dialéctica hegeliana" Chap. ii of **Método para una filosofía de la liberación. Superación analéctica de la dialéctica hegeliana** (Salamanca 1970); 2nd ed. (1974) 33-61.

0697 Eagle, M. "Privileged Access and the Status of Self-Knowledge in Cartesian and Freudian Conceptions of the Mental" **Philosophy of the Social Sciences** 12 (1982) 349-73.

0698 Eastwood, B.S. "Descartes on Refraction: Scientific Versus Rhetorical Method" **I** 75 (1984) 481-502.

0699 Eborowicz, W. "La conception augustinienne de la justice divine vindicative dans l'histoire de la théologie et de la philosophie depuis le XVIe siècle jusqu'au XVIIIe siècle" **Filosofia Oggi** 1 (1978) 37-53; 2 (1979) 141-88.

0700 Edgley, R. "Innate Ideas" **Royal Institute of Philosophy Lectures** 3 (1970) 1-33.

0701 Edie, J.M. "Descartes and the Phenomenological Problem of the Embodiment of Consciousness" **CE** (The Hague 1969) 89-115.

0702   Ehrmann, P.   "Descartes. Histoire d'une préface méconnue en France et inédite en Hollande"   **PRef** 25 (1960) 36-45.

0703* Ehrmann, P.   "Une préface méconnue en France et inédite en Hollande des Méditations de Descartes"   **Bouquiniste Français** 40 (1960).

0704   Ehrmann, P.   **Descartes. Complément à l'histoire d'une préface méconnue** (Paris 1962) [Privately printed]. Repr. in **Bouquiniste Français** 42 (1962) 98-107, 133-42.

0705   Ehrmann, P.   "Descartes. Une Edition détruite en 1667 réapparait en 1961. Conséquences"   **12CS** 1 (Louvain 1964) 282-85.

0706   Eisikovits, R.A.   "Descartes and Bertalanffy: Break or Continuity"   **JT** 19 (1984) 49-54.

0707   Elliot, R., and Smith, M.   "Descartes, God and the Evil Spirit"   **Soph** 17 (1978) No. 3, 33-36. Dis. by: O'Briant, W.H.   **Soph** 18 (1979) No. 2.

0708   Ellis, B.   "The Origin and Nature of Newton's Laws of Motion"   **Beyond the Edge of Certainty,** ed. by R.G. Colodny (Englewood Cliffs NJ 1965) 29-68.

0709   Elster, J.   "Descartes"   Chap. ii of **Leibniz et la formation de l'esprit capitaliste** (Paris 1975) 39-75.

0710* Elster, J.   **Rasjonalitet og Rasjonalisme. Okonomi, Filosofi og Vitenskap fra Descartes til Leibniz** (Oslo 1977).

0711   Elzinga, A.   "Huygens' Theory of Research and Descartes' Theory of Knowledge"   **ZAW** 2 (1971) 174-94; 3 (1972) 9-27.

0712   Engfer, H.-J.   "Widerlegt Descartes' Vierte Meditation den Gottesbeweis der Dritten? Zur Stellung Descartes' in der Philosophiegeschichte"   **SL** 16 (1984) 73-92.

0713   Equipe Descartes [Costabel, P., Armogathe, J.-R., Deschepper, J.-P., et al.].   "Bulletin Cartésien" [I] [1970]   **AP** 35 (1972) No. 2, 263-319.

0714   Equipe Descartes [Costabel, P., Armogathe, J.-R., Deschepper, J.-P., et al.].   "Bulletin Cartésien" [II] [1971]   **AP** 36 (1973) No. 4, 431-95.

0715   Equipe Descartes [Marion, J.-L., Guinamard, B., Costabel, P., et al.].   "Bulletin Cartésien III" [1972]   **AP** 37 (1974) No. 4, 453-97.

0716   Equipe Descartes [Marion, J.-L., Guinamard, B., Armogathe, J.-R., et al.].   "Bulletin Cartésien IV" [1973]   **AP** 38 (1975) No. 2, 253-309.

0717   Equipe Descartes [Marion, J.-L., Bilodeau-Guinamard, B., Armogathe, J.-R., et al.].   "Bulletin Cartésien V" [1974]   **AP** 39 (1976) No. 4, 445-94.

0718   Equipe Descartes [Marion, J.-L., Armogathe, J.-R., Buzon, C. de, et al.].   "Bulletin Cartésien VI" [1975]   **AP** 40 (1977) No. 3, 1-38.

0719 Equipe Descartes [Marion, J.-L., Armogathe, J.-R., Buzon, C. de, et al.]. "Bulletin Cartésien VII" [1976] **AP** 41 (1978) No. 4, 1-57.

0720 Equipe Descartes [Marion, J.-L., Armogathe, J.-R., Cahné, P.-A., et al.]. "Bulletin Cartésien VIII" [1977] **AP** 42 (1979) No. 4, 1-59.

0721 Equipe Descartes. "Contribution à la sémantèse d''ordre-ordo' chez Descartes" **Ordo,** ed. by M. Fattori and M. Bianchi. **2CIL** (Roma 1979) 279-328.

0722 Equipe Descartes [Rodis-Lewis, G., Marion, J.-L., Armogathe, J.-R., et al.]. "Bulletin Cartésien IX" [1978] **AP** 44 (1981) No. 1, 1-48.

0723 Equipe Descartes [Rodis-Lewis, G., Marion, J.-L., Armogathe, J.-R., et al.]. "Bulletin Cartésien X" [1979] **AP** 44 (1981) No. 4, 1-42.

0724 Equipe Descartes [Rodis-Lewis, G., Marion, J.-L., Armogathe, J.-R., et al.]. "Bulletin Cartésien XI" [1980] **AP** 45 (1982) No. 4, 1-65.

0725 Equipe Descartes [Rodis-Lewis, G., Marion, J.-L., Armogathe, J.-R., et al.]. "Bulletin Cartésien XII" [1981] **AP** 46 (1983) No. 3, 1-44.

0726 Equipe Descartes [Rodis-Lewis, G., Marion, J.-L., Armogathe, J.-R., et al.]. "Bulletin Cartésien XIII" [1982] **AP** 47 (1984) No. 3, 1-74.

0727 Equipe Descartes [Grimaldi, N., Marion, J.-L., Carraud, V., et al.] "Bulletin Cartésien XIV" [1983] **AP** 48 (1985) No. 3, 1-46.

0728 Erde, E.L. "Analyticity, the Cogito, and Self-Knowledge in Descartes' Meditations" **SwJP** 6 (1975) No. 1, 79-85.

0729 Ergetowski, R. "Liminaire II. Descartes et les polonais. Une reunion du Centre d'Histoire des Sciences Sociales (Warszawa)" **BC** 11 (1982) 33-36.

0730* Escriva de Romani, M.M. "Alejo Carpentier recurre a René Descartes" **Camp de l'Arpa: Revista de Literatura** 17-18 (1975) 49-51.

0731 Esze, J. "Deux documents inédits sur Descartes" **Acta Litteraria Academiae Scientiarum Hungaricae** 15 (1973) 230-44.

0732 Etchemendy, J. "The Cartesian Circle: Circulus ex tempore" **SC** 2 (1981) 5-42.
Dis. of: Kenny, A. **JP** 67 (1970).

0733 Etiemble. "Le sommeil de Joe Louis et de Descartes" **NRF** 12 (1964) 889-96.

0734 Evans, J.C., Jr. "Descartes" Chap. ii of **The Metaphysics of Transcendental Subjectivity: Descartes, Kant and W. Sellars** (Amsterdam 1984) 13-33.

0735 Evans, J.L. "Error and the Will" **P** 38 (1963) 136-48.

0736 Fabro, C. "Apriorismo ontologico e ateismo del cogito cartesiano"
      Pt. I, chap. i of **Introduzione all'ateismo moderno** (Roma 1964) 99-126;
      2nd ed., 2 vols. (1969).
      Trans. as "Ontological Apriorism and Atheism of the Cartesian Cogito"
      in **God in Exile: Modern Atheism. A Study of the Internal
      Dynamic of Modern Atheism, from its Roots in the Cartesian Cogito to
      the Present Day**, by A. Gibson (Westminster MD 1968) 91-119.

0737 Fafara, R.J. "An Eighth Set of Objections to Descartes' Meditations?"
      MS 57 (1979-80) 25-44.

0738 Faggiotto, P. "Deduzione matematica e argomentazione dialettica nella
      metafisica di Cartesio" **RFN** 59 (1967) 178-94.

0739 Faggiotto, P. "Renato Cartesio" Chap. iii of **Bacone - Galilei -
      Cartesio - Hobbes - Spinoza - Locke. Il problema della metafisica nel
      pensiero moderno** 1 (Padova 1969) 59-89.

0740* Faggiotto, P. "La negazione della soggettività. Note sulla critica
      empiristica al 'cogito' cartesiano" **Verifiche** 9 (1980) 159-76.

0741 Fahrenbach, H. "Endlichkeit des Bewusstseins und absolute Gewissheit
      bei Descartes" **Subjektivität und Metaphysik. Festschrift für Wolfgang
      Cramer**, ed. by D. Henrich and H. Wagner (Frankfurt 1966) 64-91.

0742 Fahrnkopf, R. "Cartesian Insanity" **A** 39 (1978-79) 68-70.
      Dis. of: DeHaven, S.   **A** 38 (1977-78).
      Dis. by: Welbourne, M.   **A** 40 (1979-80).

0743 Fahrnkopf, R. "Descartes, Welbourne, and Indubitable Beliefs" **A** 41
      (1980-81) 138-40.
      Dis. of: Welbourne, M.   **A** 40 (1979-80).
      Dis. by: Welbourne, M.   **A** 42 (1981-82).

0744 Falgueras Salinas, I. **La 'res cogitans' en Espinosa** (Pamplona 1976).

0745 Fanton d'Andon, J.-P. "Pascal et Descartes" Chapter of **L'horreur du
      vide. Expérience et raison dans la physique pascalienne** (Paris 1978).

0746 Farias, D. "Teologia e cosmologia nelle 'Meditazioni' cartesiane"
      RFN 54 (1962) 267-88.

0747 Farina, G. "Interpretazioni cartesiane" **Medicina nei Secoli** 19
      (1982) 221-24.

0748 Farina, P. "Sulla formazione scientifica di Henricus Regius: Santorio
      Santorio e il De statica medicina" **RCSF** 30 (1975) 363-99.

0749 Farina, P. "Il corpuscolarismo di Henricus Regius. Materialismo e
      medicina in un cartesiano olandese del Seicento" **Ricerche
      sull'atomismo del Seicento**, by U. Baldini et al. **Atti del Convegno
      di Studio di Santa Margherita Ligure (1976)** (Firenze 1977) 119-78.

0750   Farley, J.   "Abhorrence of Chance: The Seventeenth and Eighteenth
       Centuries"   Chap. ii of **The Spontaneous Generation Controversy from
       Descartes to Oparin** (Baltimore MD 1977) 8-30.
       Rev. by: Winsor, M.P.   **I** 71 (1980) 163-64.

0751   Faure, J.-P.   "Descartes et la naissance du matérialisme"   **Eur** 56
       (1978) 125-38.

0752   Federico, P.J.   **Descartes on Polyhedra. A Study of the De solidorum
       elementis** (Berlin 1982).

0753   Feil, E.   "Verstehen und Verständigung. Zur Problematisierung
       neuzeitlichen Wissenschaftsverständnisses"   **FZPT** 28 (1981) 206-52.

0754   Feldman, F.   "On the Performatory Interpretation of the Cogito"   **PR** 82
       (1973) 345-63.
       Dis. of: Hintikka, J.   **PR** 71 (1962).

0755   Feldman, F.   "Epistemic Appraisal and the Cartesian Circle"   **PS** 27
       (1975) 37-55.
       Dis. by: Markie, P.J.   **PS** 31 (1977).

0756   Feldman, F., and Levison, A.   "Anthony Kenny and the Cartesian Circle"
       JHP 9 (1971) 491-96.
       Dis. of: Kenny, A.   **Descartes** (1968).
       Dis. by: Kenny, A.   **JHP** 9 (1971).

0757   Felman, S.   "Madness and Philosophy or Literature's Reason"   **YFS** 52
       (1975) 206-28.
       Dis. of: Foucault, M.   **Folie et déraison** (Paris 1961).
                Derrida, J.   **RMM** 68 (1963); 69 (1964).
                Foucault, M.   **Folie et déraison** 2nd ed. (Paris
                                      1972).

0758* Fenzl, R.   "Pseudo-cartesianisches"   **Neusprachliche Mitteilungen aus
       Wissenschaft und Praxis** 20 (1967) 230-32.

0759   Fernández Rodríguez, J.L.   "La idea en Descartes"   **Anuario Filosófico**
       [Navarra] 9 (1976) No. 1, 111-61.

0760   Fernández Rodríguez, J.L.   "Las verdades eternas. Por qué Malebranche
       criticó el voluntarismo de Descartes"   **Anuario Filosófico** [Navarra]
       16 (1983) No. 2, 9-21.

0761   Ferrari, J.   "Kant, lecteur de Descartes"   Pt. I of **Les sources
       françaises de la philosophie de Kant** (Paris 1979) 22-78.

0762   Ferrari, O.   "La filosofía como liberación y el fundamento filosófico
       del cambio. Descartes-Kant-Hegel"   **Phil** 39 (1973) 85-88.

0763   Ferreras, J.I.   "La muerte di Descartes"   **Cuadernos Hispanoamericanos**
       97 (1974) 270-302.

0764   Ferrier, F. "Spontanéité et liberté: La discussion Gibieuf-Descartes" **EP** 28 (1973) 329-38.

0765   Ferrier, F. **La pensée philosophique du Père Guillaume Gibieuf (1583-1650). Etude bio-bibliographique.** 2 vols. (Lille 1976).

0766   Ferrier, F. "Dialectique de l'un et du néant chez Gibieuf" **RDS** 2 (1978) 64-71.

0767   Ferrier, F. **Un oratorien ami de Descartes. Guillaume Gibieuf et sa philosophie de la liberté** (Paris 1979).

0768   Feuer, L.S. "The Dreams of Descartes" **American Imago** 20 (1963) 3-26.

0769   Feuer, L.S. "Anxiety and Philosophy: The Case of Descartes" **American Imago** 20 (1963) 411-49.

0770   Fioravanti, L. "Il dubbio cartesiano e il realismo tomistico" **S. Tommaso nella storia del pensiero. Atti dell'VIII Congresso Tomistico Internazionale, 8. Studi Tomistici** 17 (1982) 173-80.

0771   Flage, D.E., and Glass, R.J. "Hume on the Cartesian Theory of Substance" **SJP** 22 (1984) 497-508.

0772* Flam, L. **Descartes. Het betoog over de methode (1637)** (Antwerpen 1962).

0773* Flam, L. "De ondergang van de traditionele godsverklaring van Descartes tot Kant" **Dialoog** 9 (1968-69) 320-43.

0774   Flanagan, O.J., Jr. "Minds and Bodies: René Descartes and the Possibility of a Science of Mind" Chap. i of **The Science of the Mind** (Cambridge MA 1984) 1-22.

0775   Fleckenstein, J.O. "Von Descartes zu Leibniz" **Mathematisch-Physikalische Semesterberichte zur Pflege des Zusammenhanges von Schule und Universität** 11 (1964-65) 129-43.

0776   Fleckenstein, J.O. "Die Gründung der exakten Wissenschaften im Zeitalter der Gegenreformation des Barock" Chap. ii of **Naturwissenschaft und Politik. Von Galilei bis Einstein** (München 1965) 33-89.

0777   Fleischer, M. "Die Krise der Metaphysik bei Descartes" **ZPF** 16 (1962) 68-83.

0778   Flew, A. "Descartes and the Cartesian Revolution" Chap. viii of **An Introduction to Western Philosophy** (Indianapolis IN 1971) 275-301.

0779   Flew, A. "Philosophical Doubt and Cartesian Certainty" Chap. ix of **An Introduction to Western Philosophy** (Indianapolis IN 1971) 302-30.

0780   Flores, R. "Delusions of Self: Descartes's Authorial Burden" **Kentucky Romance Quarterly** 25 (1978) 283-95.

0781 Flores, R. "Cartesian Striptease" **Sub-Stance** 12 (1983) 75-88.

0782 Flores, R. "Cartesian Striptease" Chap. iii of **The Rhetoric of Doubtful Authority: Deconstructive Readings of Self-Questioning Narratives, St. Augustine to Faulkner** (Ithaca NY 1984) 66-87.

0783 Floss, P. "Comenius und Descartes" **ZPF** 26 (1972) 231-53.

0784 Flury, V.J. "El grado cero de la interpretación" **Revista de Filosofía de la Universidad de Costa Rica** 19 (1981) 111-14.

0785 Flynn, B.C. "Descartes and the Ontology of Subjectivity" **MW** 16 (1983) 3-23.

0786 Fontan, P. "Une certaine idée de Dieu. Lecture de Descartes" **RT** 71 (1971) 349-66.

0787 Fontan, P. "Dieu, premier ou dernier connu. De Spinoza à saint Thomas d'Aquin" **RT** 74 (1974) 244-78.

0788 Fontan, P. "Du Malin Génie. Lecture de Descartes" **RT** 82 (1982) 436-48.

0789 Forbes, E.G. "Descartes and the Birth of Analytic Geometry" **Historia Mathematica** 4 (1977) 141-51.

0790 Forgie, J.W. "Frege's Objection to the Ontological Argument" **N** 6 (1972) 251-65.

0791 Forgie, J.W. "Existence Assertions and the Ontological Argument" **M** 83 (1974) 260-62.

0792 Forgie, J.W. "Is the Cartesian Ontological Argument Defensible?" **NS** 50 (1976) 108-21.

0793 Forguson, L. "Multi-Media Meditations" **Teaching Philosophy** 5 (1982) 301-09.

0794 Fortes, A. "Descartes, profeta de la revolución industrial" **Burgense. Collectanea Scientifica** 15 (1974) 207-74.

0795 Forti, U. "Le valutazioni della tecnica all'inizio dell'età moderna e il 'Discorso sul metodo' di Cartesio" **Cultura e Scuola** 5 (1966) 226-34.

0796 Fóscolo de Merckaert, N. "Les trois moments moraux du Discours de la Méthode" **RPL** 73 (1975) 607-27.

0797* Foti, V. "The Functions and Ordering of the Theistic Arguments in Descartes' 'Meditations'" **Auslegung** 4 (1976) 7-20.
      Dis. of: Kenny, A.   **FE** (Oxford 1969).
                Forgie, J.W.   **M** 83 (1974).

0798   Foucault, M. "Le grand renfermement" Chap. ii of **Folie et déraison. Histoire de la folie à l'âge classique** (Paris 1961) 56-91.
Dis. by: Derrida, J.   **RMM** 68 (1963); 69 (1964).
          Beyssade, J.-M.   **RMM** 78 (1973).
          Felman, S.   **YFS** 52 (1975).
          Giovannangeli, D.   **Cahiers Internationaux de Symbolisme** 40-41 (1980).
          D'Amico, R.   **The Structural Allegory** (Minneapolis MN 1984).

0799   Foucault, M. "Mon corps, ce papier, ce feu" App. 2 of **Folie et déraison. Histoire de la folie à l'âge classique,** 2nd ed. (Paris 1972) 583-603.
Trans. as "My Body, This Paper, This Fire" by G. Bennington. **Oxford Literary Review** 4 (1979) No. 1, 9-28
Dis. of: Derrida, J.   **RMM** 68 (1963); 69 (1964).
Dis. by: Beyssade, J.-M.   **RMM** 78 (1973).
          Felman, S.   **YFS** 52 (1975).
          B[ennington], G.P.   **Oxford Literary Review** 4 (1979) No. 1.
          Giovannangeli, D.   **Cahiers Internationaux de Symbolisme** 40-41 (1980).
          D'Amico, R.   **The Structural Allegory** (Minneapolis MN 1984).

0800* Frambourg, G. "Descartes à Suce" **Annales de Nantes et du Pays Nantais** 208 (1983) 42-43.

0801   France, P. "Descartes: La recherche de la vérité" Chap. ii, sect. 2 of **Rhetoric and Truth in France: Descartes to Diderot** (Oxford 1972) 40-67.

0802   Françon, M. "Montaigne, le Discours de la méthode de Descartes et l'humanisme" **Bulletin de la Société des Amis de Montaigne** Ser. 5 (1972) No. 1, 49-57.

0803   Frank, F.C. "Descartes' Observations on the Amsterdam Snowfalls of 4, 5, 6 and 9 February 1635" **Journal of Glaciology** 13 (1974) 535-39.

0804   Frankel, L. "Reason and Antecedent Doubt" **SJP** 22 (1984) 331-46.

0805   Frankfurt, H.G. "Memory and the Cartesian Circle" **PR** 71 (1962) 504-11.
Dis. by: Nelson, J.O.   **D** 3 (1964-65).

0806   Frankfurt, H.G. "Descartes' Validation of Reason" **APQ** 2 (1965) 149-56.
Repr. in **DCCE** (1967) 209-26.
Dis. by: Kulstad, M.   **SwJP** 8 (1977).

0807   Frankfurt, H.G. "A Reply to Mr. Nelson" **D** 4 (1965-66) 92-95.
Dis. of: Nelson, J.O.   **D** 3 (1964-65).

0808   Frankfurt, H.G. "Descartes's Discussion of His Existence in the Second Meditation" **PR** 75 (1966) 329-56.
Dis. of: Hintikka, J.   **PR** 71 (1962).
          Hintikka, J.   **PR** 72 (1963).

0809   Frankfurt, H.G.   **Demons, Dreamers, and Madmen: The Defense of Reason in Descartes' Meditations** (Indianapolis IN 1970).
Rev. by: Keefe, T.   **PB** 12 (1971) 6-10.
           Miller, L.G.   **D** 10 (1971) 839-43.
           Parsons, C.   **JP** 69 (1972) 38-46.
           A[rmogathe], J.-R. **BC** 2 (1973) 452-55.
           Sanford, D.   **PR** 82 (1973) 120-24.
           Govier, T.   **CJP** 3 (1973-74) 681-89.
           Nakhnikian, G.   **AGP** 56 (1974) 202-09.
           Watson, R.A.   **JHP** 14 (1976) 342-53.
Dis. by: Sievert, D.   **NS** 51 (1977).
           DeHaven, S.   **A** 38 (1977-78).

0810   Frankfurt, H.G.   "Descartes on the Creation of the Eternal Truths"   **PR** 86 (1977) 36-57.
Dis. by: Hauptli, B.W.   **ISP** 15 (1983).

0811   Frankfurt, H.G.   "Descartes on the Consistency of Reason"   **DCIE** (Baltimore MD 1978) 26-39.

0812   Freguglia, P.   "La 'Géométrie' di Descartes e la nascita della geometria analitica"   **Miscellanea Filosofica** (1981) 50-70.

0813* Freud, S.   "Lettre à Maxime Leroy sur quelques rêves de Descartes"   **RFP** 45 (1981) 5-7.
Dis. by: Pasche, F.   **RFP** 45 (1981) 9-30.

0814* Frutos, E.   "La moral de Séneca en Descartes"   **Actas del Congreso Internacional de Filosofía en Conmemoración de Séneca** 1 (Cordoba 1965) 137-61.

0815   Frutos, E.   "Realidad y límites de la resonancia de san Agustin en Descartes"   **Augustinus** 13 (1968) 219-48.

0816* Fullat, O., et al.   **Questions de Filosofía: Camus, Sartre, Ortega, D'Ors, Torres, Descartes, Llull** (Barcelona 1964).

0817   Funkenstein, A.   "Descartes, Eternal Truths, and the Divine Omnipotence"   **SHPS** 6 (1975) 185-99.
Repr. in **DPMP** (Brighton 1980) 181-95.

0818* Furlán, A.   "Descartes: Cuestiones gnoseológicas"   **Sapientia** 25 (1970) 209-22.

0819   Furlán, A.   "La intuición en Descartes"   **Arqué** 1 (1982) 7-39.

0820   Furth, M.   "Monadology"   **PR** 76 (1967) 169-200.

0821* G[...], J.   "Ce que fut la science pour René Descartes"   **Nature** [France] 3309 (1961) 43-44.

0822   Gabaude, J.-M.   "Descartes et la notion de nature humaine"   **EP** 16 (1961) No. 3, 277-80.

0823 Gabaude, J.-M. **Liberté et raison. La liberté cartésienne et sa**
réfraction chez Spinoza et chez Leibniz. 3 vols. (Toulouse 1970-74).
Rev. by: Etienne, J.   **RPL** 70 (1972) 144-48; 72 (1974)
781-88; 74 (1976) 114-15.
Lassègue, M.   **RP** 97 (1972) 197-98.
M[arion], J.-L.   **BC** 1 (1972) 275-82; 3 (1974) 467-68;
5 (1976) 463-64.
Quoniam, T.   **EP** (1973) 78-81.
Reix, A.   **RP** 101 (1976) 260-61.
Voisé, W.   **RS** 98 (1977) 352-54.
Goyard-Fabre, S.   **RMM** 83 (1978) 272-73.

0824 Gabaude, J.-M. "Descartes et la politique. De la conscience des
conflits à l'absence de conflit entre morale et politique" **Annales**
Publiées Trimestriellement par la Faculté des Lettres et Sciences
Humaines de Toulouse - Le Mirail 6 (1970) 19-26.

0825 Gabaude, J.-M. "Descartes-Spinoza et le mouvement historique de la
rationalité" **Pens** 194 (1977) 81-98.

0826 Gabaude, J.-M. "De quelques formes actuelles de l'anticartésianisme"
Eur 56 (1978) 106-10.

0827 Gabbey, A. "Les trois genres de découverte selon Descartes" **12CI** 2
(Paris 1970) 45-49.

0828 Gabbey, A. "Force and Inertia in Seventeenth-Century Dynamics" **SHPS**
2 (1971-72) 1-67.
Dis. by: C[ostabel], P.   **BC** 5 (1976) 489-91.

0829 Gabbey, A., ed. "Responsio ad Fragmentum Cartesii ex Epistola Henrici
Mori ad Claudium Clerselier" **Correspondance V,** ed. by C. Adam and P.
Tannery; new ed., ed. by P. Costabel, J. Beaude and A. Gabbey. Vol. 5
of **Oeuvres de Descartes** (Paris 1903); new ed. (Paris 1974) 628-47.

0830 Gabbey, A. "Appendice: Deuxième partie (Correspondance Descartes-More)"
Correspondance V, ed. by C. Adam and P. Tannery; new ed., ed. by P.
Costabel, J. Beaude and A. Gabbey. Vol. 5 of **Oeuvres de Descartes**
(Paris 1903); new ed. (Paris 1974) 668-78.

0831 Gabbey, A. "Anne Conway et Henry More. Lettres sur Descartes (1650-
1651)" **AP** 40 (1977) 379-404.

0832 G[abbey], A. "Descartes et Henry More. A propos de deux livres récents"
Review of **Cartesio in Inghilterra. Da More a Boyle,** by A. Pacchi [Roma
1973]; and of **Cartesiani e sociniani. Studio su Henry More,** by P.
Cristofolini [Urbino 1974]. **BC** 6 (1977) 2-14.

0833 Gabbey, A. "The English Fortunes of Descartes" Review of **Cartesio in**
Inghilterra. Da More a Boyle, by A. Pacchi [Roma 1973]. **BJHS** 11
(1978) 159-64.

0834 Gabbey, A. "Force and Inertia in the Seventeenth Century: Descartes and
Newton" **DPMP** (Brighton 1980) 230-320.

0835   Gabbey, A. "Philosophia Cartesiana Triumphata: Henry More (1646-1671)"
       PC (Kingston and Montreal 1982) 171-250.

0836   Gabbey, A., Marion, J.-L., et al. "Descartes" The Seventeenth
       Century: Supplement, ed. by H.G. Hall. Vol. 3A of A Critical
       Bibliography of French Literature, ed. by R.A. Brooks (Syracuse NY
       1983) 377-419.

0837   Gäbe, L. Descartes' Selbstkritik: Untersuchungen zur Philosophie des
       jungen Descartes (Hamburg 1972).
       Rev. by: Barwirsch, J.-F.   PLa 26 (1973) 9-11.
                 M[arion], J.-L.   BC 3 (1974) 468-72.
                 Caton, H.P.   PJ 37 (1975) 104-109.
                 Schmidt, G.   AGP 82 (1975) 206-09.
                 Vandenbulcke, J.   TF 57 (1975) 79-82.

0838   Gäbe, L. "Cartelius oder Cartesius. Eine Korrektur zu meinem Buche über
       'Descartes' Selbstkritik'" AGP 58 (1976) 58-59.
       Dis. of: Gäbe, L.   Descartes' Selbstkritik (Hamburg
                                         1972).

0839   Gäbe, L. "Zur Aprioritätsproblematik bei Leibniz-Locke in ihrem
       Verhältnis zu Descartes und Kant" SV (Bonn 1976) 75-106.

0840   Gäbe, L. "La Règle XIV. Lien entre géométrie et algèbre" AP 46
       (1983) 654-60.

0841   Gadoffre, G.F.A. "Le Discours de la méthode et la querelle des anciens"
       Modern Miscellany Presented to Eugène Vinaver by Pupils, Colleagues
       and Friends, ed. by T.E. Lawrenson, F.E. Sutcliffe and G.F.A. Gadoffre
       (Manchester 1969) 79-84.

0842   Gagnebin, S. "La révolution cartésienne" Pt. II, chap. i of A la
       recherche d'un ordre naturel (Neuchâtel 1971) 277-92.

0843   Gagnon, M. "Le rôle de la raison dans la morale cartésienne" Laval
       Théologique et Philosophique 25 (1969) 268-305.

0844   Galeazzi, U. "Cartesio e Kant nella 'Terminologia filosofica' di
       Adorno" RFN 76 (1984) 292-316.

0845   Galet, Y. "Passé simple et passé composé" Français Moderne 42 (1974)
       13-19.
       Dis. of: Dav, P.P.   Cahier Scientifique [Leningrad]
                                         212 (1959) 21-34.

0846   Galison, P. "Model and Reality in Descartes' Theory of Light"
       Synthesis [USA] 4 (1979) No. 4, 2-23.

0847   Galison. P. "Descartes's Comparisons: From the Invisible to the
       Visible" I 75 (1984) 311-26.

0848   Galli, G.   "Il Discorso sul metodo e le Meditazioni metafisiche de
       Cartesio"   Esposizione critica di opere filosofiche, ed. by C.
       Mazzantini et al.   Orientamenti filosofici e pedagogici 2 (Milano
       1962) 165-219.

0849   Galuzzi, M.   "Il problema delle Tangenti nella 'Géométrie' di Descartes"
       AHES 22 (1980) 37-51.

0850   Gambier, P.   "Un autre ennemi de Descartes. Le Pasteur André Rivet
       (1571-1648)"   Revue du Bas-Poitou et des Provinces de l'Ouest 75
       (1964) 184-94.

0851   Gandillac, M. de, et al.   "Discussion"   BSFP 76 (1982) 159-71.
       Dis. of: Marion, J.-L.   BSFP 76 (1982).

0852   Garagorri, P.   "Criterio y método"   Revista de Occidente 5, Tom. 16
       (1967) 277-300.

0853   Garber, D.   "Science and Certainty in Descartes"   DCIE (Baltimore MD
       1978) 114-51.

0854   Garber, D.   <Discussion of 'The Concept of Experience in Descartes'
       Theory of Knowledge'>   SC 1 (1979) 220-21.
       Dis. of: Clarke, D.M.   SL 8 (1976).

0855   Garber, D.   "Mind, Body, and the Laws of Nature in Descartes and
       Leibniz"   Contemporary Perspectives on the History of Philosophy.
       MSP 8 (1983) 105-33.

0856   Garber, D.   "Understanding Interaction: What Descartes Should Have Told
       Elisabeth"   SJP 21 Supp. (1983) 15-32.
       Dis. by: Ariew, R.   SJP 21 Supp. (1983).

0857   Garber, D., and Cohen, L.   "A Point of Order: Analysis, Synthesis, and
       Descartes's Principles"   AGP 64 (1982) 136-47.

0858   García Bacca, J.D.   "Modelo de reinterpretación sujetivista del
       universo. Renato Descartes (1596-1650)"   Dian 13 (1967) 1-54.

0859* García Bacca, J.D.   Lecciones de Historia de la Filosofía 1 (Caracas
       1972).

0860   García López, J.   El conocimiento natural de Dios. Un estudio a través
       Descartes y Santo Tomás (Murcia 1955).
       Repr. in El conocimiento de Dios en Descartes, by J. García López
       (Pamplona 1976).
       Rev. by: Dudley, J.   RPL 75 (1977) 498-500.
                  Vegas Gonzáles, S.   Arb 97 (1977) 131-32.
                  Hickman, L.A.   JHP 16 (1978) 475-76.

0861* García Suárez, A.   "Cartesianismo fuerte y cartesianismo debil a
       propósito de David Pears: Wittgenstein"   Teorema 8 (1972) 99-103.

0862* García, C.E. "La ciencia del siglo XVII y la filosofía cartesiana" **Revista de la Universidad de Caldas** 3 (1982) 54-63.

0863 Gargani, A.G. "Funzione dell'immaginazione e modelli della spiegazione scientifica in Harvey e Cartesio" **RCSF** 25 (1970) 250-74.

0864 Garin, E. "La vita e le opere di Cartesio" **Opere**, by René Descartes; tr. by E. Garin et al. 1 (Bari 1967) vii-clxxxvi. Repr. in **Vita e opere di Cartesio**, by E. Garin (Bari 1984).

0865 Garin, E. "Luca Tozzi, o la filosofia dei medici" **RCSF** 27 (1972) 75-78.

0866 Garin, E. "Lazare Meyssonnier e Descartes" **RCSF** 28 (1973) 199-201.

0867 Gaudiani, C. "La lumière cartésienne: Métaphore et phénomène optique" **Actes de New Orleans,** ed. by F.L. Lawrence. **PFSL** Supp. 5 (1982) 319-36.
Dis. by: Wolfe, P.   **PFSL** Supp. 5 (1982) 337-42.

0868 Gaudiani, C. "Light Metaphors in Pascal: The Bridge between Science and Literature" **PFSL** 10 (1983) 177-97.

0869 Gaukroger, S., ed. **Descartes: Philosophy, Mathematics and Physics** (Brighton 1980).
Rev. by: D[oney], W.   **BC** 11 (1982) 41-44.
            Millen, J.R.   **FS** 36 (1982) 198-99.
            Van de Pitte, F.P.   **Canadian Philosophical Reviews** 2 (1982) 96-99.
            Popkin, R.H.   **BJPS** 34 (1983) 182-83.

0870 Gaukroger, S. "Descartes' Project for a Mathematical Physics" **DPMP** (Brighton 1980) 97-140.

0871 Gavin, W.J. "The Meaning of a Person" **Existential Psychiatry** 7 (1969) No. 26-27, 33-35.

0872 Gawlick, G. "Die Funktion des Skeptizismus in der frühen Neuzeit" **AGP** 49 (1967) 86-97.

0873 Geach, P.T. "Omnipotence" **P** 48 (1973) 7-20.

0874 Gehin, E. "Descartes et Montesquieu: de l'objectivité de la nature à l'idée de système politique" **Revue Française de Sociologie** 14 (1973) 164-79.

0875 Gentile, L. "La scolastica, Cartesio e Bertrando Spaventa" **F** 26 (1975) 139-48.

0876 Gentils, R. "Vico, critique de Descartes" **Synthesis** [Romania] 5 (1978) 137-47.

0877 George, F. "La confirmation de l'esprit" **Liberté de l'Esprit** 7 (1984) 41-61.

0878 Gewirth, A. "The Cartesian Circle Reconsidered" **JP** 67 (1970) 668-85.
Dis. by: Kenny, A **JP** 67 (1970).

0879 Gewirth, A. "Descartes: Two Disputed Questions" **JP** 68 (1971) 288-96.
Dis. of: Kenny, A. **JP** 67 (1970).

0880 Geymonat, L. "Cartesio" Pt. IV, chap. ii of **Il Cinquecento. Il
Seicento. Storia del pensiero filosofico e scientifico** 2 (Milano
1970) 218-38.

0881 Gillispie, C.C. "The New Philosophy" Chap. iii of **The Edge of
Objectivity: An Essay in the History of Scientific Ideas** (Princeton
1960) 83-116.

0882 Gilson, E., and Langan, T. "René Descartes" Chap. vi of **Modern
Philosophy: Descartes to Kant. A History of Philosophy** 3 (New York
1963) 55-86.

0883 Gioberti, V. **Appunti inediti su Renato Cartesio. La storia della
filosofia,** ed. by E. Bocca and G. Tognon (Firenze 1981).

0884* Giordano, M. **Cartesio epistemologo. La forma cartesiana della scienza**
(Bari 1981).

0885* Giordano, M. "Cartesio e la dimensione epistemologica della filosofia"
**Vetera novis augere. Studi in onore di Carlo Giacon. 25. Convegno
degli Assistenti Universitari del Movimento di Gallarate** (Roma 1982)
309-22.

0886 Giorgiantonio, M. "Le 'nature semplici' cartesiane e la dottrina di
Epicuro" **Sop** 29 (1961) 492-94.

0887 Giorgiantonio, M. "Il problema cartesiano" **Sop** 37 (1969) 109-14.

0888 Giovannangeli, D. "La folie du cogito (Pour une lecture des
Meditations)" **Cahiers Internationaux de Symbolisme** 40-41 (1980) 59-77.
Dis. of: Foucault, M. **Folie et déraison** (Paris 1961).
Derrida, J. **RMM** 68 (1963); 69 (1964).
Foucault, M. **Folie et déraison** 2nd ed. (Paris
1972).

0889 Girolami, M. "La teoria di Cartesio dell'animale-macchina: 326 anni
dopo" **PSM** 7 (1963) No. 1, 3-24.

0890 Glenn, J.D., Jr. "Merleau-Ponty and the Cogito" **PTod** 23 (1979) 310-20.

0891* Glero, J.-P., and Le Rest, E. "La naissance du calcul infinitésimal au
XVIIe siècle" **Cahiers d'Histoire et de Philosophie des Sciences** 16
(1981).

0892 Glouberman, M. "Cartesian Substances as Modal Totalities" **D** 17
(1978) 320-43.

0893 Glouberman, M. "Conceptuality: An Essay in Retrieval" **KS** 70 (1979) 383-408.

0894 Glouberman, M. "The Dawn of Conceptuality: A Kantian Perspective" **Idealistic Studies** 9 (1979) 187-212.

0895 Glouberman, M. "Cartesian Probability and Cognitive Structure" **ZPF** 36 (1982) 564-79.

0896 Glouberman, M. "Consciousness and Cognition: From Descartes to Berkeley" **SL** 14 (1982) 244-65.

0897 Glouberman, M. "The Structure of Cartesian Scepticism" **SJP** 21 (1983) 343-57.

0898 Glouberman, M. "Mind and Body: Two Real Distinctions" **SJP** 22 (1984) 347-60.

0899 Glucksmann, A. "Pourquoi nous sommes si métaphysiques" Pt. II, chap. iv of **Les maîtres penseurs** (Paris 1977) 189-223.
Trans. as **The Master Thinkers,** by B. Pearce (New York 1980) 176-206.

0900 Gochet, P. "Le défi cybernétique" Review of **Le défi cybernétique,** by A. Robinet [Paris 1973]. **RIP** 27 (1973) 112-19.

0901 Gokieli, L.P. "Logiceskaja priroda dekartovskogo argumenta" **Voprosy Filosofii** 21 (1967) No. 3, 112-16.
Trans. as "On the Logical Character of Descartes' Argument" **Soviet Studies in Philosophy** 6 (1968) No. 4, 40-44.

0902 Goldschmidt, V. "Le paradigme platonicien et les 'Regulae' de Descartes" Chap. xiii of **Questions platoniciennes** (Paris 1970) 231-42.

0903* Golliet, P. "Descartes et les problèmes du style: La lettre latine de 1628 sur Guez de Balzac" **Handelingen van het XXVe Vlaams Filologencongres** [Antwerpen 1963] (Zellik [1965]) 199-207.

0904 Gombay, A. "'Cogito Ergo Sum': Inference or Argument?" **CS** (Oxford 1972) 71-88.

0905 Gombay, A. "Mental Conflict: Descartes" **P** 54 (1979) 485-500.

0906 Gombay, A. "Reply to F.C.T. Moore's 'Is the Intuition of Dualism Primary?'" **RIP** 37 (1983) 273-77.
Dis. of: Moore, F.C.T.   **RIP** 37 (1983).

0907 Gómez Pin, V., Le Doeuf, M., and Echeverría, J. **Conocer Descartes y su obra** (Barcelona 1979).

0908* Gómez Pin, V. **Descartes. El autor y su obra** (Barcelona 1984).

0909 Gómez, R. "La imaginación en Descartes y Kant" **Actas del Tercer Congreso Nacional de Filosofía** 2 (Buenos Aires 1982) 316-22.

0910* Gonin, A. "Descartes contre Harvey. De la circulation perpétuelle du sang aux passions de l'âme" **Mémoires de l'Académie des Sciences, Arts et Belles-Lettres de Lyon** 37 (1983) 71-87.

0911 Good, P. "Vom Schematismus einer realistischen Erkenntnistheorie" **FZPT** 24 (1977) 414-27.
Dis. of: Küng, G.   **FZPT** 24 (1977).

0912 Goode, T.M., and Wettersten, J.R. "How Do We Learn from Argument? Toward an Account of the Logic of Problems" **CJP** 12 (1982) 673-89.

0913 Goodhue, W.W. "Pascal's Theory of Knowledge: A Reaction to the Analytical Method of Descartes" **MS** 47 (1969-70) 15-35.

0914 Gordon, D. "Steiner on Cartesian Scepticism" **A** 39 (1978-79) 224.
Dis. of: Steiner, M.   **A** 39 (1978-79).

0915 Gori, G., ed. **Cartesio negli scritti di Paolo Rossi et al.** (Milano 1977).

0916 Gortari, E. de. "Oposición entre la física y la metafísica en Descartes" Chap. ii of **Siete ensayos filosóficos sobre la ciencia moderna** (México 1969) 2nd ed. (1974).

0917 Gotfredsen, E. "Corpus pineale. Cartesisk, circadisk eller hvad?" **Dansk Medicinhistorisk Arbog** (1973) 235-43.

0918 Götterbarn, D. "An Equivocation in Descartes' Proof for Knowledge of the External World" **Idealistic Studies** 1 (1971) 142-48.

0919 Götterbarn, D. "Leibniz's Completion of Descartes's Proof" **SL** 8 (1976) 105-112.
Dis. by: Doney, W.   **SC** 1 (1979).

0920 Gouhier, H. **Essais sur Descartes** (Paris 1937); 2nd ed. (1949); 3rd ed. (1973).

0921 Gouhier, H. **Les premières pensées de Descartes** (Paris 1958); 2nd ed. (1979).

0922* Gouhier, H. "L'oeuvre de Descartes et sa signification historique" **Gymnasium Helveticum** 16 (1961-62) 166-73.

0923 Gouhier, H. **La pensée métaphysique de Descartes** (Paris 1962); 2nd ed. (1969); 3rd ed. (1978).
Rev. by: Crippa, R.   **SFr** 7 (1963) 507-09.
         Rochot, B.   **RS** 84 (1963) 491-501.
         Rodis-Lewis, G.   **RP** 89 (1964) 85-89.

0924 Gouhier, H. "Les philosophes du XVIIe siècle devant l'histoire de la philosophie" **DsS** 54-55 (1962) 5-16.

0925 Gouhier, H. "Ce que le Vicaire doit à Descartes" **Présence de Jean-Jacques Rousseau. Entretiens de Genève 1962. Annales de la Société Jean-Jacques Rousseau** 35 (Paris 1963) 139-60.

0926 Gouhier, H. "Note sur G. Sebba, 'A "New" Descartes Edition?'" **JHP** 2 (1964) 71.
Dis. of: Sebba, G.   **JHP** 1 (1964).

0927 Gouhier, H. **Les grandes avenues de la pensée philosophique en France depuis Descartes** (Louvain 1966).

0928 Gouhier, H. "Le refus de la philosophie dans la nouvelle apologétique de Pascal" **Chroniques de Port-Royal** 20-21 (1972) 19-37.

0929 Gouhier, H. **Fénelon philosophe** (Paris 1977).
Rev. by: Brun, J.   **EP** (1978) 377-78.
         Kapp, V.   **Romanische Forschungen** 90 (1978) 102-05.
         Ca[hné], P.-A.   **BC** 8 (1979) 39-40.
         Orcibal, J.   **Revue d'Histoire Littéraire de la France** 80 (1980) 103-06.
         Riley, P.   **PR** 90 (1981) 285-89.

0930 Gouhier, H. "Fénelon et le cartésianisme" **Revue des Sciences Philosophiques et Théologiques** 61 (1977) 59-68.

0931 Gouhier, H. **Cartésianisme et augustinisme au XVIIe siècle** (Paris 1978).
Rev. by: Clair, P.   **SC** 1 (1979) 197-202.
         Battail, J.-F.   **SC** 1 (1979) 202-10.
         Ferrier, F.   **EP** (1980) 102-03.
         Adam, M.   **RP** 106 (1981) 351-54.
         A[rmogathe], J.-R.   **BC** 9 (1981) 34-36.

0932 Gouhier, H. "Les deux 'XVIIe siècles'" Chap. ii of **Etudes sur l'histoire des idées en France depuis le XVIIe siècle** (Paris 1980) 35-48.

0933 Gourmont, R. de. **Pour commenter Descartes** (Paris 1969).

0934 Goyard-Fabre, S. "Le problème de la matiére dans la philosophie de Descartes" **EL** 63 (1972) 31-36.

0935 Goyard-Fabre, S. "Descartes et la méthode" **EL** 63 (1972) 37-41.

0936 Goyard-Fabre, S. "L'erreur dans la philosophie de Descartes" **EL** 64 (1972) 39-42.

0937 Goyard-Fabre, S. "Descartes et Machiavel" **RMM** 78 (1973) 312-34.

0938 Gracia, J.J.E. "'A Supremely Great Being'" **NS** 48 (1974) 371-77.

0939 Grant, B. "Descartes, Belief and the Will" **P** 51 (1976) 401-19.
Dis. by: O'Hear, A.   **P** 54 (1979).

0940   Grassi, E. "G.B. Vico und das Problem des Beginns des modernen Denkens" **ZPF** 22 (1968) 491-509.

0941   Grathoff, R. "Grenze und Übergang: Bestimmungen einer cartesianischen Sozialwissenschaft" **Soziale Welt** 23 (1972) 383-400. Repr. in **Sachlichkeit. Festschrift zum 80. Geburtstag von Helmuth Plessner**, ed. by G. Dux and T. Luckmann (Opladen 1974) 223-41.

0942   Graves, J.C. "Descartes' Geometrization of Physics" Chap. vi of **The Conceptual Foundations of Contemporary Relativity Theory** (Cambridge MA 1971) 79-101.

0943   Gray, P.H. "The Problem of Free Will in a Scientific Universe: René Descartes to John Tyndall" **Journal of General Psychology** 80 (1969) 57-72.

0944   Grayeff, F. **Descartes** (London 1977).
        Rev. by: Gabaude, J.-M.   **RP** 103 (1978) 106-07.

0945   Greene, M. "Towards a Notion of Awareness" **Hegels Philosophische Psychologie**, ed. by D. Henrich. **Hegel Studien** Beih. 19 (1979) 65-80.

0946   Gregory, T. **Scetticismo ed empirismo. Studio su Gassendi** (Bari 1961).
        Rev. by: Crippa, R.   **SFr** 5 (1961) 542-43.

0947   Gregory, T. "Dio ingannatore e genio maligno. Nota in margine alle Meditationes di Descartes" **GCFI** 53 (1974) 477-516.

0948   Grene, M. "The Errors of Descartes" Chap. iii of **The Knower and the Known** (London 1966) 64-91.

0949   Grenet, C. **Descartes. Philosophe et savant** (Paris 1977).

0950   Griffin, N., and Harton, M. "Sceptical Arguments" **PQ** 31 (1981) 17-30.

0951   Grimaldi, N. "La dialectique du fini et de l'infini dans la philosophie de Descartes" **RMM** 74 (1969) 21-54.

0952   Grimaldi, N. **L'expérience de la pensée dans la philosophie de Descartes** (Paris 1978).
        Rev. by: Adam, M.   **DsS** 31 (1979) 418-19.
                  Beyssade, M.   **RP** 104 (1979) 219-21.
                  Caminade, P.   **Sud** 30 (1979) 144-45.
                  Magnard, P.   **SC** 2 (1981) 177-82.
                  M[arion], J.-L.   **BC** 9 (1981) 28-32.

0953   Grimm, R. "Cogito, ergo sum" **Theoria** 31 (1965) 159-73.

0954   Grimsley, R. "Kierkegaard and Descartes" **JHP** 4 (1966) 31-41.

0955   Grmek, M.D. "Réflexions sur des interprétations mécanistes de la vie dans la physiologie du XVIIe siècle" **Episteme** [Italia] 1 (1967) 17-30.

0956   Grmek, M.D. "Les idées de Descartes sur le prolongement de la vie et le mécanisme du vieillissement" **RHS** 21 (1968) 285-302.

0957   Grmek, M.D. "La notion de fibre vivante chez les médecins de l'école iatrophysique" **Clio Medica** 5 (1969-70) 297-318.

0958   Grmek, M.D. "Descartes gérontologiste" **12CI** 3B (Paris 1971) 25-30.

0959   Grmek, M.D. "A Survey of the Mechanical Interpretations of Life from the Greek Atomists to the Followers of Descartes" **Biology, History and Natural Philosophy,** ed. by A.D. Breck and W. Yourgrau (New York 1972) 181-95.

0960   Grmek, M.D. "Bibliographie complémentaire (Descartes et la médecine)" **BC** 9 (1981) 20-22.

0961   Groarke, L. "Descartes' First Meditation: Something Old, Something New, Something Borrowed" **JHP** 22 (1984) 281-301.

0962   Grosholz, E.R. "Descartes' Unification of Algebra and Geometry" **DPMP** (Brighton 1980) 156-68.

0963   Grosrichard, A. "'Ou suis-je?','Que suis-je?' (Réflexions sur la question de la place dans l'oeuvre de Jean-Jacques Rousseau, à partir d'un texte du Rêveries)" **Rousseau et Voltaire en 1978. Actes du Colloque International de Nice,** ed. by M.-H. Cotoni (Genève 1981) 338-65.

0964*   Grosso, G. "Il pensiero storico-filosofico di Olgiati e l'interpretazione della filosofia cartesiana" **Annali della Facoltà di Lettere e Filosofia dell'Università di Bari** 25-26 (1982-83) 503-18.

0965   Guehénno, J. "A propos de Descartes" **Entre le passé et l'avenir,** by J. Guehénno (Paris 1979) 110-15.

0966*   Guenancia, P. "Réflexions sur les rapports du mécanisme et de la finalité chez Descartes" **Cahiers Philosophiques** 2 (1980) 18-36.

0967   Guenancia, P. **Descartes et l'ordre politique: critique cartésienne des fondements de la politique** (Paris 1983).
        Rev. by: Gabaude, J.-M.   **RP** 109 (1984) 468-69.
                  Prieur, M.   **Quinzaine Littéraire** 414 (1984) 18-19.
                  Vergely, B.   **Esprit** 89 (1984) 202-04.
                  L[avigne], J.-F.   **BC** 14 (1985) 16-18.
                  Vergely, B.   **RMM** 90 (1985) 137-38.

0968   Guérin, M. "Le malin génie et l'instauration de la pensée comme philosophie" **RMM** 79 (1974) 145-76.
        Repr. in **Le génie du philosophe,** by M. Guérin (Paris 1979) 121-60.

0969   Gueroult, M. **Descartes selon l'ordre des raisons.** 2 vols. (Paris 1953); 2nd ed. (1968).
        Trans. as **Descartes' Philosophy Interpreted According to the Order of Reasons,** by R. Ariew. 2 vols. (Minneapolis MN 1984-85).

0970 Gueroult, M. "Le cogito et l'ordre des axiomes métaphysiques dans les Principia philosophiae Cartesianae de Spinoza" **AP** 23 (1960) 171-85. Repr. in **EDSM** (Hildesheim 1970) 64-78.

0971 Gueroult, M. "De la méthode prescrite par Descartes pour comprendre sa philosophie" **AGP** 44 (1962) 172-84. Repr. in **EDSM** (Hildesheim 1970) 9-21.

0972 Gueroult, M. "L'interprétation de Descartes" **Revue des Travaux de l'Académie des Sciences Morales et Politiques** 115 (1962) 239-52.

0973 Gueroult, M. "Animaux-machines et cybernétique" **Cahiers de Royaumont** 5 (1965) 7-15. Repr. in **EDSM** (Hildesheim 1970) 33-40.

0974 Gueroult, M. "La définition de la vérité (Descartes et Spinoza)" **12CS** 2 (Louvain 1965) 41-51. Repr. in **EDSM** (Hildesheim 1970) 55-63.

0975 Gueroult, M. "Note sur la première preuve 'a posteriori' chez Descartes" **RP** 91 (1966) 487-88.

0976 Gueroult, M. "The History of Philosophy as a Philosophical Problem" **Mon** 53 (1969) 563-87.

0977 Gueroult, M. **Etudes sur Descartes, Spinoza, Malebranche et Leibniz. Studien und Materialien zur Geschichte der Philosophie** 5 (Hildesheim 1970).
Rev. by: Specht, R. **PRu** 22 (1976) 71-77.

0978 Gueroult, M. "A propos du 'Rôle de l'idée de l'instant dans la philosophie de Descartes'" **RMM** 75 (1970) 354.
Dis. of: Wahl, J. **Du rôle de l'idée de l'instant dans la philosophie de Descartes** (Paris 1920).

0979 Gueroult, M. "Spinoza et les lois cartésiennes du mouvement" App. 4 of **L'âme (Ethique II). Spinoza** 2 (Paris 1974) 552-54.

0980 Gueroult, M. "Le schéma neuro-cérébral cartésien et le schéma spinoziste" App. 9 of **L'âme (Ethique II). Spinoza** 2 (Paris 1974) 570-71.

0981 Gueroult, M. "La doctrine cartésienne du libre arbitre et la critique de Spinoza" App. 19 of **L'âme (Ethique II). Spinoza** 2 (Paris 1974) 619-25.

0982 Gueroult, M. "L'excommunication majeure: Descartes et le cartésianisme" Chap. vii of **En Occident, des origines jusqu'à Condillac. Dianoematique. Livre I: Histoire de l'histoire de la philosophie** 1 (Paris 1984) 171-93.

0983* Guerrieri, L. "Cartesio, maestro di Cristina di Svezia" **CNSM** (Roma 1967) 260-80.

0984* Guerrieri, L. "Iatromeccanica e iatrochimica in Cartesio" **CNSM** (Roma 1967) 341-62.

0985 Guibert, A.J. **Bibliographie des oeuvres de René Descartes publiées au XVIIe siècle** (Paris 1976).
Rev. by: Arnoult, J.-M.   **Bulletin des Bibliothèques de France**
                           22 (1977) 787-88.
        Kirsop, W.   **BC** 7 (1978) 20-21.

0986 Gullace, G. "Sartre et Descartes. Le problème de la liberté" **Revue de l'Université Laval** 21 (1966) 107-25.

0987 Gumppenberg, R. von. "Uber die Seinslehre bei Descartes. Eine Untersuchung des Seinsbegriffes in den Meditationes de prima philosophia" **SbJP** 12-13 (1968-69) 131-39.

0988 Gunderson, K. "Descartes, La Mettrie, Language and Machines" **P** 39 (1964) 193-222.
Repr. in **Mentality and Machines,** by K. Gunderson (Garden City NY 1971) 1-38.

0989 Günther, O. "Die Weiterentwicklung des copernicanischen Weltbildes und seine Stellung in den Auseinandersetzungen am Ende des 16. und während des 17. Jahrhunderts" **Nicolaus Copernicus, 1473-1973. Das Bild vom Kosmos und die copernicanischen Revolution in den gesellschaftlichen und geistigen Auseinandersetzungen. Studien zum Copernicus-Jahr 1973,** ed. by J. Herrmann (Berlin 1973) 133-46.

0990* Gupta, S. **The Origin and Theories of Linguistic Philosophy: A Marxist Point of View** (New Delhi 1983).

0991 Gurwitsch, A. "Towards a Theory of Intentionality" **PPR** 30 (1969-70) 354-67.

0992 Gustafsson, L. "Die Wege der Freiheit bei Luther, Descartes und Sartre" **Schweizer Monatshefte** 64 (1984) 613-19.

0993 Guthke, K.S. "Das Risiko der Vernunft: Descartes und Cyrano de Bergerac" Chap. iii, sect. 5 of **Der Mythos der Neuzeit. Das Thema der Mehrheit der Welten in der Literatur- und Geistesgeschichte von der kopernikanischen Wende bis zur Science Fiction** (Bern 1983) 164-79.

0994 Gutteridge, J.D. "Coleridge and Descartes's 'Meditations'" **Notes and Queries** 20 (1973) 45-46.

0995 Guzzoni, G. "La metafisica di Cartesio" **Pensiero** 20 (1975) 1-38, 161-88.

0996 Gysi, L. **Platonism and Cartesiansim in the Philosophy of Ralph Cudworth** (Bern 1962).

0997 Haack, S. "Descartes, Peirce and the Cognitive Community" **Mon** 65 (1982) 156-81.

0998   Hacking, I.   "Leibniz and Descartes: Proof and Eternal Truths"
       Proceedings of the British Academy 59 (1973) 175-88.
       Repr. in **DPMP** (Brighton 1980) 169-80.

0999   Hacking, I.   "Five Parables" **Philosophy in History: Essays on the**
       Historiography of Philosophy, ed. by R. Rorty, J.B. Schneewind and Q.
       Skinner (Cambridge 1984) 103-24.

1000   Hahn, A.   "De Descartes à Claude Bernard. L'évolution du concept de
       méthode en médecine" **Humanisme actif. Mélanges d'art et de**
       littérature offerts à Julien Cain, ed. by E. Dennery.   2 (Paris 1968)
       335-48.

1001   Hahn, R.   **The Anatomy of a Scientific Institution: The Paris Academy of**
       Sciences, 1666-1803 (Berkeley CA 1971).

1002   Haight, J.   **The Concept of Reason in French Classical Literature 1635-**
       1690 (Toronto 1982).
       Rev. by: Doney, W.   **JHP** 22 (1984) 478-80.

1003   Halbfass, W.   **Descartes' Frage nach der Existenz der Welt.**
       Untersuchungen über die cartesianische Denkpraxis und Metaphysik
       (Meisenheim 1968).
       Rev. by: Klemmt, A.   **Eras** 21 (1969) 257-60.
                 Röd, W.   **PLa** 22 (1969) 273-77.
                 Corr, C.   **JHP** 8 (1970) 343-45.
                 Röd, W.   **PRu** 18 (1971) 78-92.

1004   Halbwachs, F.   "Le problème de la découverte des 'possibles' dans
       l'élaboration des lois du choc au XVIIe siècle" **Bulletin de**
       Psychologie 30 (1977) 240-46.

1005   Hall, A.R.   **From Galileo to Newton 1630-1720. The Rise of Modern**
       Science 3 (New York 1963).

1006   Hall, A.R., and Hall, M.B.   "Le monde scientifique à l'époque de
       Spinoza" **RS** 99 (1978) 19-32.

1007   Hall, M.B.   "Matter in Seventeenth Century Science" **The Concept of**
       Matter, ed. by E. McMullin (Notre Dame IN 1963) 344-67.
       Repr. in **The Concept of Matter in Modern Philosophy,** ed. by E.
       McMullin (Notre Dame IN 1978) 76-99.

1008   Hall, R.A.   "Cartesian Dynamics" **AHES** 1 (1960-62) 172-78.

1009   Hall, T.S.   "Microbiomechanics" Chap. iv of **Ideas of Life and Matter**
       1 (Chicago IL 1969) 250-63.

1010   Hall, T.S.   "Descartes's Physiological Method: Position, Principles,
       Examples" **Journal of the History of Biology** 3 (1970) 53-79.

1011   Hall, T.S.   "The Physiology of Descartes" **Treatise of Man,** by René
       Descartes; ed. and tr. by T.S. Hall (Cambridge MA 1972) xxvi-xxxiii.

1012   Hall, T.S.   <Notes>   **Treatise of Man,** by René Descartes; ed. and tr. by T.S. Hall (Cambridge MA 1972) passim.

1013   Haller, R.   "Das cartesische Dilemma"   **ZPF** 18 (1964) 369-85.

1014   Hallie, P.P.   "Montaigne and Descartes"   App. of **The Scar of Montaigne: An Essay in Personal Philosophy** (Middletown CT 1966) 157-75.

1015   Hamlyn, D.W.   "The Rationalists"   Chap. v of **Sensation and Perception: A History of the Philosophy of Perception** (London 1961) 62-92.

1016   Hammacher, K.   "Einige methodische Regeln Descartes' und das erfindende Denken"   **ZAW** 4 (1973) 203-23.
       Dis. by: Rathmann, B.   **PFSL** 7 (1980).

1017   Hammacher, K.   "La raison dans la vie affective et sociale selon Descartes et Spinoza"   **EP** (1984) 73-81.

1018   Hammer, F.   "Personale Leiblichkeit"   **SbJP** 19 (1974) 199-218.

1019   Han, P.   "The Passions in Descartes and Racine's Phèdre"   **Romance Notes** 11 (1969-70) 107-09.

1020   Hanfling, O.   "Can There be a Method of Doubt?"   P 59 (1984) 505-11.

1021   Hankins, T.L.   **Jean d'Alembert: Science and Enlightenment** (Oxford 1970).
       Dis. by: Cane, E.   I 67 (1976).

1022   Hankins, T.L.   "Response"   I 67 (1976) 276-78.
       Dis. of: Cane, E.   I 67 (1976).

1023   Harms, J.   "Sein und Zeit bei Cartesius"   **Neue Zeitschrift für Systematische Theologie und Religionsphilosophie** 18 (1976) 277-94.

1024   Haroche, C.   "Lecture dialectique du cartésianisme"   **Eur** 56 (1978) 110-24.

1025   Haroche, M.-P.   "Philosophie et religion chez Daniel-Paul Schreber"   **Liberté de l'Esprit** 1 (1982) 31-86.

1026   Harré, R.   "Powers"   **BJPS** 21 (1970) 81-101.

1027   Harries, K.   "Irrationalism and Cartesian Method"   **Journal of Existentialism** 6 (1965-66) 295-304.

1028   Harries, K.   "Descartes, Perspective, and the Angelic Eye"   **YFS** 49 (1973) 28-42.

1029   Harris, E.E.   "Materialism and Existentialism"   Review of **The Phenomenon of Life,** by H. Jonas [New York 1966].   **Human Context** 4 (1972) 339-49.

1030 Harrison, J. Review of **Descartes: The Project of Pure Enquiry**, by B. Williams [Harmondsworth 1978]. **M** 90 (1981) 122-35.

1031 Harrison, J. "The Incorrigibility of the Cogito" **M** 93 (1984) 321-35.

1032 Hart, A. "Descartes' 'Notions'" **PPR** 31 (1970-71) 114-22.

1033 Hart, A. "Descartes on Re-identification" **JHP** 13 (1975) 17-26.

1034 Harth, E. **Cyrano de Bergerac and the Polemics of Modernity** (New York 1970).

1035 Harth, E. "Classical Innateness" **YFS** 49 (1973) 212-30.

1036 Harth, E. "Exorcising the Beast: Attempts at Rationality in French Classicism" **PMLA** 88 (1973) 19-24.

1037 Hartmann, O.J. "Mensch, Maschine, Lebewesen. Problematik der 'res cogitans' und 'res extensa'" **Scheidewege** 3 (1973) 533-44.

1038 Hartnack, J. "Descartes" Chapter of **History of Philosophy** (Odense 1973) 84-95.

1039 Hartnack, J. "A Note on the Logic of One of Descartes' Arguments" **IPQ** 15 (1975) 181-84.

1040 Hatfield, G.C. "Force (God) in Descartes' Physics" **SHPS** 10 (1979) 113-40.
      Dis. by: C[ostabel], P. **BC** 10 (1981) 35-37.

1041 Hauptli, B.W. "Doubting 'Descartes' Self-Doubt'" **PRA** 6 (1980) No. 1399.
      Dis. of: Sievert, D. **PR** 84 (1975).

1042 Hauptli, B.W. "Frankfurt on Descartes: Consistency or Validation of Reason?" **ISP** 15 (1983) 59-70.
      Dis. of: Frankfurt, H.G. **Demons, Dreamers, and Madmen** (Indianapolis IN 1970).
               Frankfurt, H.G. **DCIE** (Baltimore MD 1978).

1043 Hausman, A. "Innate Ideas" **Studies in Perception: Interrelations in the History of Philosophy and Science,** ed. by P.K. Machamer and R.G. Turnbull (Columbus OH 1978) 200-30.

1044 Hayward, S. "'Res brutae' and Diderot's Nun, Suzanne Simonin" **Diderot Studies** 20 (1981) 109-23.

1045 Heckmann, H.-D. "What a Res Cogitans is - and Why I am One" **R** 25 (1983) 121-36.

1046 Heidegger, M. "Der europäische Nihilismus" Chap. v of **Nietzsche** 2 (Pfullingen 1961) 31-256.
      Trans. as "Le nihilisme européen" in Vol. 2 of **Nietzsche,** by P. Klossowski (Paris 1971) 31-203.

Trans. as "European Nihilism" in **Nihilism,** by F.A. Capuzzi. Vol. 4 of **Nietzsche,** ed. and tr. by D.F. Krell (San Francisco CA 1982) 1-196. Rev. by: M[arion], J.-L. **BC** 2 (1973) 455-59.

1047 Heidegger, M. "Einleitung zu 'Was ist Metaphysik?' Der Rückgang in den Grund der Metaphysik" **Wegmarken,** by M. Heidegger (Frankfurt 1967) 195-211.
Trans. in **Questions I,** by H. Corbin et al. (Paris 1968) 23-45.

1048 Heidsieck, F. "Honor and Nobility of Soul: Descartes to Sartre" **IPQ** 1 (1961) 569-92.

1049 Heidsieck, F. "L'amour selon Descartes d'après la lettre à Chanut du 1er février 1647 (Commentaire)" **RP** 97 (1972) 421-36.

1050 Heil, J. "Doxastic Incontinence" **M** 93 (1984) 56-70.
Dis. by: Vinci, T. **M** 94 (1985).

1051 Heimsoeth, H. "Die dualistische Substanzen-Ontologie. Descartes' als Dualismus in der Weltstruktur" Chap. viii of **Atom, Seele, Monade. Historische Ursprünge und Hintergrunde von Kants Antinomie der Teilung** (Mainz 1960) 319-25.

1052 Heinekamp, A. "Ein ungedrückter Brief Descartes' an Roderich Dotzen" **SL** 2 (1970) 1-12.

1053 Henley, K. "Cartesian Ethics" **PF** 9 (1977-78) 429-39.

1054 Hennigfeld, J. "Zweifel und Uberzeugung. Peirces Kritik an der Cartesischen Zweifelsargumentation" **Perspektiven der Philosophie** 9 (1983) 235-52.

1055 Henrich, D. **Der ontologische Gottesbeweis. Sein Problem und seine Geschichte in der Neuzeit** (Tübingen 1960).

1056 Henry, M. "Sur l'ego du cogito" **PaRa** (Paris 1983) 97-112.

1057 Henson, J.R. "Descartes and the ECG Lettering Series" **Journal of the History of Medicine** 26 (1971) 181-86.

1058 Henze, D.F. "Descartes on Other Minds" **APQ** Mon. 6 (Oxford 1972) 41-56.
Dis. by: Van de Pitte, F.P. **PPR** 35 (1974-75).

1059 Henze, D.F. "Descartes vs. Berkeley: A Study in Early Modern Metaphilosophy" **Met** 8 (1977) 147-63.

1060 Hepp, N. "Humanisme et cartésianisme: La guerre ou la paix?" **TLL** 13 (1975) No. 2, 451-61.

1061* Herrera Restrepo, D. "El Discurso del Método 'Primer manifiesto' de la ciencia moderna" **Revista de Filosofía** [México] 9 (1976) 7-20.

1062* Herrlinger, R. "Auf der Suche nach dem Sitz der Seele" **Zeitschrift für Arztliche Fortbildung** 54 (1965) 798-805.

1063 Herrmann, F.-W. von. "Sein und Cogitationes - Zu Heideggers Descartes-Kritik" **Durchblicke: Martin Heidegger zum 80. Geburtstag,** ed. by V. Klostermann (Frankfurt 1970) 235-54.

1064 Herrmann, F.-W. von. **Husserl und die Meditationen des Descartes** (Frankfurt 1971).

1065 Herrmann, R.-D. "Descartes' Scheme of a Machine in the 'Traité de l'homme'" **SL** Supp. 13 (1974) 115-19.

1066 Her[r]mann, R.-D. "Newton, Descartes, and the Cogitationes" **Theoria cum praxi. Zum Verhältnis von Theorie und Praxis im 17. und 18. Jahrhundert, IV. SL** Supp. 22 (1982) 143-48.

1067 Hesse, M.B. "The Corpuscular Philosophy" Chap. v of **Forces and Fields: The Concept of Action at a Distance in the History of Physics** (London 1961) 98-125.

1068 Heyd, M. "Jean-Robert Chouet et l'introduction du cartésianisme à l'Académie de Genève" **Bulletin de la Société d'Histoire et d'Archéologie de Genève** 15 (1972-75) 125-53.

1069 Heyd, M. "From a Rationalist Theology to Cartesian Voluntarism: David Derodon and Jean-Robert Chouet" **JHI** 40 (1979) 527-42.

1070 Heyd, M. **Between Orthodoxy and the Enlightenment: Jean-Robert Chouet and the Introduction of Cartesian Science in the Academy of Geneva** (The Hague 1982).
Rev. by: Watson, R.A. **JHP** 23 (1985) 259-60.

1071 Heyndels, R. "Le Voyage du Monde de Descartes, du Père Gabriel Daniel. Présentation générale." **Annales de l'Institut de Philosophie** [Bruxelles] (1976) 67-95; (1977) 43-61.

1072 Heyndels, R. "Un jésuite dans la lune à la fin du XVIIème siècle" **RDS** 2 (1978) 17-31.

1073 Hickerson, S.R. "Complexity and the Meaning of Freedom" **American Journal of Economics and Sociology** 43 (1984) 91-101.

1074 Hill, C. "Why Cartesian Intuitions are Compatible with the Identity Thesis" **PPR** 42 (1981-82) 254-65.

1075 Hilton, P., and Pedersen, J. "Descartes, Euler, Poincaré, Polya - and Polyhedra" **Enseignement Mathématique** 27 (1981) 327-43.

1076 Hinman, L.M. "Descartes' Children: The Skeptical Legacy of Cartesianism" **NS** 56 (1982) 355-70.

1077 Hintikka, J. "Cogito, Ergo Sum: Inference or Performance?" PR 71 (1962) 3-32.
Repr. in DCCE (Garden City NY 1967) 108-39.
Repr. in Knowledge and the Known, by J. Hintikka (Dordrecht 1974) ch. v.
Dis. by: Weinberg, J.R. PR 71 (1962).
Carney, J.D. PR 71 (1962).
Leyden, W. von AS 63 (1962-63).
Frankfurt, H.G. PR 75 (1966).
Booth, C.S. Journal of Critical Analysis 4 (1972).
Mitton, R. M 81 (1972).
Feldman, F. PR 82 (1973).
Dunlap, J.T. Per 57 (1976).
Walton, D. D 16 (1977).

1078 Hintikka, J. "Cogito, Ergo Sum as an Inference and a Performance" PR 72 (1963) 487-96.
Dis. of: Weinberg, J.R. PR 71 (1962).
Carney, J.D. Pr 71 (1962).
Dis. by: Frankfurt, H.G. PR 75 (1966).
Feldman, F. PR 82 (1973).

1079 Hintikka, J. "A Discourse on Descartes's Method" DCIE (Baltimore MD 1978) 74-88.

1080 Hintikka, J., and Remes, U. "On the Significance of the Method of Analysis in Early Modern Science" Chap. ix of The Method of Analysis (Dordrecht 1974) 105-17.

1081 Hinton, J.M. "Quantification, Meinongism and the Ontological Argument" PQ 22 (1972) 97-109.
Dis. of: Kenny, A. Descartes (New York 1967).

1082 Hirsch, W. "Die Aporie des Willens" Sein und Geschichtlichkeit. Karl-Heinz Volkmann-Schluck zum 60. Geburtstag, ed. by I. Schüssler and W. Janke (Frankfurt 1974) 177-94.

1083 Hobart, M.E. "'Number' and 'Substance' in Descartes" Chap. ii of Science and Religion in the Thought of Nicolas Malebranche (Chapel Hill NC 1982) 23-45.
Rev. by: Watson, R.A. JHP 21 (1983) 570-71.

1084 Hobson, M. "Du Theatrum Mundi au Theatrum Mentis" RSH 167 (1977) 379-94.

1085 Hodgson, F. "A Notion of Reading Process in Early French Essays" French Literature Series 9 (1982) 1-8.

1086 Hoeven, P. van der. Metafysica en fysica bij Descartes (Gorinchem 1961).

1087 Hoeven, P. van der. Descartes. Wetenschap en wijsbegeerte (Baarn 1972).

1088 Hoeven, P. van der. **De cartesiaanse fysica in het denken van Spinoza** (Leiden 1973).

1089 Hoeven, P. van der. "Over Spinoza's interpretatie van de cartesiaanse fysica, en de betekenis daarvan voor het systeem der ethica" **TF** 35 (1973) 27-86.

1090 Hoeven, P. van der. "The Significance of Cartesian Physics for Spinoza's Theory of Knowledge" **Spinoza on Knowing, Being and Freedom,** ed. by J.G. van der Bend (Assen 1974) 114-25.

1091 Hoeven, P. van der. "Filosoferen over de methode. De manier waarop Descartes en Pascal over de wiskundige methode denken, brengt enkele centrale inzichten van hun gehele filosoferen aan het licht" **TF** 38 (1976) 54-97.

1092 Hofer, H. "Der Weg der Philosophie von Descartes zu Pascal" **Reformatio** 13 (1964) 33-42, 116-20.

1093 Hoffmann, P. "Féminisme cartésien" **TLL** 7 (1969) 83-105.

1094 Hoffmann, P. "Modèle mécaniste et modèle animiste. De quelques aspects de la représentation du vivant chez Descartes, Borelli et Stahl" **RSH** 186-87 (1982) 199-211.

1095* Hofmann, J.E. "Descartes und das debeaunesche Problem" **Humanismus und Technik** 15 (1973) 3-5.

1096 Holland, A.J. "Scepticism and Causal Theories of Knowledge" **M** 86 (1977) 555-73.

1097 Hommes, U. "Sicherheit als Mass der Freiheit? Descartes' Idee der mathesis universalis und die praktische Philosophie der Neuzeit" **Gegenwart und Tradition. Strukturen des Denkens. Eine Festschrift für Bernhard Lakebrink,** ed. by C. Fabro (Freiburg 1969) 105-24.

1098 Hommes, U. "Der Begriff des Unendlichen im Denken der Neuzeit" **Wissenschaft und Weltbild** 25 (1972) 96-112.

1099 Hooker, M. "Descartes' Argument for the Claim that his Essence is to Think" **Grazer Philosophische Studien** 1 (1975) 143-63.

1100 Hooker, M., ed. **Descartes: Critical and Interpretive Essays** (Baltimore MD 1978).
Rev. by: Cavallo, G.   **F** 30 (1979) 585-92.
           Powell, B.   **PQ** 30 (1980) 149-50.
           Clarke, D.M.   **PB** 22 (1981) 12-14.
           B[rykman], G.   **BC** 10 (1981) 12-15.
           Sievert, D.   **SC** 2 (1981) 183-88.

1101 Hooker, M. "Descartes's Denial of Mind-Body Identity" **DCIE** (Baltimore MD 1978) 171-85.

1102 Hooker, M. "De Re Belief" **Dia** 13 (1978) 59-71.

1103   Hooker, M.   "The Deductive Character of Spinoza's Metaphysics"   **PBS**
(Washington DC 1980) 17-34.

1104*   Hooker, M.   "René Descartes (1596-1650)"   Chap. i of **The Age of Reason and the Enlightenment: René Descartes to Montesquieu**, ed. by G. Stade. **European Writers** 3 (New York 1984) 1-22.

1105*   Hoorn, W. van.   "Descartes en de psychologie van vandaag"   **Wijsgerig Perspectief op Maatschappij en Wetenschap** 12 (1971-72) 295-307.

1106   Horowitz, L.K.   **Love and Language: A Study of the Classical French Moralist Writers** (Columbus OH 1977).

1107   Horowitz, T.   "Stipulation and Epistemological Privilege"   **PS** 44 (1983) 305-18.

1108   Horst, R. ter.   "Calderonian Cartesianism: The Iconography of the Mind in La Exaltación de la Cruz"   **Esprit Créateur** 15 (1975) 286-304.

1109   Hottois, G.   "Miroirs historiques de la contemporanéité langagière" Review of **Le langage à l'âge classique**, by A. Robinet [Paris 1978]. **RIP** 33 (1979) 570-86.

1110   Hubbeling, H.G.   "Spinoza comme précurseur du reconstructivisme logique dans son livre sur Descartes"   **SL** 12 (1980) 88-95.

1111   Hubbeling, H.G.   "Arnold Geulincx, origineel vertegenwoordiger van het Cartesio-Spinozisme"   **ANTW** 75 (1983) 70-80.

1112   Hubener, W.   "Descartes-Zitate bei Clauberg. Zum Quellenwert frühcartesianischer Kontroversliteratur für die Descartesforschung" **SL** 5 (1973) 233-39.

1113   Hübner, K.   "Descartes' Rules of Impact and Their Criticism. An Example of the Structure of Processes in the History of Science"   **Essays in Memory of Imre Lakatos**, ed. by R.S. Cohen. (Dordrecht 1976) 299-310.

1114   Hughes, R.D., III.   "Descartes' Ontological Argument as Not Identical to the Causal Arguments"   **NS** 49 (1975) 473-85.
Dis. of: Imlay, R.A.   **NS** 43 (1969).
                Humber, J.M.   **NS** 44 (1970).
                Imlay, R.A.   **NS** 45 (1971).

1115   Hughes, R.D., III.   "Liminaire. Le 'cercle' des Méditations: un état des recherches récentes"   **BC** 7 (1978) 1-12.

1116   Humber, J.M.   "Descartes' Ontological Argument as Non-Causal"   **NS** 44 (1970) 449-59.
Dis. of: Imlay, R.A.   **NS** 43 (1969).
Dis. by: Imlay, R.A.   **NS** 45 (1971).
                Hughes, R.D., III   **NS** 49 (1975).

1117 Humber, J.M. "Doubts about 'Descartes's Self-Doubt'" **PR** 87 (1978) 253-58.
Dis. by: Sievert, D.   **PR** 84 (1975).

1118 Humber, J.M. "Recognizing Clear and Distinct Perceptions" **PPR** 41 (1980-81) 487-507.

1119 Humphrey, T.B. "How Descartes Avoids the Hidden Faculties Trap" **JHP** 12 (1974) 371-77.
Dis. of: Norton, D.F.   **JHP** 6 (1968).
Dis. by: Norton, D.F.   **JHP** 12 (1974).

1120 Humphrey, T.B. "Schopenhauer and the Cartesian Tradition" **JHP** 19 (1981) 191-212.

1121 Hund, J. "A Crack in the Foundations of Descartes's Theory of Knowledge" **South African Journal of Philosophy** 3 (1984) 125-29.

1122 Hunter, J.A. "Descartes' Skepticism: A New Criticism" **SwJP** 8 (1977) No. 1, 109-17.

1123 Hunter, J.F.M. "The Difference between Dreaming and Being Awake" **M** 92 (1983) 80-93.

1124 Hurtado, G.C. "Analitica del Recurso del Método" **Revista de Filosofía de la Universidad de Costa Rica** 17 (1979) 57-61.

1125 Hussain, S. "Locke on Personal Identity" **PPJ** 10 (1971) No. 1, 112-19.

1126 Hussain, S. "Descartes' Concept of a Person" **PPJ** 11 (1973) No. 2, 108-18.

1127 Hutchison, K. "What Happened to Occult Qualities in the Scientific Revolution?" **I** 73 (1982) 233-53.

1128 Hutin, S. **Henry More. Essai sur les doctrines théosophiques chez les Platoniciens de Cambridge** (Hildesheim 1966).

1129 Idoniboye, D.E. "Descartes and His Clear and Distinct Ideas" **Cahiers Philosophiques Africains** 5 (1974) 25-35.

1130 Ijsseling, S. "Francis Bacon, René Descartes and the New Science" Chap. ix of **Rhetoric and Philosophy in Conflict: An Historical Survey** (The Hague 1976) 60-70.

1131 Iltis, C. "Leibniz and the Vis Viva Controversy" **I** 62 (1971) 21-35.

1132 Iltis, C. "The Decline of Cartesianism in Mechanics: The Leibnizian-Cartesian Debates" **I** 64 (1973) 356-73.

1133 Imlay, R.A. "Descartes' Ontological Argument" **NS** 43 (1969) 440-48.
Dis. by: Humber, J.M.   **NS** 44 (1970).
          Hughes, R.D., III   **NS** 49 (1975).

1134 Imlay, R.A. "Descartes' Ontological Argument: A Causal Argument" **NS**
      45 (1971) 348-51.
      Dis. of: Humber, J.M.   **NS** 44 (1970).
      Dis. by: Hughes, R.D., III   **NS** 49 (1975).

1135 Imlay, R.A. "Intuition and the Cartesian Circle" **JHP** 11 (1973) 19-27.

1136 Imlay, R.A. "Science, Necessity and the Cartesian Circle" **SL** 9
      (1977) 255-65.

1137 Imlay, R.A. "Arnauld on Descartes' Essence: A Misunderstanding" **SL**
      11 (1979) 134-45.

1138 Imlay, R.A. "Descartes' Two Hypotheses of the Evil Genius" **SL** 12
      (1980) 205-14.

1139 Imlay, R.A. "Descartes and Indifference" **SL** 14 (1982) 87-97.

1140 Immerwahr, J. "Descartes' Two Cosmological Proofs" **NS** 56 (1982)
      346-54.

1141 Ishiguro, H. "Reply to Jacques Bouveresse" **RIP** 37 (1983) 311-18.
      Dis. of: Bouveresse, J.   **RIP** 37 (1983).

1142 Isolle, J. "Un disciple de Descartes: Louis de La Forge" **DsS** 92
      (1971) 99-131.

1143 Itard, J. "Descartes ou le triomphe de l'algèbre" **Atomes** 21 (1966)
      59-64.

1144 Itard, J. "La lettre de Torricelli à Roberval, d'octobre 1643" **RHS**
      28 (1975) 113-24.

1145 Jacob, P. "La politique avec la physique à l'âge classique. Principe
      d'inertie et conatus: Descartes, Hobbes et Spinoza" **Dialectiques** 6
      (1974) 99-121.

1146 Jaffé-Freem, E. "Amsterdam vu par quelques écrivains français"
      Septentrion [Nederland] 4 (1975) 5-17.

1147 Jager, B. "The Three Dreams of Descartes: A Phenomenological
      Exploration" **Review of Existential Psychology and Psychiatry** 8 (1968)
      195-213.

1148* Jaki, S.L. "The Milky Way from Galileo to Wright" **Journal of the
      History of Astronomy** 26 (1972) 199-204.

1149 Jamieson, K.M. "Pascal vs. Descartes: A Clash over Rhetoric in the
      Seventeenth Century" **Communication Monographs** 43 (1976) 44-50.

1150 Jandin, P.-P. "L'oblique" **Exercices de la Patience** 2 (1981) 167-80.

1151 Janik, L.G. "A Renaissance Quarrel: The Origin of Vico's Anti-
      Cartesianism" **New Vico Studies** 1 (1983) 39-50.

1152   Janke, W.   Review of **Commercium mentis et corporis,** by R. Specht
       [Stuttgart 1966]. **PRu** 18 (1971) 92-105.

1153   Jankowitz, W.-G.   "Der Cartesianische Zweifel als Versuch einer
       Grundlegung vorurteilsfreien Wissenschaft" Chap. ii of **Philosophie und
       Vorurteil. Untersuchung zur Vorurteilshaftigkeit von Philosophie als
       Propädeutik einer Philosophie des Vorurteils** (Meisenheim 1975) 25-43.

1154* Janne, H.   "René Descartes, la médecine et la 'morale'" **Revue de
       l'Institut de Sociologie** No. 3-4 (1983) 289-92.

1155   Jarrett, C.   "Cartesian Pluralism and the Real Distinction" **SJP** 19
       (1981) 347-60.

1156   Jarrety, M.   "La voix de Descartes et la main de Pascal: Note sur Valéry
       et l'écriture philosophique" **NRF** No. 375 (1984) 62-71.

1157   Jaynes, J.   "The Problem of Animate Motion in the Seventeenth Century"
       JHI 31 (1970) 219-34.

1158   Jean, B., and Mouret, F.   Chaps. i-x of **Montaigne, Descartes et Pascal
       par la dissertation,** by B. Jean and F. Mouret (Manchester 1971) 61-124.
       Rev. by: Topliss, P.   **FS** 27 (1973) 450-51.

1159* Jervis, G.   **Presenza e identità. Lezioni di psicologia** (Milano 1984).

1160   Johanson, A.E.   "Paper Doubt, Feigned Hesistancy, and Inquiry"
       Transactions of the Charles S. Peirce Society 8 (1972) 214-30.

1161   Johnson, B.T.   "A Dialogue on Epistemology between René Descartes and
       Henri Poincaré" **Di** 25 (1982-83) 41-47.

1162   Johnston, J.M.   "Cartesian Lucidity" **F** 19 (1968) 663-70.

1163   Joja, A.   "Descartes et le modèle mathématique" **Analele Universitatii
       Bucuresti. Acta Logica** 14 (1971) 5-27.

1164   Joja, A.   "Les entités abstraites chez Galilée, Descartes et Leibniz"
       Revue Roumaine des Sciences Sociales. Série Philosophie et Logique 17
       (1973) 3-35, 307-14.

1165   Jolibert, B.   "L'enfance des philosophes" Chapter of **L'enfance au
       XVIIe siècle,** (Paris 1981) 75-101.
       Rev. by: Millet, L.   **EP** (1984) 120-21.

1166   Jolley, N.   "Leibniz and Descartes: God and Creation" **TKR** (1981) 56-66.

1167   Joly, A.   "Cartésianisme et linguistique cartésienne: mythe ou realité?"
       Beiträge zur Romanischen Philologie 11 (1972) 86-94.
       Dis. of: Chomsky, N.   **Cartesian Linguistics** (New York 1966).

1168   Jones, H.   "Descartes" Pt. II, ch. iii of **Pierre Gassendi 1592-1655:
       An Intellectual Biography** (Nieuwkoop 1981) 135-203.

1169   Jones, W.T.   "Somnio ergo sum: Descartes's Three Dreams" [OWith an appendix: Descartes's Olympica, tr. by J.F. Benton]   PL 4 (1980) 145-66.

1170   Joulia, P.   Descartes et la sagesse mésoccidentale (Torino 1960).

1171* Joulia, P.   "Vingt ans d'histoire à Descartes. Création et organisation du Musée Descartes (1960-1980)"   Revue de l'Enseignement Philosophique 12 (1980) 82-83.

1172   Joyce, W.B., and Joyce, A.   "Descartes, Newton, and Snell's Law" Journal of the Optical Society of America 66 (1976) 1-8.

1173   Judge, B.   "Thoughts - And Their Contents"   APQ 20 (1983) 365-74.

1174   Judovitz, D.   "Autobiographical Discourse and Critical Praxis in Descartes"   PL 5 (1981) 91-107.

1175   Judovitz, D.   "Le Discours de la méthode: théorie du sujet comme pratique littéraire"   Actes de New Orleans, ed. by F.L. Lawrence. PFSL Supp. 5 (1982) 343-62.
       Dis. by: Battail, J.-F.   PFSL Supp. 5 (1982) 363-68.

1176   Judrin, R.   "Sur Descartes"   NRF 15 (1967) 128-31.

1177   Jurgens, M., and Mesnard, J.   "Quelques pièces exceptionnelles découvertes au Minutier central des notaires de Paris 1600-1650, II" Revue d'Histoire Littéraire de la France 79 (1979) 739-54.

1178   Kadler, E.H.   "Descartes, Malherbe, Madame de Sévigné, Fénelon, Mademoiselle de Scudéry, Scarron, Saint-Evremond" Chap. i of Literary Figures in French Drama (1784-1834) (The Hague 1969) 13-27.

1179   Kahan, T.   "Descartes, Pascal et la physique moderne"   Sciences et l'Enseignement des Sciences 21-22 (1962) 56-62.

1180   Kahl-Furthmann, G.   "Philosophische Interpretation. Ein Wort zur dritten Auflage zu Karl Jaspers' Schrift 'Descartes and die Philosophie'" ZPF 14 (1960) 127-38.
       Dis. of: Jaspers, K.   Descartes und die Philosophie
                                     (Berlin 1937); 3rd ed. (1956).

1181   Kalin, M.G.   "Freedom and Authority: A Look Back at Descartes" Listening 17 (1982) 120-25.

1182   Kalocsai, D.   "A propos de la morale 'définitive' de Descartes"   Etudes sur Descartes, by E. Rozsnyai, D. Kalocsai and Z. Tordai (Budapest 1964) 65-133.

1183   Kalocsai, D.   "Uber Descartes' moralische Ansichten"   Deutsche Zeitschrift für Philosophie 12 (1964) 290-309.

1184   Kalocsai, D.   Le problème des règles de la morale 'provisoire' de Descartes (Budapest 1973).
       Rev. by: Migasiński, J.   Etyka 13 (1974) 260-62.

1185 Kaloyeropoulos, N.A. "Le principe de la distinction chez Descartes"
RMM 83 (1978) 333-58.

1186 Kamiya, M. **La théorie cartésienne du temps** (Tokyo 1982).

1187 Kamlah, W. "Der Anfang der Vernunft bei Descartes--autobiographisch und
historisch" **AGP** 43 (1961) 70-84.

1188 Kane, G.S. "The Beginnings of Modern Thought: Philosophy and Theology
in the 17th Century" **Illinois Quarterly** 34 (1971) No. 2, 28-51.

1189 Kaplan, F. "La récusation probabiliste du cogito" **RP** 97 (1972) 401-19.

1190* Karling, S. "The Descartes Monument in the Adolf Fredrik Church,
Stockholm" **Nationalmuseum Bulletin** Fasc. 4 (1981) 145-64.

1191 Kaulbach, F. "Beschreibung und Mathesis Universalis. Descartes" Chap.
iii of **Philosophie der Beschreibung** (Köln 1968) 147-53.

1192 Kearns, E.J. "Descartes" Chap. ii of **Ideas in Seventeenth-Century
France** (Manchester 1979) 32-81.
Rev. by: Clair, P.   **SC** 2 (1981) 202-08.
          Assaf, F.   **PFSL** 16 (1982) 386-88.

1193 Keaton, A.E. "Descartes' Method" **SwJP** 5 (1974) No. 1, 89-95.

1194 Keefe, T. "Descartes's 'Morale Provisoire': A Reconsideration" **FS** 26
(1972) 129-42.

1195 Keefe, T. "Descartes's 'Morale Définitive' and the Autonomy of Ethics"
Romanic Review 64 (1973) 85-98.

1196 Keeling, S.V. **Descartes** (London 1934); 2nd ed. (1968).
Rev. by: Keefe, T.   **PB** 10 (1969) 14-15.

1197* Keezer, W.S. "Historical and Philosophical Aspects of Iatrochemistry
and Iatromechanics. Part III: René Descartes: Dualist Mechanist"
Texas Journal of Medicine 61 (1965) 52-56.

1198* Kelly, M.J. "The Cartesian Circle: Descartes' Response to Scepticism"
JT 5 (1970) 64-71.

1199 Kelly, M.J. "Are Egos but Modes in Descartes?" **PF** 11 (1979-80) 80-85.

1200 Kennington, R. "Descartes' 'Olympica'" **Social Research** 28 (1961)
171-204.

1201 Kennington, R. "René Descartes 1596-1650" **History of Political
Philosophy,** ed. by L. Strauss and J. Cropsey (Chicago IL 1963) 379-96;
2nd ed. (1972) 395-414.

1202 Kennington, R. "The Finitude of Descartes' Evil Genius" **JHI** 32
(1971) 441-46.
Dis. by: Caton, H.P.   **JHI** 34 (1973).

1203 Kennington, R. "The 'Teaching of Nature' in Descartes' Soul Doctrine" **RM** 26 (1972-73) 86-117.

1204 Kennington, R. "Reply to Caton" **JHI** 34 (1973) 641-43.
Dis. of: Caton, H.P.   **JHI** 34 (1973).
Dis. by: Caton, H.P.   **JHI** 34 (1973).

1205 Kennington, R. "Descartes and Mastery of Nature" **Organism, Medicine, and Metaphysics: Essays in Honor of Hans Jonas on his 75th Birthday,** ed. by S.F. Spicker (Dordrecht 1978) 201-23.

1206 Kennington, R., ed. **The Philosophy of Baruch Spinoza** (Washington DC 1980).

1207 Kennington, R. "Analytic and Synthetic Methods in Spinoza's Ethics" **PBS** (Washington DC 1980) 293-318.

1208 Kenny, A. "Cartesian Privacy" **Wittgenstein: The Philosophical Investigations,** ed. by G. Pitcher (Garden City NY 1966) 352-70. Repr. in **The Anatomy of the Soul,** by A. Kenny (Oxford 1973) 113-28.
Dis. by: Solomon, R.C.   **SJP** 12 (1974).
        Davies, K.   **PQ** 31 (1981).

1209 Kenny, A. "Descartes on Ideas" **DCCE** (Garden City NY 1967) 227-49. Repr. in **Descartes: A Study of His Philosophy,** by A. Kenny (New York 1968) 96-125.

1210 Kenny, A. **Descartes: A Study of his Philosophy** (New York 1968).
Rev. by: Halbfass, W.   **JHP** 7 (1969) 210-12.
        Henderson, G.P.   **PQ** 19 (1969) 81-83.
        Röd, W.   **PRu** 18 (1971) 82-84.
        Nakhnikian, G.   **AGP** 56 (1974) 202-09.

1211 Kenny, A. "Descartes' Ontological Argument" **FE** (Oxford 1969) 18-36.
Dis. by: Malcolm, N.   **FE** (Oxford 1969).
        Penelhum, T   **FE** (Oxford 1969).
        Sosa, E.   **FE** (Oxford 1969).
        Williams, B.   **FE** (Oxford 1969).
        Brecher, R.   **Soph** 14 (1975) No. 3.

1212 Kenny, A. "Reply" **FE** (Oxford 1969) 58-62.
Dis. of: Malcolm, N.   **FE** (Oxford 1969).
        Penelhum, T.   **FE** (Oxford 1969).
        Sosa, E.   **FE** (Oxford 1969).
        Williams, B.   **FE** (Oxford 1969).

1213 Kenny, A. "The Cartesian Circle and the Eternal Truths" **JP** 67 (1970) 685-700.
Dis. of: Gewirth, A.   **JP** 67 (1970).
Dis. by: Gewirth, A.   **JP** 68 (1971).
        Montague, R.   **AGP** 59 (1977).
        Etchemendy, J.   **SC** 2 (1981).

1214 Kenny, A. "A Reply by Anthony Kenny" **JHP** 9 (1971) 497-98.
Dis. of: Feldman, F.,
and Levison, A. **JHP** 9 (1971).

1215 Kenny, A. "Descartes on the Will" **CS** (Oxford 1972) 1-31.
Repr. in **The Anatomy of the Soul,** by A. Kenny (Oxford 1973) 81-112.
Dis. by: Caton, H.P. **JP** 72 (1975).

1216 Kenny, A. "R.C. Solomon's 'On Cartesian Privacy'" **SJP** 12 (1974)
537-38.
Dis. of: Solomon, R.C. **SJP** 12 (1974).

1217 Kenny, A. "'The First Person'" **Intention and Intentionality,** ed. by
C. Diamond (Ithaca NY 1979) 3-13.
Dis. of: Anscombe, G.E.M. **Mind and Language** (Oxford 1975).

1218 Kenny, A. "The Cartesian Spiral" **RIP** 37 (1983) 247-56.
Dis. by: Bouveresse, J. **RIP** 37 (1983).

1219 Kenshur, O. "Fiction and Hypothesis in Voltaire" **Eighteenth Century**
24 (1983) 39-50.

1220 Keohane, N.O. "A Variety of Loves and the Sovereignty of Will" Chap.
vi of **Philosophy and the State in France: The Renaissance to the
Enlightenment** (Princeton NJ 1980) 183-212.
Rev. by: Major, J.R. **Renaissance Quarterly** 34 (1981)
234-36.

1221 Kern, R. "Bacon, Descartes and the Background of Music" **Centennial
Review** 22 (1978) 231-54.

1222* Khan, Q. "Ghazali and Descartes" **PPC** 12 (1965) 389-93.

1223 Kim, C.-T. "Cartesian Dualism and the Unity of a Mind" **M** 80 (1971)
337-53.

1224 Kimmerle, G. **Kritik der identitätslogischen Vernunft. Untersuchung zur
Dialektik der Wahrheit bei Descartes und Kant** (Königstein 1982).

1225 King-Farlow, J. "Myths of the Given and Cogito Proofs" **PS** 12 (1961)
49-53.

1226 Kirkinen, H. **Les origines de la conception moderne de l'homme-machine.
Le problème de l'âme en France à la fin du règne de Louis XIV (1670-
1715)** (Helsinki 1960).
Rev. by: Rochot, B. **RS** 82 (1961) 143-45.
Raven, F. **Eras** 16 (1962) 129-33.
Spink, J.S. **FS** 16 (1962) 275-76.

1227 Kirsop, W. "Les Meditationes de prima philosophia de Descartes"
Chapter of **Bibliographie matérielle et critique textuelle** (Paris 1970)
61-67.

1228 Kirwan, C.A. "Truth and Universal Assent" **CJP** 11 (1981) 377-94.

1229* Klein, T. "The Problem of Abnormality" **Philosophical Topics** Supp.
      (1982) 7-22.

1230 Klemmt, A. **Descartes und die Moral** (Meisenheim 1971).
      Rev. by: Vandenbulcke, J.   **TF** 37 (1975) 96-100.

1231 Klever, W.N.A. "Spinoza's methodebegrip" **ANTW** 74 (1982) 28-49.
      Dis. by: Bobeldijk, H.   **ANTW** 74 (1982).

1232 Klever, W.N.A. "Spinoza geen Cartesiaan" **ANTW** 74 (1982) 197-98.
      Dis. of: Bobeldijk, H.   **ANTW** 74 (1982).

1233 Kline, G.L. "Randall's Reinterpretation of the Philosophies of
      Descartes, Spinoza, and Leibniz" **Naturalism and Historical
      Understanding: Essays on the Philosophy of John Herman Randall, Jr.,**
      ed. by J.P. Anton (Buffalo NY 1967) 83-93.

1234 Kline, M. "Coordinate Geometry" Chap. xv of **Mathematical Thought from
      Ancient to Modern Times** (New York 1972) 302-24.

1235 Kline, M. "The Mathematization of Science" Chap. xvi of **Mathematical
      Thought from Ancient to Modern Times** (New York 1972) 325-41.

1236 Kluge, E. "Cartesianische Anthropologie" **Münchener Medizinische
      Wochenschrift** 115 (1973) 946-49.

1237 Knapp, B.L. "Descartes, 'The Dreams Came from Above'" Chap. i of
      Dream and Image (Troy NY 1977) 25-60.

1238 Knowlson, J. "The Philosophical Language" Chap. iii of **Universal
      Language Schemes in England and France, 1600-1800** (Toronto 1975) 65-111.

1239 Knudsen, O., and Moller Pedersen, K. "The Link between 'Determination'
      and Conservation of Motion in Descartes' Dynamics" **Centaurus** 13
      (1968) 183-86.

1240* Köhler, H. "Wo aber bleibt der Mensch? Von der cartesianischen
      Kürzungsregel und der Mathematisierung der Welt" **Zeitschrift für
      Ganzheitsforschung** 28 (1984) 163-82.

1241* Köhler, H. "Wo aber bleibt der Mensch? Von der cartesianischen
      Kürzungsregel und der Mathematisierung der Welt" **Vierteljahrsschrift
      für Wissenschaftliche Padagogik** (1984) 332-55.

1242 Kojima, H. "Zur philosophischen Erschliessung der religiösen Dimension.
      Uberlegungen im Anschluss an Descartes, Husserl und den Zen-Buddhismus"
      PJ 85 (1978) 56-70.

1243 Köpeczi, B. "La Politique des cartésiens en Hongrie et en Transylvanie
      au XVIIe siècle et au début du XVIIIe siècle" **Studia Historica
      Academiae Scientiarum Hungaricae** 103 (1975) 3-21.
      Repr. in **Eur** 56 (1978) 87-105.

1244   Kopper, J.   "Descartes und Crusius über 'Ich denke' und leibliches Sein des Menschen"   **KS** 67 (1976) 339-52.

1245   Körner, F.   "Das cartesische Grundprinzip der neuzeitlichen Philosophie und seine gnoseologische Fragwürdigkeit: Eine historisch-kritische Voruntersuchung zur reflexionsphänomenologischen Erkenntniskritik" **SbJP** 17-18 (1973-74) 93-120.

1246   Kottukapally, J.   "Husserl's Critique of his Cartesian Way"   **IPQ** 22 (1982) 145-56.

1247   Kourim, Z.   "Le nouveau 'Discours de la méthode' de Condillac"   **RMM** 79 (1974) 177-95.

1248   Kouznetsov, B.   "La notion cartésienne de l'inertie et la science moderne"   **MAK** 1 (Paris 1964) 361-66.

1249   Koyré, A.   "Newton and Descartes"   Chap. iii of **Newtonian Studies** (Cambridge MA 1965) 53-200. Trans. in **Etudes newtoniennes** (Paris 1968) 85-242.

1250   Krailsheimer, A.J.   "Descartes"   Chap. ii of **Studies in Self-Interest from Descartes to La Bruyère** (Oxford 1962) 31-46.

1251   Kraus, P.A.   "From Universal Mathematics to Universal Method: Descartes's 'Turn' in Rule IV of the Regulae" **JHP** 21 (1983) 159-74.

1252   Krejtman, C.   **Pour Descartes. Le processus logique de la pensée confuse** (Paris 1982).

1253   Kremer-Marietti, A.   "La philosophie cartésienne vue par Auguste Comte" **RDS** 1 (1976) 140-50.

1254   Kretzmann, N.   "On Rose's 'Cartesian Circle'"   **PPR** 26 (1965-66) 90-92.
Dis. of: Rose, L.E.   **PPR** 26 (1965-66).
Dis. by: Rose, L.E.   **PPR** 26 (1965-66).

1255   Krieger, L.   "The One that Got Away"   **Proceedings of the American Philosophical Society** 128 (1984) 248-51.

1256* Kruck, G.   **René Descartes: 1596-1650. Eine Auseinandersetzung mit seiner Philosophie im Vergleich zu Kant und aus heutiger Sicht** (Zürich 1983).

1257   Krutch, J.W.   "One of the Greatest of Men Who Made One of the Greatest of Mistakes"   Chap. v of **And Even If You Do: Essays on Man, Manners, and Machines** (New York 1967) 289-95.

1258   Kuhns, R.   "Metaphor as Plausible Inference in Poetry and Philosophy" **PL** 3 (1979) 225-38.

1259   Kujawski, G. de Mel[l]o.   **Descartes existencial** (São Paulo 1969).

1260 Kujawski, G. de Mello. "Descartes e o Brasil" **Convivium** [Brasil] 9 (1970) 409-12.

1261 Kuklick, B. "Seven Thinkers and How They Grew: Descartes, Spinoza, Leibniz; Locke, Berkeley, Hume; Kant" **Philosophy in History: Essays on the Historiography of Philosophy,** ed. by R. Rorty, J.B. Schneewind and Q. Skinner (Cambridge 1984) 125-39.

1262 Kulstad, M. "Frankfurt's Interpretation of Descartes' Validation Of Reason" **SwJP** 8 (1977) No. 2, 7-16.
       Dis. of: Frankfurt, H.G.   **APQ** 2 (1965).

1263 Kumar, D. "Doubt and Descartes' Method" **Visva-Bharati Journal of Philosophy** 3 (1966-67) 101-11.
       Dis. of: Sibajiban   **PPR** 24 (1963-64).

1264 Küng, G. "Pouvons-nous connaître les choses telles qu'elles sont? L'anticartésianisme contemporain et ses limites" **FZPT** 24 (1977) 397-413.
       Dis. by: Good, P.   **FZPT** 24 (1977).

1265 Kunkel, J. "Dreams, Metaphors and Scepticism" **PTod** 25 (1981) 307-16.

1266 Kuntz, P.G. "The Dialectic of Historicism and Anti-historicism" **Mon** 53 (1969) 656-69.

1267 Kurrik, M.J. "The Genealogy of Negation" Chap. i of **Literature and Negation** (New York 1979) 1-81.

1268 Kuspit, D.B. "Epoché and Fable in Descartes" **PPR** 25 (1964-65) 30-51.

1269 La Croix, R.R. "Descartes on God's Ability to Do the Logically Impossible" **CJP** 14 (1984) 455-75.

1270* Labastida, J. **Producción, ciencia y sociedad de Descartes a Marx** (México 1969); 9th ed. (1980).

1271 Lachterman, D.R. "Descartes and the Philosophy of History" **IJP** 4 (1983) 31-46.
       Dis. by: Rosen, S.   **IJP** 4 (1983).

1272 Lafleur, L.J. "Descartes' Place in History" **CE** (The Hague 1969) 3-13.

1273* Lafrance, Y. "O Discurso do método de René Descartes" **Revista da Universidade Católica de São Paulo** 23 (1962) 391-433.

1274* Lamacchia, A. "Il problema dell'anima nelle Meditazioni metafisiche di Cartesio" **Annali della Facoltà di Lettere e Filosofia dell'Università di Bari** 7 (1961) 5-39.
       Repr. in **L'uomo e il suo destino** (Padova 1963) 44-66.

1275 Lamanna, E.P. "Renato Cartesio" Chap. ii, sect. 1 of **Da Cartesio a Kant. Storia della filosofia** 3 (Firenze 1961) 52-76; 2nd ed. (1966).

1276 Lambert des Cilleuls, J. "Le cartésianisme en Anjou et particulièrement à Saumur et ses protagonistes au XVIIe siècle" **Comptes Rendus du 97e Congrès National des Sociétés Savantes. Section des Sciences** 1 (1976) 111-21.

1277 Lamizet, G. "Alain et les sciences" **Alain philosophe de la culture et théoricien de la démocratie,** ed. by G. Kahn. **Actes du Colloque "Vigueur d'Alain, Rigueur de Simone Weil"** (Paris 1976) 61-75. Dis. by: Coulomb, J., et al. **Alain philosophe de la culture et théoricien de la démocratie** (Paris 1976).

1278 Lana, R.E. "Giambattista Vico and the History of Social Psychology" **Journal for the Theory of Social Behavior** 9 (1979) 251-63.

1279 Land, S.K. "The Cartesian Language Test and Professor Chomsky" **Linguistics** 122 (1974) 11-24. Dis. of: Chomsky, N. **Cartesian Linguistic** (New York 1966).

1280 Landucci, S. "La creazione delle verità eterne in Descartes" **Annali della Scuola Normale Superiore di Pisa** 10 (1980) 233-81.

1281 Landucci, S. "Per la storia della teodicea nell'età cartesiana" **RCSF** 36 (1981) 401-37.

1282 Landucci, S. "Noterelle cartesiane" **RCSF** 38 (1983) 318-24.

1283 Laporte, J.-M. "Husserl's Critique of Descartes" **PPR** 23 (1962-63) 335-52.

1284* Largeault, J. "Platon, Aristote, Descartes, sur l'espace" **Langage et philosophie des sciences** (Grenoble 1984) 57-78.

1285 Larmore, C. "Descartes' Empirical Epistemology" **DPMP** (Brighton 1980) 6-22.

1286 Larmore, C. "Descartes' Psychologistic Theory of Assent" **HPQ** 1 (1984) 61-74.

1287 Larmore, C. Review of **Sur la théologie blanche de Descartes,** by J.-L. Marion [Paris 1981]. **JP** 81 (1984) 156-62.

1288* Larsen, E. "Descartes et la conception visuelle de la nature" Chapter of **Frans Post, interprète du Bresil** (Amsterdam 1962).

1289 Larsen, E. "Descartes and the Rise of Naturalistic Landscape Painting in 17th Century Holland" **Art Journal** 24 (1963-64) 12-17.

1290 Larsen, E. "Le Baroque et l'esthétique de Descartes" **Baroque** 6 (1973) 69-73.

1291 Laruelle, F. **Descartes, mission terminée, retour impossible. Pourquoi pas la philosophie?** 1 (Paris 1983).

1292 Lascola, R.A. "Descartes' Unsound Argument" **NS** 52 (1978) 41-53.

1293 Lattre, A. de. "Perception et réflexion chez Descartes et Bergson" **EP** 27 (1972) 179-99.

1294 Laudan, L. "The Clock Metaphor and Probabilism: The Impact of Descartes on English Methodological Thought, 1650-1665" **ASc** 22 (1966) 73-104.

1295 Laudan, L. "The Clock Metaphor and Hypotheses: The Impact of Descartes on English Methodological Thought, 1650-1670" Chap. iv of **Science and Hypothesis: Historical Essays on Scientific Methodology** (Dordrecht 1981) 27-58.

1296 Lauer, H. "Descartes' Concept of Number" **SC** 2 (1981) 137-42.

1297 Lauth, R. "Der Entwurf der neuzeitlichen Philosophie durch Descartes" Chap. i of **Zur Idee der Transzendentalphilosophie** (München 1965) 11-41.

1298 Lauth, R. "La constitution du texte des Regulae de Descartes" **AP** 31 (1968) 648-56.
      Dis. of: Weber, J.-P.   **La constitution du texte des Regulae** (Paris 1964).

1299 Laymon, R. "Transubstantiation: Test Case for Descartes's Theory of Space" **PC** (Kingston and Montréal 1982) 149-70.

1300 Le Guern, M. **Pascal et Descartes** (Paris 1971).

1301 Leary, D.E. "The Intentions and Heritage of Descartes and Locke: Toward a Recognition of the Moral Basis of Modern Psychology" **Journal of General Psychology** 102 (1980) 283-310.

1302 Lebrun, G. "La notion de 'ressemblance' de Descartes à Leibniz" **SV** (Bonn 1976) 39-57.

1303 Leclerc, I. "The Ontology of Descartes" **RM** 34 (1980-81) 297-323.

1304 Lécrivain, A. "Spinoza et la physique cartésienne" **Cahiers Spinoza** 1 (1977) 235-65; 2 (1978) 93-206.
      Dis. by: Caveing, M.   **Raison Présente** 43 (1977).
                C[ostabel], P.   **BC** 8 (1979) 36-38.

1305 Leduc-Fayette, D. "Une lecture de Descartes au XVIIIe siècle: L'essai sur Descartes du Comte Algarotti (1754)" **EP** 26 (1971) 165-73.

1306 Leduc-Fayette, D. "La Mettrie et Descartes" **Eur** 56 (1978) 37-48.

1307 Leduc-Fayette, D. "La Mettrie et 'le labyrinthe de l'homme'" **RP** 105 (1980) 343-64.

1308 Leduc-Fayette, D. "Liminaire. 'Perinde ac cadaver'" **RP** 105 (1980) 275-85.

1309 Leduc-Fayette, D. "D'une raison, l'autre. Remarques sur Coste et l'essai d'une histoire cartésienne de la philosophie" **PaRa** (Paris 1983) 287-302.

1310* Lefèvre, L.J. "Nos actes nous suivent. Notes sur Descartes et sur Bergson" **PCa** 28 (1974) 67-79.

1311 Lefèvre, R. **La métaphysique de Descartes** (Paris 1959); 2nd ed. (1966); 3rd ed. (1972).
Rev. by: Salomon-Bayet, C.   **EP** 15 (1960) 114-15.
          Röd, W.   **PLa** 14 (1961) 24-26.

1312 Lefèvre, R. **La bataille du "Cogito"** (Paris 1960).
Rev. by: Röd, W.   **AGP** 44 (1962) 214-20.

1313 Lefèvre, R. "Le procès Biran-Descartes" **RSH** 101 (1961) 13-22.

1314 Lefèvre, R. "Quand Descartes dîne à Douai" **RSH** 107 (1962) 313-26.

1315 Lefèvre, R. **La pensée existentielle de Descartes** (Paris 1965).

1316 Lefèvre, R. "La méthode cartésienne et les passions" **RSH** 142 (1971) 283-301.

1317 Lefèvre, R. "Descartes contre Galilée" **Saggi su Galileo Galilei**, ed. by C. Maccagni. 2 (Firenze 1972) 297-308.

1318 Lefèvre, R. "Descartes, maître en son siecle" **RSH** 149 (1973) 5-16.

1319 Lefèvre, R. **La structure du cartésianisme** (Lille 1978).
Rev. by: Adam, M.   **SC** 2 (1981) 188-89.
          Beyssade, J.-M.   **SC** 2 (1981) 189-92.
          Beyssade, J.-M.   **RMM** 86 (1981) 126-27.
          Buzon, F. de   **BC** 10 (1981) 21-22.
          Gabaude, J.-M.   **Pens** 220 (1981) 141-43.

1320* Lefèvre, R. "Méthode cartésienne et modèle mathématique" **Modèles et interprétation,** ed. by L. Bescond et al. **Centre de Recherches sur l'Analyse et Théorie des Savoirs** (Lille 1978) 89-116.

1321 [Lefranc, A.]. "Explication d'un texte du 'Discours de la méthode'" **Revue de l'Enseignement Philosophique** 5 (1973) 18-25.

1322 Legros, R. "La métaphysique de Descartes et la pensée technicienne" **Annales de l'Institut de Philosophie et de Sciences Morales** (1983) 77-92.

1323 Lehrer, K. "Skepticism and Prior Probabilities" **Phi** 11 (1982) 89-93.

1324 Leibowitz, F. "Inference to the Best Explanation and Descartes' Conception of Matter" **Nature and System** 3 (1981) 81-89.
Dis. of: Buchdahl, G.   **Scientific Change** (New York 1963).

1325 Lennon, T.M. "Occasionalism and the Cartesian Metaphysic of Motion" **CJP** Supp. 1 (1974) 29-40.

1326 Lennon, T.M. "The Inherence Pattern and Descartes' Ideas" **JHP** 12 (1974) 43-52.

1327   Lennon, T.M.   "La logique janseniste de la liberté" **Revue d'Histoire et de Philosophie Religieuses** 59 (1979) 37-44.

1328   Lennon, T.M.   "Philosophical Commentary" **The Search after Truth and Elucidations of the Search after Truth,** by Nicolas Malebranche; tr. by T.M. Lennon and P.J. Olscamp (Columbus OH 1980) 757-848.

1329   Lennon, T.M.   "Representationalism, Judgement and Perception of Distance: Further to Yolton and McRae" **D** 19 (1980) 151-62.
       Dis. of: Yolton, J.W.   **D** 14 (1975).
                  McRae, R.   **D** 14 (1975).

1330   Lennon, T.M.   "The Leibnizian Picture of Descartes" **NM** (Dordrecht 1983) 215-26.

1331   Lennon, T.M., Nicholas, J.M., and Davis, J.W., edd. **Problems of Cartesianism** (Kingston and Montréal 1982).
       Rev. by: Phillips, M.   **RP** 109 (1985) 471-74.

1332   Lenoir, T.   "Descartes and the Geometrization of Thought: The Methodological Background of Descartes' Géométrie" **Historia Mathematica** 6 (1979) 355-79.

1333   Lenzen, W.   "Die Verwirrung des Skeptizismus. Descartes und seine Folgen" **Grazer Philosophische Studien** 18 (1982) 123-35.

1334* Leonard, D.C.   "Descartes, Melville and the Mardian Vortex" **South Atlantic Bulletin** 45 (1980) 13-25.

1335* Leopoldo e Silva, F.   "Por que ler Descartes hoje" **O Estado de São Paulo** Supp. (29 May 1983).

1336   Lepenies, W.   "'Interesting Questions' in the History of Philosophy and Elsewhere" **Philosophy in History: Essays on the Historiography of Philosophy,** ed. by R. Rorty, J.B. Schneewind and Q. Skinner (Cambridge 1984) 141-71.

1337   Letts, J.T.   **Le Cardinal de Retz historien et moraliste du possible** (Paris 1966).

1338   Levene, J.R.   "Sources of Confusion in Descartes's Illustrations, With Reference to the History of Contact Lenses" **HSc** 6 (1967) 90-96.

1339   Levert, P.   "'Ici' et 'ailleurs'. Quelques questions à propos de l'espace sensible" **AP** 45 (1982) 109-31.

1340   Levi, A.   "Medicine and Morals" Chap. ix of **French Moralists: The Theory of the Passions, 1585 to 1649** (Oxford 1964) 234-56.

1341   Levi, A.   "The Topmost Branch" Chap. x of **French Moralists: The Theory of the Passions, 1585 to 1649** (Oxford 1964) 257-98.

1342   Levi, A.W.   "Modern Philosophy: The Age of the Gentleman. Descartes" Chap. iv of **Philosophy as Social Expression** (Chicago IL 1974) 165-231.

1343 Levin, M.E. "Descartes' Proof that He is Not His Body" **AJP** 51 (1973)
115-23.

1344 Levinas, E. **Totalité et infini. Essai sur l'extériorité** (The Hague
1961).
Rev. by: Kaplan, F.　　　　**RP** 88 (1963) 127-31.
　　　　　Lauer, Q.　　　　　**Eras** 15 (1963) 65-68.
　　　　　Peursen, C.A. van　**PRu** 12 (1964-65) 10-12.

1345 Levron, J. "Une défense de René Fede, éditeur de Descartes" **Mercure
de France** 338 (1960) 354-56.

1346* Lévy, D. "Descartes et les femmes" **Discours Psychanalytique** (1983)
45-52.

1347 Lewin, B.D. "Psychoanalytic Comments on a Meditation of Descartes"
Chap. vii of **The Image and the Past** (New York 1968) 87-102.

1348 Leyden, W. von. "Cogito, Ergo Sum" **AS** 63 (1962-63) 67-82.
Dis. of: Hintikka, J.　　　　**PR** 71 (1962).

1349 Leyden, W. von. **Seventeenth-Century Metaphysics: An Examination of
Some Main Concepts and Theories** (London 1968).

1350 Lichtenstein, A. **Henry More: The Rational Theology of a Cambridge
Platonist** (Cambridge MA 1962).

1351 Limbrick, E. "Franciscus Sanchez 'Scepticus': un médecin philosophe
précurseur de Descartes (1550-1623)" **Renaissance and Reformation** 6
(1982) 264-72.

1352 Limonta, A. "Il criterio prassista nel pensiero di Cartesio" **Teoria e
prassi**, ed. by B. D'Amore and A. Giordano. **Atti del VI Congresso
Internazionale del Centro Internazionale di Studi e di Relazioni
Culturali** (Napoli 1979) 401-07.

1353 Lindborg, R. **Descartes i Uppsala. Striderna om 'nya filosofien' 1663-
1689** (Stockholm 1965).
Rev. by: Rosenfeld, L.　　　　**I** 58 (1967) 136-38.

1354 Lindborg, R. **René Descartes** (Stockholm 1968).

1355 Lindeboom, G.A. "The Impact of Descartes on Seventeenth Century Medical
Thought in the Netherlands" **Janus** 58 (1971) 201-06.
Repr. in **13CI** 9 (Moscow 1974) 243-49.

1356 Lindeboom, G.A. "Florentius Schuyl und seine Bedeutung für die
Verbreitung des Cartesianismus in den Niederlanden" **Janus** 59 (1972)
25-37.

1357* Lindeboom, G.A. "In de ochtendschemering van de moderne fysiologie:
Henricus Regius' Physiologia (1641) - en een eigentijds oordeel
daarover" **Nederlands Tijdschrift voor Geneeskunde** 116 (1972) 1124-29.

1358* Lindeboom, G.A. "Nog een exemplar van Henricus Regius' Physiologia (1641)" **Nederlands Tijdschrift voor Geneeskunde** 116 (1972) 1750.

1359 Lindeboom, G.A. **Florentius Schuyl (1619-1669). En zijn betekenis voor het Cartesianisme in de geneeskunde** (The Hague 1974).

1360 Lindeboom, G.A. **Descartes and Medicine** (Amsterdam 1978).
Rev. by: Collins, J.   **MS** 58 (1980-81) 133-34.
          Bernstein, H.R.   **JHP** 20 (1982) 309-12.

1361* Lindner, H. "Die Klassengrundlage des Zweifels in der Philosophie Descartes'" **Wissenschaftliche Zeitschrift der Friedrich-Schiller-Universität Jena. Gesellschafts- und Sprachwissenschaftliche Reihe** 9 (1959-60) 277-82.

1362 Lindner, H. "Die Klassengrundlage des Zweifels in der Philosophie Descartes'" **Deutsche Zeitschrift für Philosophie** 8 (1960) 720-29.

1363 Link, C. **Subjectivität und Wahrheit: die Grundlegung der neuzeitlichen Metaphysik durch Descartes** (Stuttgart 1978).

1364 Lions, P., and Lagny, J. "René Descartes à Poissy (Juillet 1623)" **Revue de l'Histoire de Versailles et de Seine-et-Oise** 61 (1973-75) 111-12.

1365 Lissa, G. **Cartesianesimo e anticartesianesimo in Fontanelle** (Napoli 1971).
Rev. by: Namer, E.   **RMM** 78 (1973) 235-36.
          Corsano, A.   **GCFI** 53 (1974) 308-10.

1366* Lissa, G. **Fontanelle. Tra scetticismo e nuova critica** (Napoli 1973).

1367* Little, I. "Freedom, Determinism, and Reason" **Proceedings of the New Mexico-West Texas Philosophical Society** (1974) 21-27.

1368 Livet, P. "Le traitement de l'information dans le 'Traité des Passions'" **RP** 103 (1978) 3-35.

1369 Llano, A. **El problema del voluntarismo en Descartes** (Bahia Blanca 1960).

1370 Lledó, E. "Semántica cartesiana" **Convivium** [España] 31 (1970) 47-67.

1371 Lloyd, G. "The Man of Reason" **Met** 10 (1979) 18-37.

1372 Lloyd, G. "Reason as Attainment" Chap. iii of **The Man of Reason: 'Male' and 'Female' in Western Philosophy** (Minneapolis MN 1984) 38-56.

1373* Lluberes, P. "Descartes y el argumento sobre la existencia" **Revista Venezolana de Filosofia** 2 (1975) 83-119.

1374 Lo Giudice, F. **Il problema morale nella filosofia di Cartesio, Spinoza e Croce** (Cosenza 1970).

1375 Locke, D. "Mind, Matter, and the Meditations" **M** 90 (1981) 343-66.

1376 Loeb, L.E. **From Descartes to Hume: Continental Metaphysics and the Development of Modern Philosophy** (Ithaca NY 1981).
Rev. by: Yolton, J.W.   **PB** 23 (1982) 155-57.
          Bolton, M.B.   **PR** 92 (1983) 89-92.
          Lennon, T.M.   **JHP** 21 (1983) 276-78.
          Norman, R.   **M** 93 (1984) 301-03.
          Watson, R.A.   **ISP** 16 (1984) 98-99.

1377 Loewer, B. "Descartes' Skeptical and Antiskeptical Arguments" **PS** 39 (1981) 163-82.

1378 Lohmann, J. "Descartes' 'Compendium musicae' und die Entstehung des neuzeitlichen Bewusstseins" **Archiv für Musikwissenschaft** 36 (1979) 81-104.

1379 Lojacono, E. "Science et coupures epistémiques" **15CS** (Montréal 1971) 174-80.

1380 Long, D.C. "Descartes' Argument for Mind-Body Dualism" **PF** 1 (1968-69) 259-73.

1381* Loparic, Z. "A procura de um Descartes segundo a ordem das dificuldades" **Revista Discurso** 6 (1975) 151-85.

1382 López Quintás, A. "Dos líneas de interpretación del pensamiento cartesiano" **Arb** 86 (1973) 17-28.

1383 López, A. "La cinemática del XVII frente a la física Aristotélica" **Salmanticensis** 18 (1971) 351-76.

1384 Loptson, P.J. "Cartesian Dualism" **Idealistic Studies** 7 (1977) 50-60.

1385 Losee, J. "Descartes" Chap. vii of **A Historical Introduction to the Philosophy of Science** (Oxford 1972) 70-79.

1386 Lot, G. **Descartes** (Paris 1966).

1387* Louise, G. "Une oeuvre poétique de Descartes. Les vers du ballet La Naissance de Paix" **Mémoires de l'Académie Nationale des Sciences, Arts et Belles-Lettres de Caen** 20 (1982) 175-203.

1388 Love, H., and Love, R. "A Cartesian Allusion in Dryden and Lee's 'Oedipus'" **Notes and Queries** 25 (1978) 35-37.

1389 Love, R. "Revisions of Descartes's Matter Theory in Le Monde" **BJHS** 8 (1975) 127-37.

1390 Löwith, K. **Das Verhältnis von Gott, Mensch und Welt in der Metaphysik von Descartes und Kant** (Heidelberg 1964).

1391 Löwith, K. "Descartes" Chap. i of **Gott, Mensch und Welt in der Metaphysik von Descartes bis zu Nietzsche** (Göttingen 1967) 24-40.

1392   Löwith, K.   "Valérys Cartesianismus"   Chap. i of **Paul Valéry. Grundzüge seines philosophischen Denkens** (Göttingen 1971) 9-25.

1393   Lüth, P.   "René Descartes in der modernen Naturwissenschaft und Medizin" **Verhandlungen des XX. Internationalen Kongresses für Geschichte der Medizin** (Hildesheim 1968) 802-12.

1394   Lynes, J.W.   "Descartes' Theory of Elements: From Le Monde to the Principes" **JHI** 43 (1982) 55-72.

1395   Lyons, J.D.   "The Cartesian Reader and the Methodic Subject" **Esprit Créateur** 21 (1981) 37-47.

1396   Lyons, J.D.   "Subjectivity and Imitation in the Discours de la méthode" **Neophilologus** 66 (1982) 508-24.

1397   Macey, S.L.   "The Impact of Horology in Literature, 1660-1760" **Expression, Communication and Experience in Literature and Language,** ed. by R.G. Popperwell.   **Proceedings of the XII Congress of the International Federation for Modern Languages and Literatures** ([London] 1973) 209-12.

1398   Machamer, P.K.   "Causality and Explanation in Descartes' Natural Philosophy" **Motion and Time, Space and Matter,** ed. by P.K. Machamer and R.G. Turnbull (Columbus OH 1976) 168-99.

1399   Machamer, P.K.   "The Harmonies of Descartes and Leibniz" **Contemporary Perspectives on the History of Philosophy. MSP** 8 (1983) 135-42.

1400   MacIntosh, J.J.   "Perception and Imagination in Descartes, Boyle and Hooke" **CJP** 13 (1983) 327-52.

1401   Mackenzie, A.W.   "A Word About Descartes' Mechanistic Conception of Life" **Journal of the History of Biology** 8 (1975) 1-13.

1402   Magnard, P.   "Le discours de la machine" **RMM** 79 (1974) 108-17.

1403   Magnard, P.   "L'intuitus mentis et la vision aveugle" **PaRa** (Paris 1983) 79-95.

1404   Magnus, B.   "The Modalities of Descartes' Proofs for the Existence of God" **CE** (The Hague 1969) 77-87.

1405   Magnus, B., and Wilbur, J.B., edd.   **Cartesian Essays: A Collection of Critical Studies** (The Hague 1969).
        Rev. by: Röd, W.   **PLa** 24 (1971) 355-59.

1406   Mahnke, D.   **Der Aufbau des philosophischen Wissens nach René Descartes** (München 1967).
        Rev. by: Röd, W.   **PRu** 18 (1971) 78-92.

1407   Mahoney, M.S.   "Descartes: Mathematics and Physics" **Dictionary of Scientific Biography,** ed. by C.C. Gillispie.   4 (New York 1971) 55-61.

1408   Mahoney, M.S.   "Die Anfange der algebräischen Denkweise im 17.
       Jahrhundert"   **Rete** 1 (1971) 15-31.
       Trans. as "The Beginnings of Algebraic Thought in the Seventeenth
       Century"   in **DPMP** (Brighton 1980) 141-55.

1409   Mahoney, M.S.   "Introduction"   **Le Monde, ou Traité de la Lumière,** by
       René Descartes; ed. and tr. by M.S. Mahoney (New York 1979) vii-xxvi.

1410   Malbreil, G.   "L'occasionalisme d'Arnold Geulincx"   **AP** 37 (1974) 77-105.

1411   Malcolm, N.   **Dreaming** (London 1959).
       Dis. by: Curley, E.M.   **AJP** 53 (1975).

1412   Malcolm, N.   "Descartes's Proof that His Essence Is Thinking"   **PR** 74
       (1965) 315-38.
       Repr. in **DCCE** (Garden City NY 1967) 312-37.
       Repr. in **Thought and Knowledge,** by N. Malcolm (Ithaca NY 1977) 15-39.

1413   Malcolm, N.   "Descartes' Ontological Proof"   **FE** (Oxford 1969) 36-43.
       Dis. of: Kenny, A.   **FE** (Oxford 1969).
       Dis. by: Kenny, A.   **FE** (Oxford 1969).

1414   Malcolm, N.   "Mind and Body"   Chap. i of **Problems of Mind: Descartes to
       Wittgenstein** (New York 1971) 1-59.
       Rev. by: Mayberry, T.C.   **PFo** 14 (1975) 289-95.
                  Largeault, J.   **RS** 99 (1978) 372-78.

1415   Malcolm, N.   "Thoughtless Brutes"   **Proceedings and Addresses of the
       American Philosophical Association** 46 (1972-73) 5-20.
       Repr. in **Thought and Knowledge,** by N. Malcolm (Ithaca NY 1977) 40-57.

1416   Malcolm, N.   "Author's Response"   **PFo** 14 (1975) 296-305.
       Dis. of: Mayberry, T.C.   **PFo** 14 (1975).

1417   Malcolm, N.   **Thought and Knowledge: Essays** (Ithaca NY 1977).

1418   Malcolm, N.   "Descartes' Proof that He Is Essentially a Non-Material
       Thing"   **Thought and Knowledge,** by N. Malcolm (Ithaca NY 1977) 58-84.

1419   Mamiani, M.   "La teoria dello spazio di Descartes"   Chap. i of **Teorie
       dello spazio da Descartes a Newton** (Milano 1980) 15-56.

1420   Mamiani, M.   "Henry More: la discussione sullo spazio nella
       corrisponzenza con Descartes"   Chap. ii of **Teorie dello spazio da
       Descartes a Newton** (Milano 1980) 59-89.

1421   Mandrou, R.   "Sur l'influence de Comenius en France au XVIIe siècle"
       Acta Comeniana 3 (1972) 235-38.

1422   Manteau-Bonamy, H.-M.   "Réflexions critiques sur les Méditations de
       Descartes"   **RT** 63 (1963) 37-72.

1423* Manzana Martínez de Marañón, J. "'Cogito ergo Deus est'. La aportación de Descartes al problema de la existencia de Dios" **Scriptorium Victoriense** 7 (1960) 181-206.

1424* Manzi, L. "'Le passioni dell'anima' di Renato Cartesio" **CNSM** (Roma 1967) 168-75.
Repr. in **PSM** 11 (1967) No. 1, 56-63.

1425* Manzoni, C. **I cartesiani italiani (1660-1760)** (Udine 1984).

1426 Marc-Wogau, K. "The Cartesian Doubt and the Cogito Ergo Sum" **Philosophical Essays,** by K. Marc-Wogau (Lund 1967) 41-60.

1427 Marcantonantos, L.G. "Les traductions du 'Discours de la méthode' de Descartes en grec moderne" **Balkan Studies** 22 (1981) 275-88.

1428 Marcial de Alcaide, M.T. **La filosofía de Descartes** (Santiago del Estero 1967).

1429 Marcil-Lacoste, L. "Dieu garant de veracité ou Reid critique de Descartes" **D** 14 (1975) 584-605.

1430 Marcil-Lacoste, L. "La notion d'évidence et le sens commun: Fénelon et Reid" **JHP** 15 (1977) 293-307.

1431 Marciszewski, W. "The Cartesian Concept of Conviction" **Poznan Studies** 1 (1975) No. 4, 27-55.

1432 Marciszewski, W. "Epistemological Foundations of Democratism in Cartesian Philosophy" **Poznan Studies** 5 (1979) 77-86.

1433 Marciszewski, W. "A Rationalistic Interpretation of 'Reasons of the Heart': A Study in Pascal" **Dialectics and Humanism** 7 (1980) 155-62.

1434 Marello, J.-R. "La croyance, la raison et la foi chez Descartes" **La croyance,** ed. by J. Greisch (Paris 1982) 161-87.

1435* Margat-Barbéris, C. "Mais où sont les guerres d'antan?" **Oui la Philosophie** 2 (1984) 16-23.

1436 Margolis, J. "'I exist'" **M** 73 (1964) 571-74.
Dis. of: Ayer, A.J.   **The Problem of Knowledge** (1956).
Dis. by: Deutscher, M.   **M** 76 (1967).

1437 Margolis, J., ed. **Fact and Existence** (Oxford 1969).

1438* Margot, J.-P. "L'analyse et la synthèse chez Descartes" **De Philosophia** 3 (1982) 33-44.

1439* Margot, J.-P. "La lecture foucaldienne de Descartes. Ses présupposés et ses implications" **Philosophiques** 11 (1984) 3-39.

1440 Marignac, P. "Descartes et ses concepts de la substance" **RMM** 85 (1980) 298-314.

1441 Marin, L. "Sur une société de machines dans la Logique de Port-Royal" RSH 186-87 (1982) 159-69.

1442 Marion, J.-L. "A propos d'une sémantique de la méthode" RIP 27 (1973) 37-48.
Dis. by: Crapulli, G.   BC 4 (1975) 280-85.

1443 Marion, J.-L. "Ordre et relation. Sur la situation aristotelicienne de la théorie cartésienne de l'ordre selon les Regulae V et VI" AP 37 (1974) 243-74.

1444 Marion, J.-L. Sur l'ontologie grise de Descartes. Science cartésienne et savoir aristotelicien dans les Regulae (Paris 1975); 2nd ed. (1981).
Rev. by: Beyssade, J.-M.   RMM 81 (1976) 566-68.
         Martineau, E.   EP (1976) 475-94.
         Clarke, D.M.   SL 9 (1977) 120-22.
         Deprun, J.   BC 6 (1977) 17-25.
         Deschepper, J.-P.   RPL 75 (1977) 500-04.
         Röd, W.   ZPF 32 (1978) 146-49.
         Garber, D.   Revista Venezolana de Filosofía 11
                                (1979) 164-69.
         Marshall, D.J., Jr.   PRu 31 (1984) 126-39.

1445 Marion, J.-L. "De la divinisation à la domination: Etude sur la sémantique de capable/capax chez Descartes" RPL 73 (1975) 263-93.

1446 M[arion], J.-L. "Heidegger et la situation métaphysique de Descartes" BC 4 (1975) 253-65.

1447 Marion, J.-L. "L'ambivalence de la métaphysique cartésienne" EP (1976) 443-60.
Dis. by: Courtine, J.-F.   BC 7 (1978) 42-44.

1448 Marion, J.-L. "Introduction" Règles utiles et claires pour la direction de l'esprit en la recherche de la vérité, by René Descartes; tr. by J.-L. Marion (The Hague 1977) ix-xvi.

1449 Marion, J.-L. "Annotations" Règles utiles et claires pour la direction de l'esprit en la recherche de la vérité, by René Descartes; tr. by J.-L. Marion (The Hague 1977) 85-294.

1450 Marion, J.-L. "Annexes I, II" Règles utiles et claires pour la direction de l'esprit en la recherche de la vérité, by René Descartes; tr. by J.-L. Marion (The Hague 1977) 295-309.

1451 Marion, J.-L. "Les chemins de la recherche sur le jeune Descartes: notes bibliographiques sur quelques ouvrages récents (1966-1977)" 08CM (Marseille 1979) 173-79.

1452 Marion, J.-L. "L'instauration de la rupture: Gilson à la lecture de Descartes" Etienne Gilson et nous: La philosophie et son histoire, ed. by M. Couratier (Paris 1980) 13-34.

1453   Marion, J.-L. **Sur la théologie blanche de Descartes. Analogie,**
       création des vérités éternelles et fondement (Paris 1981).
       Rev. by: Ashworth, E.J.   **SC** 2 (1981) 219-24.
                  Garceau, B.   **Canadian Philosophical Reviews** 2
                                          (1982) 117-20.
                  Marty, F.   **BC** 12 (1983) 1-17.
                  Armogathe, J.-R.   **DsS** 36 (1984) 385-87.
                  Canziani, G.   **Rivista di Storia della Filosofia**
                                          1 (1984) 91-106.
                  Larmore, C.   **JP** 81 (1984) 156-62.
                  Marshall, D.J., Jr.   **PRu** 31 (1984) 126-39.

1454   Marion, J.-L. "Descartes et l'onto-théologie" **BSFP** 76 (1982) 117-58.
       Dis. by: Gandillac, M. de,
                  et al.   **BSFP** 76 (1982).
                  B[eyssade], J.-M.   **BC** 13 (1984).

1455   Marion, J.-L. "Les trois songes ou l'éveil du philosophe" **PaRa**
       (Paris 1983) 55-78.

1456   Marion, J.-L. "Descartes et l'onto-théologie" **GM** 6 (1984) 3-49.

1457   Marion, J.-L. "Die Cartesianische Onto-Theo-Logie" **ZPF** 38 (1984)
       349-80.

1458   Marion, J.-L., and Deprun, J., edd. **La passion de la raison. Hommage à**
       Ferdinand Alquié (Paris 1983).

1459* Marion, M. "Logique et cogito cartésien" **Phi Zéro** 10 (1982) 3-17.
       Dis. of: Hintikka, J.   **PR** 71 (1962).

1460   Maritain, J. "Il n'y a pas de savoir sans intuitivité" **RT** 70 (1970)
       30-71.

1461   Mark, T.C. "Descartes Proof in Meditation III" **ISP** 7 (1975) 69-88.

1462   Mark, T.C. "Truth and Adequacy in Spinozistic Ideas" **SwJP** 8 (1977)
       No. 3, 11-34.
       Repr. in **Spinoza: New Directions,** ed. by R.W. Shahan and J.I. Biro
       (Norman OK 1978) 11-34.

1463   Markie, P.J. "Fred Feldman and the Cartesian Circle" **PS** 31 (1977)
       429-32.
       Dis. of: Feldman, F.   **PS** 27 (1975).

1464   Markie, P.J. "Clear and Distinct Perception and Metaphysical Certainty"
       M 88 (1979) 97-104.

1465   Markie, P.J. "Dreams and Deceivers in Meditation One" **PR** 90 (1981)
       185-209.
       Dis. by: White, C.J.,
                  and Gillespie, T.C.   **PS** 42 (1982) 287-95.

1466   Markie, P.J. "The Cogito Puzzle" **PPR** 43 (1982-83) 59-81.

1467   Markie, P.J.   "Descartes' Theory of Judgment"   **SJP** 21 Supp. (1983)
       101-10.
       Dis. of: Tlumak, J.   **SJP** 21 Supp. (1983).

1468   Marlies, M.   "Doubt, Reason, and Cartesian Therapy"   **DCIE** (Baltimore
       MD 1978) 89-113.

1469   Marshall, D.J., Jr.   **Prinzipien der Descartes-Exegese** (Freiburg 1979).
       Rev. by: Caton, H.P.   **JHP** 22 (1984) 480-82.

1470   Marshall, D.J., Jr.   Review of **Sur l'ontologie grise de Descartes**, by
       J.-L. Marion [Paris 1975]; and of **Sur la théologie blanche de
       Descartes**, by J.-L. Marion [Paris 1981].   **PRu** 31 (1984) 126-39.

1471   Martano, G.   "La conoscenza sensibile nel pensiero di Cartesio"   Chap. i
       of **La conoscenza sensibile nel razionalismo moderno (da Cartesio a
       Baumgarten)** (Napoli 1960) 17-46.

1472   Martin, B.D.   "Descartes' Use of 'Nature' in the Meditations"   **Di** 23
       (1980-81) 37-42.

1473   Martineau, E.   "L'ontologie de l'ordre"   Review of **Sur l'ontologie
       grise de Descartes**, by J.-L. Marion [Paris 1975].   **EP** (1976) 475-94.

1474   Martinet, M.   "Science et hypothèses chez Descartes"   **AIHS** 24 (1974)
       319-39.

1475   Martinet, M.   "La théorie de la lumière selon Descartes"   **RDS** 1 (1976)
       92-110.

1476   Martinet, M.   "Apologie de la 'Briève description des principaux
       phénomènes' introduite par Descartes dans la IIIème partie des
       Principes"   **RDS** 2 (1978) 32-43.

1477   Martinet, M.   "Un manuel subversif. La 'Somme philosophique' de René
       Descartes"   **Eur** 56 (1978) 28-36.

1478   Martinet, M.   "La séduisante théorie des tourbillons cartésiens"   **RDS**
       4 (1980) 21-35.

1479   Martinet, S.   "Descartes et Copernic"   **Avant, avec, après Copernic. La
       représentation de l'Univers et ses conséquences épistémologiques**, ed.
       by S. Delorme.   **31me Semaine de Synthèse au Centre International de
       Synthèse** (Paris 1975) 231-39.

1480   Martinet, S.   "Rôle du problème de la lumière dans la construction de la
       science cartésienne"   **DsS** 34 (1982) 285-309.

1481   Martorana, A.L.   "Il valore del dato storico in Cartesio e la sua
       conseguente ambiguità: L'antistoricismo come 'remedium' al naturalismo"
       Sop 40 (1972) 281-89.

1482   Martos, J.   "The Cartesian Constellation"   **Kinesis** 3 (1970-71) 63-80.

1483   Marty, F.   "Liminaire I. L'analogie perdue. La métaphysique sur les chemins de la science de Descartes à Kant"   Review of **Sur la théologie blanche de Descartes,** by J.-L. Marion [Paris 1981].   **BC** 12 (1983) 1-17.

1484   Masi, S.   "La storiografia filosofica da Cartesio a Brucker"   Review of **Dall'età cartesiana a Brucker,** by F. Bottin, M. Longo and G. Piaia [Brescia 1979].   **RF** 72 (1981) 165-69.

1485   Masterson, P.   "Modern Science and the Cartesian Cogito"   Chap. i of **Atheism and Alienation: A Study of the Philosophical Sources of Contemporary Atheism** (Dublin 1971) 1-13.

1486   Matheron, A.   "Psychologie et politique: Descartes. La noblesse du chatouillement"   **Dialectiques** 6 (1974) 79-98.

1487   Mathrani, G.N.   "Descartes' Idea of God as the Cause of his God-Idea: A Critical Analysis"   **Philosophical Quarterly** [India] 33 (1960-61) 249-54.

1488   Mathrani, G.N.   "An Analytic Scrutiny of Descartes' Theory of Self"   **Journal of the Indian Academy of Philosophy** 11 (1972) 11-18.

1489   Matsuo, Y.   "'A Digression of the Animale Spirits': the Changes of the Concept of 'Spirit' in the Seventeenth-Century Science (I)"   **Historia Scientiarum** 25 (1983) 1-15.

1490   Mattern, R.   "Descartes's Correspondence with Elizabeth: Concerning Both the Union and Distinction of Mind and Body"   **DCIE** (Baltimore MD 1978) 212-22.

1491   Matthews, G.   "Consciousness and Life"   **P** 52 (1977) 13-26.

1492   Matthews, G.   "Animals and the Unity of Psychology"   **P** 53 (1978) 437-54.

1493   Matthews, H.E.   "Descartes and Locke on the Concept of a Person"   **Locke Newsletter** 8 (1977) 9-34.

1494* Mattos, C. Lopes de.   "Dialogando com Descartes"   **Revista Brasileira de Filosofia** 10 (1960) 471-82.

1495   Maull, N.L.   "Perception and Primary Qualities"   **PSA 1978. Proceedings of the 1978 Biennial Meeting of the Philosophy of Science Association** 1 (1978) 3-17.

1496   Maull, N.L.   "Cartesian Optics and the Geometrization of Nature"   **RM** 32 (1978-79) 253-73.
       Repr. in **DPMP** (Brighton 1980) 23-40.

1497   Mauriac, P.   "Comment peut-on être cartésien?"   **Presse Médicale** 68 (1960) 125-26.

1498   Mavrodes, G.I.   "Solving a Cartesian Conundrum"   **PPQ** 64 (1983) 351-53.
       Dis. of: Oakes, R.   **PPQ** 64 (1983) 144-50.

1499   Mayberry, T.C.   Review of **Problems of Mind: Descartes to Wittgenstein,**
       by N. Malcolm [New York 1971].   **PFo** 14 (1975) 289-95.
       Dis. by: Malcolm, N.   **PFo** 14 (1975).

1500* Mayer, R. "Gott und Substanz. Zur Gottesproblematik bei Descartes und
       ihren philosophischen und religionskritischen Konsequenzen"
       Wissenschaftliche Zeitschrift der Friedrich-Schiller-Universität Jena.
       Gesellschafts- und Sprachwissenschaftliche Reihe 29 (1980) 337-41.

1501* Mayer, R. "Der Substanzbegriff in der cartesianischen Philosophie und
       seine Kritik durch Spinoza und Leibniz" **Wissenschaftliche Zeitschrift**
       der Martin-Luther-Universität Halle-Wittenberg. Gesellschafts- und
       Sprachwissenschaftliche Reihe 30 (1981) 93-99.

1502* Mazzalomo, U.L. "Filosofía y matematica en Descartes" **Phil** 41-42
       (1979-80) 63-92.

1503   Mazzeo, J.A. "Bacon: The New Philosophy" Chap. iv of **Renaissance and**
       Revolution: The Remaking of European Thought (New York 1965) 161-234.

1504   McBride, R. "Doubt and Certainty in Cartesianism" Chap. vi of **Aspects**
       of Seventeenth-Century French Drama and Thought (London 1979) 147-64.

1505   McClaughlin, T. "Censorship and Defenders of the Cartesian Faith in
       Mid-Seventeenth Century France" **JHI** 40 (1979) 563-81.
       Dis. by: Girbal, F.   **SC** 2 (1981) 225-29.

1506   McClaughlin, T., and Picolet, G. "Un exemple d'utilisation du Minutier
       central de Paris: La bibliothèque et les instruments scientifiques du
       physicien Jacques Rohault selon son inventaire après décès" **RHS** 29
       (1976) 3-20.

1507   McGuire, J.E. "Atoms and the 'Analogy of Nature': Newton's Third Rule
       of Philosophizing" **SHPS** 1 (1970-71) 3-58.

1508   McGuire, J.E. "Space, Geometrical Objects and Infinity: Newton and
       Descartes on Extension" **NM** (Dordrecht 1983) 69-112.

1509   McKenna, A. "L'argument 'Infini-Rien'" **Méthodes chez Pascal. Colloque**
       C.C. Fernand, ed. by T. Goyet et al. (Paris 1979) 497-508.

1510   McKinnon, A. "Some Conceptual Ties in Descartes' Meditations" **D** 18
       (1979) 166-74.

1511* McLane, B. "Les premières idées de Simone Weil sur la perception.
       Simone Weil et Jean-Paul Sartre" **Cahiers Simone Weil** 5 (1982) 22-45.

1512   McMullen, W.A. **Posthumous Meditations: A Dialogue in Three Acts**
       (Indianapolis IN 1982).

1513   McMullin, E. "Empiricism and the Scientific Revolution" **Art, Science,**
       and History in the Renaissance, ed. by C.S. Singleton (Baltimore MD
       1967) 331-69.

1514 McMullin, E. "Introduction: The Concept of Matter in Transition" **The Concept of Matter in Modern Philosophy,** ed. by E. McMullin (Notre Dame IN 1978) 1-55.

1515 McNiven Hine, E. "Criticism of Seventeenth-Century Metaphysical Systems: Descartes, Malebranche and Boursier" Chap. iii of **A Critical Study of Condillac's Traité des systèmes** (The Hague 1979) 48-82.

1516 McRae, R. "Descartes: The Project of a Universal Science" Chap. iii of **The Problem of the Unity of the Sciences: Bacon to Kant** (Toronto 1961) 46-68.

1517 McRae, R. "'Idea' as a Philosophical Term in the Seventeenth Century" **JHI** 26 (1965) 175-90.

1518 McRae, R. "Descartes' Definition of Thought" **CS** (Oxford 1972) 55-70.

1519 McRae, R. "Innate Ideas" **CS** (Oxford 1972) 32-54.

1520 McRae, R. "On Being Present to the Mind: A Reply" D 14 (1975) 664-66. Dis. of: Yolton, J.   D 14 (1975). Dis. by: Lennon, T.M.   D 19 (1980).

1521 McRae, R. "Descartes and Locke" Chap. ii of **Leibniz: Perception, Apperception, and Thought** (Toronto 1976) 8-18.

1522 McRae, R. "Life, Vis inertiae, and the Mechanical Philosophy" **Pragmatism and Purpose: Essays Presented to Thomas A. Goudge,** ed. by L.W. Sumner, J.G. Slater and F. Wilson (Toronto 1981) 189-98.

1523* Meattini, V. **Il fondamento nel pensiero di Cartesio e di Berkeley. Aspetti del problema della certezza** (Pisa 1982).

1524 Meisel, J.M. "On the Possibility of Non-Cartesian Linguistics" **Linguistics** 122 (1974) 25-38. Dis. of: Chomsky, N.   **Cartesian Linguistics** (New York 1966).

1525 Melchiorre, V. "L'interpretazione di Cartesio nel pensiero di E. Mounier" **RFN** 53 (1961) 298-313. Repr. in **La coscienza utopica,** by V. Melchiorre (Milano 1970) 147-69.

1526 Melis, P. "Spazio e tempo nella fisica di Cartesio" **Annali delle Facultà di Lettere Filosofia e Magistero dell'Università di Cagliari** 30 (1966-67) 185-308.

1527* Melis, P. "L'ottica di Cartesio" **Annali della Facoltà di Magistero dell'Università di Cagliari** 7 (1983) Pt. 3, 243-407.

1528 Mendenhall, V. "Reinterpreting First Evidence: Around the Cogito with Jean Nabert" **PTod** 20 (1976) 327-40.

1529 Mendus, S. "Kant's Doctrine of the Self" **KS** 75 (1984) 55-64.

1530   Menezes Veloso, A.   "Do pensamento à comunicação: o problema da inter-
       relação na filosofia cartesiana"   **Actas do 1 Congresso Luso-Brasileiro
       de Filosofia. Revista Portuguesa de Filosofia** 38 (1982) No. 4, 241-54.

1531* Merlotti, E.   "A propos de Vico et Descartes"   **Notiziario Culturale
       Italiano** 10 (1969) 46-50.

1532   Merrill, K.R.   "Did Descartes Misunderstand the 'Cogito'?"   **SC** 1
       (1979) 111-20.

1533   Mesnage, M.   "Vico et le concept cartésien de culture"   **Actes du
       Colloque Franco-italien de Philosophie, Ecole Normale d'Instituteurs de
       Nice** (Paris 1977) 90-108.

1534   Mesnard, J.   "Entre Pascal et Descartes: Jacques Habert de Saint-
       Léonard"   **TLL** 13 (1975) No. 2, 103-115.

1535   Mesnard, P.   "Le point de vue génétique dans la physiologie cartésienne"
       Revue Générale des Sciences Pures et Appliquées 72 (1965) 379-82.

1536   Mesnard, P.   **Descartes ou le Combat pour la Vérité** (Paris 1966); 2nd
       ed. (1974).
       Rev. by: Tillmann, A.   **EP** 21 (1966) 391-94.

1537* Messeri, M.   "Il corpo singolo nella teoria fisica della materia di
       Spinoza e in quella di Descartes"   **Annali della Scuola Normale
       Superiore di Pisa** 14 (1984) 771-95.

1538   Metz, A.   "Descartes et Leibniz. Note sur leurs conceptions de la force
       et du mouvement, à la lumière de la science actuelle"   **AP** 31 (1968)
       473-76.

1539   Meyer, H.   "Mensch und Tier aus der Sicht der Aufklärung"   **Philosophia
       Naturalis** 18 (1980-81) 493-514.

1540   Meyers, R.G.   "Peirce on Cartesian Doubt"   **Transactions of the Charles
       S. Peirce Society** 3 (1967) 13-23.

1541   Michaud, Y.   "La formation de la problématique de la substance
       spirituelle chez Berkeley"   **RMM** 79 (1974) 63-83.

1542   Michel, A.   "Saint Augustin et la rhétorique pascalienne: La raison et
       la beauté dans l''Apologie de la religion chrétienne'"   **DsS** 34 (1982)
       133-48.

1543   Michel, E.   "Descartes und Prinzessin Elisabeth von Böhmen"
       Sudetenland 22 (1980) 250-54.

1544   Micheli, G.   "Il 'Traité de l'homme' e una supposita crisi della
       filosofia cartesiana"   Review of **L'uomo,** by René Descartes; tr. by G.
       Cantelli [Torino 1960].   **RCSF** 16 (1961) 315-20.

1545 Miel, J. "Pascal, Port-Royal, and Cartesian Linguistics" **JHI** 30 (1969) 261-71.
Dis. of: Chomsky, N. **Cartesian Linguistics** (New York 1966).

1546 Miethe, T.L. "The Ontological Argument: A Research Bibliography" **MS** 54 (1976-77) 148-66.

1547 Mijuskovic, B. "Descartes's Bridge to the External World: The Piece of Wax" **SIF** 3 (1971) 65-81.

1548 Mijuskovic, B.L. **The Achilles of Rationalist Arguments: The Simplicity, Unity, and Identity of Thought and Soul from the Cambridge Platonists to Kant** (The Hague 1974).

1549 Miles, M.L. "Condensation and Rarefaction in Descartes' Analysis of Matter" **Nature and System** 5 (1983) 169-80.

1550 Miles, M.L. "Psycho-Physical Union: The Problem of the Person in Descartes" **D** 22 (1983) 23-46.

1551 Milhaud, G. "La Fontaine à l'avant-garde des sciences et de la philosophie" **Eur** 50 (1972) 73-83.

1552 Milhaud, G., ed. **Descartes. Eur** 56 (Paris 1978) 3-155.

1553 Milhaud, G. "Descartes à sa juste place" **Eur** 56 (1978) 3-4.

1554 Milhaud, G. "Chronologie de Descartes" **Eur** 56 (1978) 147-55.

1555 Miller, R.P., and Miller, V.R. "Descartes' Principia philosophiae: Some Problems of Translation and Interpretation" **SC** 2 (1981) 143-54.

1556 Millet, L. "Man and Risk" **IPQ** 2 (1962) 417-27.

1557 Mimoune, R. "Le XVIIe siècle et la non-raison dans la pensée de Jean Wahl" **Revue des Sciences Philosophiques et Théologiques** 67 (1983) 595-602.

1558 Mimoune, R. "Vision de Descartes dans la pensée arabe contemporaine" **RDS** 7 (1984) 91-103.

1559* Miranda, P. de. "Meditações anticartesianos" **Revista Brasileira de Filosofia** 31 (1981) 3-13.

1560 Misenga, N. "Apport de la Méthodologie Cartésienne dans le Discours et dans les Règles au problème de l'existence d'une philosophie africaine traditionnelle" **Revue Philosophique de Kinshasa** 1 (1983) 97-122.

1561 Mittelstrass, J. "Die Idee einer Mathesis universalis bei Descartes" **Perspektiven der Philosophie** 4 (1978) 177-92.

1562 Mittelstrass, J. "The Philosopher's Conception of Mathesis Universalis from Descartes to Leibniz" **ASc** 36 (1979) 593-610.

1563 Mitton, R. "Professor Hintikka on Descartes' 'Cogito'" **M** 81 (1972)
407-08.
Dis. of: Hintikka, J.   **PR** 72 (1963).

1564 Molland, A.G. "Shifting the Foundations: Descartes's Transformation of
Ancient Geometry" **Historia Mathematica** 3 (1976) 21-49.

1565 Molnar, T. "A Commentary on Prof. H.M. Curtler on Descartes" **MA** 18
(1974) 440-41.
Dis. of: Curtler, H.M.   **MA** 18 (1974).

1566 Monasterio, X.O. "On Macintyre, Rationality, and Dramatic Space"
ACPA 58 (1984) 151-64.

1567 Monro, D.H. "The Sonneteer's History of Philosophy" **P** 55 (1980)
363-75.

1568 Montague, R. "Descartes' Circle Recycled?" **AGP** 59 (1977) 167-180.
Dis. of: Kenny, A.   **JP** 67 (1970).

1569 Montias, H. **Descartes** (Paris 1969).

1570 Moore, F.C.T. "Is the Intuition of Dualism Primary?" **RIP** 37 (1983)
265-72.
Dis. by: Gombay, A.   **RIP** 37 (1983).

1571 Moraes, M. "O cartesianismo de António Cordeiro" **Revista Portuguesa
de Filosofia** 22 (1966) 3-27.

1572 Moreau, J. "Présentation de Descartes" **Miscelânea de Estudos a
Joaquim de Carvalho** 8 (1962) 816-28.

1573 Moreau, J. "Sanchez, précartésien" **RP** 92 (1967) 264-70.

1574 Moreau, J. "Examen de la philosophie de Descartes" **EP** 26 (1971) 57-66.

1575 Moreau, P.-F. "Saisset lecteur de Spinoza" **RDS** 4 (1980) 85-98.

1576 Morick, H. "Cartesian Privilege and the Strictly Mental" **PPR** 31
(1970-71) 546-51.

1577 Morot-Sir, E. "Le Français est-il toujours cartésien?" **Bulletin de la
Société des Professeurs Français en Amérique** (1965) 5-9.

1578 Morot-Sir, E. "Samuel Beckett and Cartesian Emblems" **Symposium on
Samuel Beckett: The Art of Rhetoric,** ed. by E. Morot-Sir, H. Harper and
D. McMillan III (Chapel Hill NC 1976) 25-104.

1579 Morris, J.M. "A Plea for the French Descartes" **D** 6 (1967-68) 236-39.
Dis. of: Nelson, J.O.   **D** 3 (1964-65).

1580 Morris, J.M. "Raison, Connaissance and Conception in Descartes'
'Meditations'" **Sop** 36 (1968) 265-72.

1581 Morris, J.M. "A Computer-Assisted Study of a Philosophical Text" **Computers and the Humanities** 3 (1968-69) 175-78. Dis. by: Robinet, A. **EP** (1970).

1582 Morris, J.M. "Cartesian Certainty" **AJP** 47 (1969) 161-68. Dis. by: Schouls, P.A. **AJP** 48 (1970).

1583 Morris, J.M. "Pattern Recognition in Descartes' Automata" **I** 60 (1969) 451-60.

1584 Morris, J.M. "Descartes and Probable Knowledge" **JHP** 8 (1970) 303-12.

1585 Morris, J.M. **Descartes Dictionary** (New York 1971). Rev. by: Dubois, P. **RP** 97 (1972) 189-90.

1586 Morris, J.M. "The Essential Incoherence of Descartes" **AJP** 50 (1972) 20-29.

1587 Morris, J.M. "Descartes' Natural Light" **JHP** 11 (1973) 169-87.

1588 Morris, J.M. "Descartes on Tendencies" **PF** 5 (1973-74) 572-83.

1589 Morris, J.M. "What the Skeptic Cannot Doubt" **PF** 11 (1979-80) 363-88.

1590 Morrison, J.C. "Vico's Principle of Verum is Factum and the Problem of Historicism" **JHI** 39 (1978) 579-95.

1591 Morrissey, R. "Vers un topos littéraire: La préhistoire de la rêverie" **Modern Philology** 77 (1979-80) 261-90.

1592 Morscher, E. "Ist Existenz immer noch kein Prädikat?" **Philosophia Naturalis** 19 (1982) 163-99.

1593 Morstein, P. von. "Descartes: Theory and Practice of Knowledge" **Theoria cum praxi. Zum Verhältnis von Theorie und Praxis im 17. und 18. Jahrhundert, III.** **SL** Supp. 21 (1980) 101-11.

1594 Mortureux, M.-F. "A propos du vocabulaire scientifique dans la seconde moitié du XVIIe siècle" **Langue Française** 17 (1973) 72-80.

1595 Mortureux, M.-F. "Mondes et/ou Tourbillons" Chap. vi of **La formation et le fonctionnement d'un discours de la vulgarisation scientifique au XVIIIe siècle à travers l'oeuvre de Fontenelle** (Lille 1983) 389-429.

1596 Moser, P.R. "Anotações sôbre o ideal cartesiano de conhecimento" **Convivium** [Brasil] 10 (1971) 462-69.

1597 Mosley, J. "Boardman's Dreams and Dramas" **PQ** 31 (1981) 158-62. Dis. of: Boardman, W.S. **PQ** 29 (1979).

1598 Mounier, E. "Le conflit de l'anthropocentrisme et du théocentrisme dans la philosophie de Descartes" **EP** 21 (1966) 319-24.

1599 Mourant, J.A. "The Cogitos: Augustinian and Cartesian" **Augustinian Studies** 10 (1979) 27-42.

1600* Mout, N. "Comenius, Descartes and Dutch Cartesianism" **Acta Comeniana** 27 (1972) 239-43.

1601 Mouton, D.L. "Hume and Descartes on Self-Acquaintance" **D** 13 (1974) 255-69.

1602* Mullatti, L.C. "Descartes' Philosophy of Nature" **Journal of the Karnatak University** 3 (1967) 24-34; 4 (1968) 1-8.

1603 Muller, A. "Descartes(1596-1650)" Chapter of **De Rabelais à Paul Valéry. Les grands écrivains devant le christianisme** (Paris 1969) 40-44.

1604 Mumford, L. "Reflections: The Megamachine - II" **New Yorker** 46 (17 October 1970) 48-141.

1605 Munkácsy, G. "Die kartesianische Metaphysik und die Profanisation der Philosophie: I. Descartes und die Welt der Substanzen; II. Die Welt des 'positiv Unendlichen'" **Annales Universitatis Scientiarum Budapestinensis de Rolando Eötvös Nominatae. Sectio Philosophica et Sociologica** 16 (1982) 91-109; 17 (1983) 199-215.

1606 Munot, P. "Un extrait du Discours de la méthode" **Cahiers d'Analyse Textuelle** 16 (1974) 48-60.

1607 Münzenmayer, H.P. "Der Calculus Situs und die Grundlagen der Geometrie bei Leibniz" **SL** 11 (1979) 274-300.

1608 Muralt, A. de. "Epoché--Malin Génie--Théologie de la toute-puissance divine. Le concept objectif sans objet. Recherches d'une structure de pensée" **Studia Philosophica** 26 (1966) 159-91.

1609 Muralt, A. de. "La doctrine médiévale des distinctions et l'intelligibilité de la philosophie moderne" **Revue de Théologie et de Philosophie** 112 (1980) 113-32; 217-40.

1610 Nádor, G. "L'importance de la doctrine heuristique de Descartes dans l'histoire de la science" **Dialectica** 16 (1962) 25-38.

1611 Nádor, G. "Métaphores de chemins et de labyrinthes chez Descartes" **RP** 87 (1962) 37-51.

1612 Nádor, G. "Scientia mirabilis. Descartes et Leibniz" **Dialectica** 19 (1965) 144-57.

1613 Nádor, G. "Eine heraklitische Denkform in Descartes' Werk" **Antike und Abendland** 13 (1967) 96-100.

1614* Nagasaki, H. "Notes philosophiques" **Revue de l'Université d'Hiroshima** 16 (1970) 61-160.

1615   Najm, S.M.   "The Place and Function of Doubt in the Philosophies of
        Descartes and al-Ghazali"   **Philosophy East and West** 16 (1966) 133-41.

1616   Nakamura, T.   "How and Why did Descartes Support the Theory of Blood
        Circulation?"   **Japanese Studies in the History of Science** 13 (1974)
        75-80.

1617   Nakamura, T.   "T. Willis' and Lower's Physiology with Special Reference
        to the Theory of Heart Movement"   **Japanese Studies in the History of
        Science** 16 (1977) 23-41.

1618   Nakamura, Y., Tokoro, T., et al., edd.   **Bibliographie chronologique des
        publications en langue japonaise sur Descartes et le cartésianisme
        1951-1979. Analecta Cartesiana 1.** SC Supp. (Amsterdam 1981).

1619   Nakhnikian, G.   "Descartes and the Theory of Knowledge: Meditations on
        First Philosophy, I-II"   Pt. II of **An Introduction to Philosophy** (New
        York 1967) 63-164.
        Rev. by: Röd, W.   **PRu** 18 (1971) 78-92.

1620   Nakhnikian, G.   "Descartes and the Problem of God: Meditations on First
        Philosophy, III-VI"   Pt. III of **An Introduction to Philosophy** (New
        York 1967) 165-241.
        Rev. by: Röd, W.   **PRu** 18 (1971) 78-92.

1621   Nakhnikian, G.   "The Cartesian Circle Revisited"   **APQ** 4 (1967) 251-55.

1622   Nakhnikian, G.   "Incorrigibility"   **PQ** 18 (1968) 207-15.

1623   Nakhnikian, G.   "On the Logic of Cogito Propositions"   **N** 3 (1969)
        197-209.

1624   Nakhnikian, G.   Review of **Demons, Dreamers, and Madmen,** by H.G.
        Frankfurt [Indianapolis IN 1970]; and of **Descartes: A Study of his
        Philosophy,** by A. Kenny [New York 1968]. **AGP** 56 (1974) 202-09.

1625   Nakhnikian, G.   "Comments"   **N** 10 (1976) 15-17.
        Dis. of: Wilson, M.D.   **N** 10 (1976).

1626   Nakhnikian, G.   "Descartes's Dream Argument"   **DCIE** (Baltimore MD 1978)
        256-86.

1627   Namer, E.   **Le beau roman de la physique cartésienne et la science
        exacte de Galilée** (Paris 1979).
        Rev. by: Cavallo, G.   **F** 30 (1979) 585-92.
                 Finocchiaro, M.A.   **JHP** 20 (1982) 95-96.

1628   Namer, E.   Review of **Itinéraire du jeune Descartes,** by A. Tillmann
        [Lille 1976].   **RMM** 84 (1979) 560-61.

1629   Nancy, J.-L.   "Larvatus pro Deo"   **Glyph** 2 (1977) 14-36.
        Repr. in **Ego Sum,** by J.-L. Nancy (Paris 1979) 63-94.

1630   Nancy, J.-L.   "Dum scribo"   **Oxford Literary Review** 3 (1978) No. 2, 6-21.
       Repr. in **Ego Sum,** by J.-L. Nancy (Paris 1979) 41-60.

1631   Nancy, J.-L.   "Mundus est fabula"   **MLN** 93 (1978) 635-53.
       Repr. in **Ego Sum,** by J.-L. Nancy (Paris 1979) 97-127.

1632   Nancy, J.-L.   **Ego sum** (Paris 1979).
       Rev. by: Madou, J.-P.   **NRF** 334 (1980) 139-43.
                Judovitz, D.   **MLN** 96 (1981) 916-17.
                M[arion], J.-L.   **BC** 10 (1981) 38-40.

1633   Nardi, A.   "Descartes e Galileo"   Review of **Le beau roman de la
       physique cartésienne et la science exacte de Galilée,** by E. Namer
       [Paris 1979].   **GCFI** 60 (1981) 129-48.

1634   Nardi, A.   "La luce e la favola del mondo. Descartes 1629-1633"   **Annali
       dell'Istituto di Filosofia** [Firenze] 3 (1981) 103-45.

1635   Nathan, E.   "Apuntes para una visión externalista de la filosofía de
       Descartes"   **Dian** 28 (1982) 199-212.

1636   Natoli, S.   **Soggetto e fondamento. Studi su Aristotele e Cartesio**
       (Padova 1979).

1637* Navarro Cordón, J.M.   "Método y filosofía en Descartes"   **ASM** 7 (1972)
       39-63.

1638   Ndiaye, A.-R.   "Le concept d'étendue intelligible: Influences
       gassendistes sur Malebranche d'après Arnauld"   **RDS** 4 (1980) 99-113.

1639   Needham, P.   **Descartes: An Introduction to the Philosophy of Mind**
       (Stockholm 1981).

1640   Negri, A.   **Descartes politico o della ragionevole ideologia** (Milano
       1970).

1641   Neisser, H.   "The Phenomenological Basis of Descartes' Doubt"   **PPR** 25
       (1964-65) 572-74.
       Dis. of: Sibajiban.   **PPR** 24 (1963-64).

1642   Nelli, S., ed.   **Determinismo e libero arbitrio da Cartesio a Kant**
       (Torino 1982).

1643   Nelson, J.O.   "In Defence of Descartes: Squaring a Reputed Circle"   **D**
       3 (1964-65) 262-72.
       Dis. of: Frankfurt, H.G.   **PR** 71 (1962).
       Dis. by: Frankfurt, H.G.   **D** 4 (1965-66).
                Morris, J.M.   **D** 6 (1967-68).

1644   Neuenschwander, U.   "Der Gott der zweifelnden und sebstgewissen
       Vernunft. René Descartes" Pt. II, chap. ii of **Gott im neuzeitlichen
       Denken** 1 (Gütersloh 1977) 96-106.

1645 Neville, R.C. "Some Historical Problems about the Transcendence of God" **Journal of Religion** 47 (1967) 1-9.

1646 Nicolosi, S. "Presenza e assenza di Dio nel sistema cartesiano" **Aquinas** 24 (1981) 175-200.

1647* Nicolosi, S. "Il sorgere della scienza sperimentale e la crisi della metafisica" **Metafisica e scienze dell'uomo**, ed. by B. D'Amore and A. Ales Bello. **Atti del VII Congresso Internazionale del Centro Internazionale di Studi e di Relazioni Culturali** 1 (Roma 1982) 131-59.

1648 Nicolosi, S. "La morale provvisoria di Cartesio" **Studia Patavina** 30 (1983) 323-46.

1649 Nicolosi, S. "La psicologia cartesiana tra dualismo ed unità sostanziale" **Aquinas** 26 (1983) 35-52.

1650 Niebel, W.F. **Das Problem des 'cogito, ergo sum'.** Beitr. 22 of **Philosophie als Beziehungswissenschaft. Festschrift für Julius Schaaf,** ed. by W.F. Niebel and D. Leisegang (Frankfurt 1972). Repr. in **Philosophie als Beziehungswissenschaft. Festschrift für Julius Schaaf,** ed. by W.F. Niebel and D. Leisegang (Frankfurt 1974).

1651 Niebel, W.F. "Scire, Scientia, Scientia generalis: Die Neu-Begründung des Wissens als Wissenschaft bei Descartes" **Sprache und Begriffe. Festschrift für Bruno Liebrucks,** ed. by H. Röttger, B. Scheer and J. Simon (Meisenheim 1974) 67-85.

1652 Niebel, W.F. "Scientia, Experientia und Sapientia beim frühen Descartes" **Theoria cum Praxi. Zum Verhältnis von Theorie und Praxis im 17. und 18. Jahrhundert,** I. **SL** Supp. 19 (1980) 144-57.

1653 North, J.D. "Finite and Otherwise: Aristotle and Some Seventeenth Century Views" **NM** (Dordrecht 1983) 113-48.

1654 Norton, D.F. "Descartes on Unknown Faculties: An Essential Inconsistency" **JHP** 6 (1968) 245-56.
     Dis. by: Brewster, L.E.   **JHP** 12 (1974).
              Humphrey, T.B.   **JHP** 12 (1974).
              Stevens, J.C.   **JHP** 16 (1978).

1655 Norton, D.F. "Descartes' Inconsistency: A Reply" **JHP** 12 (1974) 509-20.
     Dis. of: Brewster, L.E.   **JHP** 12 (1974).
              Humphrey, T.B.   **JHP** 12 (1974).
     Dis. by: Stevens, J.C.   **JHP** 16 (1978).

1656 Norton, D.F. "A Reply to Professor Stevens" **JHP** 16 (1978) 338-41.
     Dis. of: Stevens, J.C.   **JHP** 16 (1978).

1657 Norton, D.F. "The Myth of 'British Empiricism'" **History of European Ideas** 1 (1980-81) 331-44.

1658 Noussan-Lettry, L. "Experiencia y trascendencia ontológica en las meditaciones cartesianas" **Phil** 26 (1962) 24-49.

1659 Noussan-Lettry, L. "La crítica de las humanidades en Descartes (Discurso, I, párrafos 7o y 8o)" **Actas de las Segundas Jornadas Universitarias de Humanidades** (Mendoza 1964) 207-17.

1660 Noussan-Lettry, L. "Die Anerkennung des Historischen in der Lebenserfahrung und der Weg des Denkens bei Descartes" **PJ** 80 (1973) 15-37.

1661 Noussan-Lettry, L. "Para una interpretación temática de la moral provisoria. Descartes, Discurso, III" **Phil** 39 (1973) 47-61.

1662 Noussan-Lettry, L. "Lebenserfahrung und Denken, Frage und Antwort in Descartes' Meditationen" **Wiener Jahrbuch für Philosophie** 7 (1974) 242-71.

1663 Nuchelmans, G. "Idea and Judgment in Descartes" Chap. ii of **Judgment and Proposition: From Descartes to Kant** (Amsterdam 1983) 36-54.
Rev. by: Yolton, J.W.   **PB** 25 (1984) 200-02.

1664 Nuchelmans, G. "Repercussions of Descartes's Theory of Judgment" Chap. iii of **Judgment and Proposition: From Descartes to Kant** (Amsterdam 1983) 55-69.
Rev. by: Yolton, J.W.   **PB** 25 (1984) 200-02.

1665* Nuti, F. "Una lettera di Descartes riflessa in una lirica di Baudelaire" **Annuario dell'Istituto Tecnico Commerciale Gattapone di Gubbio** (1972) 1961-71.

1666 Nuzzetti, M. "Sulla fondazione dell'etica cartesiana" **Sapienza** 34 (1981) 328-38.

1667* Nykrog, P. "Ud fra en side af Descartes" **(Pré)Publications** 28 (1976) 31-54.

1668 Nykrog, P. "The Literary Cousins of the Stock Market: On Mystification and Demystification in the Baroque Age" **Stanford French Review** 7 (1983) 57-71.

1669 O'Briant, W.H. "Doubting the Truths of Mathematics in Descartes' Meditations" **SJP** 15 (1977) 527-35.

1670 O'Briant, W.H. "The Malignant Demon and Mathematics" **SL** 10 (1978) 101-12.
Dis. of: Cottingham, J.G.   **SL** 8 (1976).
Dis. by: Cottingham, J.G.   **SL** 10 (1978).

1671 O'Briant, W.H. "Is Descartes' Evil Spirit Finite or Infinite?" **Soph** 18 (1979) No. 2, 28-32.
Dis. of: Elliot, R.,
          and Smith, M.   **Soph** 17 (1978) No. 3.

1672 O'Hear, A. "Belief and the Will" **P** 47 (1972) 95-112.

1673 O'Hear, A. "Was Descartes a Voluntarist?" **P** 54 (1979) 105-07.
Dis. of: Grant, B. **P** 51 (1976).

1674 O'Kelley, T.A. "Locke's Doctrine of Intuition was not Borrowed from Descartes" **P** 46 (1971) 148-51.

1675 O'Neil, B.E. "Cartesian Simple Natures" **JHP** 10 (1972) 161-79.

1676 O'Neil, B.E. **Epistemological Direct Realism in Descartes' Philosophy** (Albuquerque NM 1974).
Rev. by: Wilson, M.D. **PR** 85 (1976) 408-10.
Watson, R.A. **JHP** 15 (1977) 342-43.

1677 O'Neill, W. "Augustine's Influence upon Descartes and the Mind-Body Problem" **Revue des Etudes Augustiniennes** 12 (1966) 255-60.

1678 O'Neill, W. "The Love of Wisdom" **Per** 52 (1971) 459-82.

1679 O'Shaughnessy, B. "The Given" Chap. v of **The Will: A Dual Aspect Theory** 1 (Cambridge 1980) 143-66.

1680 O'Shaughnessy, B. "The Striving Nature of All Action" Chap. xi of **The Will: A Dual Aspect Theory** 2 (Cambridge 1980) 75-112.

1681 O'Shaughnessy, B. "The Ontological Status of Physical Action (1): Defining the Psychological and the Mental" Chap. xiv of **The Will: A Dual Aspect Theory** 2 (Cambridge 1980) 133-92.

1682 Oakes, R. "Material Things: A Cartesian Conundrum" **PPQ** 64 (1983) 144-50.
Dis. by: Mavrodes, G.I. **PPQ** 64 (1983) 351-53.

1683 Obersteiner, J. "Der Weg zur Gotteserkenntnis bei Augustinus und Descartes" **Augustinus** 13 (1968) 283-305.

1684 Obertello, L. Review of **Descartes. Die innere Genesis des cartesianischen Systems,** by W. Röd [München 1964]. **F** 17 (1966) 397-401. Repr. as **Un libro su Descartes** (Torino 1966).

1685 Odegard, D. "Escaping the Cartesian Circle" **APQ** 21 (1984) 167-73.

1686 Oegema van der Wal, T. **De mens Descartes** (Brussel 1960).
Dis. by: Closset, F. **Revue des Langues Vivantes** 26 (1960).

1687 Oeing-Hanhoff, L. "Descartes und das Problem der Metaphysik. Zu F. Alquiés Descartes-Interpretation" Review of **La découverte métaphysique de l'homme chez Descartes,** by F. Alquié [Paris 1950]. **KS** 51 (1959-60) 196-217.

1688 Oeing-Hanhoff, L. "Der Mensch in der Philosophie Descartes'" **Die Frage nach dem Menschen: Aufriss einer philosophischen Anthropologie. Festschrift für Max Müller zum 60. Geburtstag,** ed. by H. Rombach (Freiburg 1966) 375-409.

1689 Oeing-Hanhoff, L. "Descartes' Lehre von der Freiheit" **PJ** 78 (1971) 1-16.

1690 Oeing-Hanhoff, L. "Note sur l'argument ontologique chez Descartes et Bonaventure" **AP** 36 (1973) 643-55.

1691 Oeing-Hanhoff, L. "Der sogenannte ontologische Gottesbeweis bei Descartes und Bonaventura" **Die Wirkungsgeschichte Anselms von Canterbury. Akten der ersten Internationalen Anselm-Tagung. 1: Das ontologische Argument in der Geschichte der Philosophie**, ed. by H. Kohlenberger. **Analecta Anselmiana** 4 (1975) 211-20.

1692 Oeing-Hanhoff, L. "René Descartes. Neugründung der Metaphysik" Chap. iii of **Philosophie der Neuzeit I**, ed. by J. Speck. **Grundprobleme der grossen Philosophen** (Göttingen 1979) 35-73.

1693 Oeing-Hanhoff, L. "Liminaire I. Descartes et la Princesse Elisabeth" **BC** 11 (1982) 1-33. Trans. as "Descartes und Elisabeth von der Pfalz" **PJ** 91 (1984) 82-106.

1694 Oetjens, H. "Descartes' Konzept einer allgemeinen Methodologie als Alternative zur traditionellen Ontologie" **Sprache und Ontologie. Akten des 6. Internationalen Wittgenstein-Symposium**, ed. by W. Leinfellner et al. (Wien 1982) 71-74.

1695 [Ogonowski, Z.]. "Liminaire II. Descartes et la réception du cartésianisme. Les études polonaises récentes" **BC** 12 (1983) 18-20.

1696 Ohana, J. "Note sur la théorie cartésienne de la direction du mouvement" **EP** 16 (1961) No. 3, 313-16.

1697 Ohana, J. "Le sophisme de l'évidence ex terminis. A propos de l'opposition Descartes-Spinoza au sujet de la liberté" **RP** 90 (1965) 151-68.

1698 Olaso, E. de. "La distinción entre el alma y el cuerpo" **Revista de Filosofía** [Argentina] 15 (1964) 43-49.

1699 Olaso, E. de. "Leibniz y la duda metódica" **Revista de Filosofía** [Argentina] 14 (1964) 37-56.

1700 Olaso, E. de, ed. and tr., and Zwanck, T.E., tr. "Advertencias a la parte general de los Principios de Descartes" **Dia** 13 (1978) 129-71.

1701* Oliveira Torres, J.C. de. "Descartes e las ciências sociais" **RBF** 23 (1973) 190-92.

1702 Oliver, W.D. "A Sober Look at Solipsism" **APQ** Mon. 4 (Oxford 1970) 30-39.

1703 Olivetti, M. "Riforma cattolica e filosofica moderna" Review of **Cartesio. Riforma cattolica e filosofia moderna, 1**, by A. Del Noce [Bologna 1965]. **Archivio di Filosofia** 38 (1969) 153-87.

1704 Olscamp, P.J. "Introduction" **Discourse on Method, Optics, Geometry, and Meteorology,** by René Descartes; tr. by P.J. Olscamp (Indianapolis IN 1965) ix-xxxiv.

1705* Orenduff, J.M. "The Cartesian Circle" **Philosophical Topics** Supp. (1982) 109-13.

1706 Orenstein, A. "I Think, Therefore I am Not" **ILR** 6 (1975) 166.
Dis. by: Ratzsch, D.   **ILR** 8 (1977).
         Cobb-Stevens, V.   **ILR** 11 (1980).

1707 Orr, L. "Descartes à la Mode: Nietzsche and Valéry on Cognition" **Neohelicon** 10 (1983) 165-76.

1708 Osler, M.J. "Descartes and Charleton on Nature and God" **JHI** 40 (1979) 445-56.

1709 Ostrowski, A.M. "On Descartes' Rule of Signs of Certain Polynomial Developments" **Journal of Mathematics and Mechanics** 14 (1965) 195-209.

1710 Oudemans, T.C.W. "Relativiteit en volstrektheid van de kennis. Een overdenking bij de opvattingen van Descartes en Wittgenstein" **TF** 44 (1982) 53-103.

1711 Pacchi, A. "Henry More cartesiano" **RCSF** 26 (1971) 3-19, 115-140.

1712 Pacchi, A. **Cartesio in Inghilterra. Da More a Boyle** (Roma 1973).
Rev. by: Sina, M.   **RFN** 66 (1974) 183-87.
         Gabbey, A.   **BC** 6 (1977) 2-14.
         Gabbey, A.   **BJHS** 11 (1978) 159-64.

1713* Pacchi, A. **Il razionalismo del Seicento** (Torino 1982).

1714 Pacho, J. **Ontologie und Erkenntnistheorie: Eine Erörterung ihres Verhältnisses am Beispiel des Cartesianischen Systems** (München 1980).
Rev. by: M[arion], J.-L.   **BC** 11 (1982) 44-45.
         Schneider, M.   **RM** 36 (1982-83) 943-45.

1715 Pacho, J. "Uber einige erkenntnistheoretische Schwierigkeiten des klassischen Rationalismus. Uberlegungen anhand eines cartesianischen Beispiels" **ZPF** 38 (1984) 561-81.

1716* Padovani, U. "Descartes (il mondatore del pensiero moderno)" **Vidyá** 5 (1967) 1-25.

1717 Paisse, J.-M. "Socrate et Descartes" **Bulletin de l'Association de Guillaume Budé** 27 (1968) 241-57; 28 (1969) 89-100.

1718 Palacz, R. "La filosofía de la naturaleza en la Universidad de Cracovia en el siglo XV" **Pensamiento** 39 (1983) 449-76.

1719 Palmer, H. "Must Clocks be Material?" **R** 14 (1972) 36-44.

1720 Palmer, H. "The Cogito is Semi-circular" **ILR** 12 (1981) 5-15.

1721* Pandit, G.L. "The Cartesian Questions of Methodology and Against Psychologism" **Indian Philosophical Quarterly** 8 (1980-81) 299-304.

1722* Panou, S. "Doute et réflexion. Descartes et Husserl" **Philosophia** [Greece] 12 (1982) 326-37.

1723 Papineau, D. "The <u>Vis Viva</u> Controversy: Do Meanings Matter?" **SHPS** 8 (1977) 111-42.
Dis. by: C[ostabel], P.   **BC** 8 (1979) 57-58.

1724 Paré, F. "Descartes et Montaigne, autobiographes" **Etudes Littéraires** 17 (1984) 381-94.

1725 Parkinson, G.H.R. "From Descartes to Collingwood: Recent Work on the History of Philosophy" **P** 50 (1975) 205-20.

1726 Parkinson, G.H.R., ed. **Truth, Knowledge and Reality: Inquiries into the Foundations of Seventeenth Century Rationalism. SL** Sonderh. 9 (1981).

1727* Pasche, F. "Métaphysique et inconscient" **RFP** 45 (1981) 9-30.
Dis. of: Freud, S.   **RFP** 45 (1981) 5-7.

1728 Pastine, D., ed. "Caramuel contro Descartes. Obiezioni inedite alle Meditazioni" **RCSF** 27 (1972) 177-221.

1729 Pastore, N. "Descartes" Chap. ii of **Selective History of Theories of Visual Perception: 1650-1950** (London 1971) 18-40.

1730 Pastore, N., and Klibbe, H. "The Orientation of the Cerebral Image in Descartes' Theory of Visual Perception" **Journal of the History of the Behavioral Sciences** 5 (1969) 385-89.

1731 Patten, S.C. "Kant's <u>Cogito</u>" **KS** 66 (1975) 331-41.

1732 Pav, P.A. "Eighteenth Century Optics: The Cartesian-Newtonian Conflict" **Applied Optics** 14 (1975) 3102-08.

1733 Pavan, A. "Appunti di storiografia cartesiana" **Scritti in onore di Carlo Giacon** (Padova 1972) 383-408.

1734 Pavan, A. **All'origine del progetto borghese. Il giovane Descartes** (Brescia 1979).

1735 Payot, R. "L'argument ontologique et le fondement de la métaphysique" **AP** 39 (1976) 227-68, 427-44.

1736 Pearl, L. **Descartes** (Boston 1977).
Rev. by: Hodgson, F.   **FR** 52 (1978-79) 482-83.

1737 Pellecchia, P. "Il principio del 'passo indietro' del pensiero" **Aquinas** 27 (1984) 343-72.

1738   Peltz, R.W.   "The Logic of the Cogito"   **PPR** 23 (1962-63) 256-62.
       Dis. of: Bar-Hillel, Y.   **PS** 11 (1960).

1739   Peltz, R.W.   "Indexical Sentences and Cartesian Rationalism"   **PPR** 27
       (1966-67) 80-84.

1740   Peña García, V.   "Descartes, razón y metáfora"   **Arb** 108 (1981) 175-83.

1741   Peña García, V.   "Acerca de la razón en Descartes: reglas de la moral y
       reglas del metodo"   **Arb** 112 (1982) 167-83.

1742   Penelhum, T.   "Descartes' Ontological Argument"   **FE** (Oxford 1969) 43-55.
       Dis. of: Kenny, A.   **FE** (Oxford 1969).
       Dis. by: Kenny, A.   **FE** (Oxford 1969).

1743* Pepe, L.   "Note sulla diffusione della Géométrie di Descartes in Italia
       nel secolo XVII"   **Bollettino di Storia delle Scienze Matematiche** 2
       (1982) 249-88.

1744   Percival, W.K.   "On the Non-existence of Cartesian Linguistics"   **CS**
       (Oxford 1972) 137-45.
       Dis. of: Chomsky, N.   **Cartesian Linguistics** (New York 1966).

1745   Perelman, C.   "Analogie et métaphore en science, poésie et philosophie"
       RIP 23 (1969) 3-15.

1746* Peres, A.   "Etude d'une oeuvre. Descartes' Règles pour la direction de
       l'esprit"   **EL** 72 (1981) 43-50; 73 (1982) 43-51.

1747* Peres, A.   "L'affectivité chez Descartes et Spinoza"   **EL** 75 (1984)
       39-50.

1748   Pérez, J.   "Descartes et Saint Jean de la Croix"   **Les cultures
       ibériques en devenir. Essais publiés en hommage à la mémoire de Marcel
       Bataillon (1895-1977)**, ed. by G. Duby (Paris 1979) 197-207.

1749   Perini, R.   "Mathesis universalis e metafisica nel metodo cartesiano"
       GM 28 (1973) 159-207.

1750* Perini, R.   "Naturae simplices e 'intuitus' nelle Regulae ad directionem
       ingenii"   **Annali della Facoltà di Lettere e Filosofia dell'Università
       di Perugia** 16-17 (1979-80) 241-79.

1751   Perini, R.   "La fondazione del sapere nella 'scientia' cartesiana"
       Annali della Facoltà di Lettere e Filosofia dell'Università di Perugia
       18 (1980-81) 35-70.

1752* Perini, R.   **Il problema della fondazione nelle Regulae di Descartes**
       (Rimini 1983).

1753   Perkinson, H.J.   "Descartes's Method"   **Since Socrates: Studies in the
       History of Western Educational Thought**, by H.J. Perkinson (New York
       1980) 74-88.

1754 Perrot, J. "Le Descartes Dostoïvskien de La Chute d'Albert Camus" **Revue des Lettres Modernes** 315-22 (1972) 129-53.

1755 Perrot, M. "Descartes, Saumaise et Christine de Suède. Une lettre inédite de Christine à Saumaise du 9 mars 1650" **EP** (1984) 1-9.

1756 Peters, K., Schmidt, W., and Holz, H.H. **Erkenntnisgewissheit und Deducktion: zum Aufbau der philosophischen Systeme bei Descartes, Spinoza, Leibniz** (Darmstadt 1975).

1757 Petit, L. "Descartes en Italie sur les pas de Montaigne" **Bulletin de la Société des Amis de Montaigne** Ser. 3 (1960) No. 13, 22-33.

1758* Petit, L. "Un roman d'amour: Descartes et la princesse Elizabeth" **Cerf-volant** 36 (1961) 59-63; 38 (1962) 21-24; 39 (1962) 31-33; 40 (1962) 12-14.

1759 Petit, L. **Descartes et la Princesse Elisabeth. Roman d'amour vécu** (Paris 1969).
Rev. by: [Rizza, C.]   **SFr** 14 (1970) 148-49.
          Sabatier, R.   **Figaro Littéraire** (9-15 Feb. 1970) 24.
          Sartenaer, J.   **Lettres Romanes** 27 (1973) 85-87.

1760 Petruzzellis, N. "Le passioni nel pensiero di Tommaso d'Aquino, di R. Descartes e di B. Spinoza" **Rassegna di Scienze Filosofiche** 25 (1972) 253-86, 381-405.

1761* Pétry, M.J. "De Regenboog" Chap. iii of **Spinoza. Kernmomenten in zijn Denken**, by F.D.A. Vleeskens et al. (Baarn 1977).

1762 Peukert, K.W. "Der Wille und die Selbstbewegung des Geistes in Descartes Meditationen" **ZPF** 19 (1965) 87-109, 224-47.

1763* Peursen, C.A. van. "'Waarheid' bij Descartes" **Wijsgerig Perspectief op Maatschappij en Wetenschap** 19 (1978-79) 70-73.

1764* Peursen, C.A. van. **Wetenschappelijke openheid en metafysische kwetsbaarheid** (Kampen 1982).

1765 Pfeiffer, M.L. "El límite de la duda" **RLF** 4 (1978) 75-80.
Dis. of: Sosa, E.   **RLF** 2 (1976).
Dis. by: Sosa, E.   **RLF** 4 (1978).

1766 Pflug, G. "Descartes und das mechanistische Menschenbild" **Medizinhistorisches Journal** 17 (1982) 3-19.

1767* Philippe, M.-D. "La preuve de l'existence de Dieu chez Descartes" **Bulletin du Cercle Thomiste St-Nicolas de Caen** 97 (1983) 9-36.

1768 Phillips, M. "La Causa Sive Ratio chez Descartes" **EP** (1984) 11-21.

1769 Philonenko, A. "Le cartésianisme de Malebranche suivant Ferdinand Alquié" Review of **Le cartésianisme de Malebranche**, by F. Alquié [Paris 1974]. **RMM** 80 (1975) 209-39.

1770   Philonenko, A.   "Une lecture fichtéenne du cartésianisme n'est-elle pas nécessaire?"   **PaRa** (Paris 1983) 341-57.

1771   Picardi, F.   **Il concetto di metafisica nel razionalismo cartesiano** (Milano 1971).
       Rev. by: Cartechini, S.   **Gregorianum** 53 (1972) 595-97.
                 Nicolaci, G.   **GM** 29 (1974) 295-96.

1772* Piccolomini, M.   **Il pensiero estetico di Gianvincenzo Gravina** (Ravenna 1984).

1773   Piclin, M.   "Descartes et la première certitude"   **EP** (1984) 23-36.

1774* Pies, E.   "Der (Mord-)+Fall René Descartes. Kapitalverbrechen vor 333 Jahre begangen, heute aufgeklärt"   **Mitteilungen der Westdeutschen Gesellschaft für Familienkunde** 31 (1983) 35-41.

1775* Pignoloni, E.   "Gioberti e il pensiero moderno"   **Rivista Rosminiana di Filosofia e di Cultura** 64 (1970) 155-75.

1776   Pilon, J.G.   "Cartesian Roots of the Ontological Principle"   **Process Studies** 6 (1976) 249-54.

1777   Pizzorusso, A.   "L'idea di 'letteratura' nel seicento francese"   **Belfagor** 38 (1983) 1-15.

1778   Plaisance, D.   "Corbinelli auteur de comptes rendus de séances cartésiennes?"   **TLL** 19 (1981) 39-52.

1779   Plante, R.   "Cybernétique et dualisme cartésien"   **D** 10 (1971) 743-50.

1780   Plante, R.   "Le dépistage automatique des structures de surface et l'analyse des textes philosophiques"   **Cirpho** 3 (1976) 57-79.

1781   Plantinga, A.   "Alston on the Ontological Argument"   **DCCE** (Garden City NY 1967) 303-11.
       Repr. in **God and Other Minds,** by A. Plantinga (Ithaca NY 1967) 47-63.
       Dis. of: Alston, W.P.   **PR** 69 (1960).

1782   Plantinga, A.   "World and Essence"   **PR** 79 (1970) 461-92.
       Dis. by: Carter, W.R.   **PR** 81 (1972).

1783   Plantinga, A.   "Could Socrates have been an Alligator?"   Chap. iv, sect. 12 of **The Nature of Necessity** (Oxford 1974) 65-69.

1784   Plantinga, A.   "Descartes and Possibilism"   Sect. 4A of **Does God Have a Nature?** (Milwaukee WI 1980) 95-126.

1785   Pochtar, R.   "El _Examen de Ingenios_ y la 'linguistica cartesiana'"   **RLF** 2 (1976) 179-85.
       Dis. of: Chomsky, N.   **Cartesian Linguistics** (New York 1966).

1786   Podestá, R.   "La concepción cartesiana de la ciencia"   **Revista de Filosofía de la Universidad de Costa Rica** 14 (1976) No. 39, 75-83.

1787 Poirier, J.-L. **"Méditations métaphysiques" de Descartes: commentaire** (Paris 1980).

1788 Polin, R. "Descartes et la philosophie politique" **MAK** 2 (Paris 1964) 381-99.

1789 Polo, L. **Evidencia y realidad en Descartes** (Madrid 1963).

1790 Pomian, K. "De l'animal comme être philosophique" **Débat** 27 (1983) 127-42.

1791 Pompa, L. "The Incoherence of the Cartesian Cogito" **Inquiry** 27 (1984) 3-21.

1792 Popkin, R.H. "Descartes: Conqueror of Scepticism" Chap. ix of **The History of Scepticism from Erasmus to Descartes** (Assen 1960); rev. ed. (New York 1964) 175-96.
Rev. by: Tonelli, G. **F** 15 (1964) 327-32.

1793 Popkin, R.H. "Descartes: Sceptique Malgré lui" Chap. x of **The History of Scepticism from Erasmus to Descartes** (Assen 1960); rev. ed. (New York 1964) 197-217.
Rev. by: Tonelli, G. **F** 15 (1964) 327-32.

1794 Popkin, R.H. "The High Road to Pyrrhonism" **APQ** 2 (1965) 18-32.

1795 Popkin, R.H. "Cartesianism and Biblical Criticism" **PC** (Kingston and Montréal 1982) 61-81.
Dis. by: Rex, W.E. **PC** (Kingston and Montréal 1982).

1796 Porschnew, B.F. "Descartes und die Fronde" **Beiträge zur französischen Aufklärung und zur spanischen Literatur. Festgabe für Werner Krauss zum 70. Geburtstag**, ed. by W. Bahner (Berlin 1971) 281-87.

1797 Poser, H. "Zum Verhältnis von Beobachtung und Theorie bei Descartes, Spinoza und Leibniz" **TKR** (1981) 115-46.

1798 Poulet, G. "La 'Nausée' de Sartre et le 'Cogito' cartésien" **SFr** 5 (1961) 452-62.

1799 Pousa, N. **Moral y libertad en Descartes** (La Plata 1960).

1800* Pousseur, J.-M. "La distinction de la ratio et de la methodus dans le Novum Organum et ses prolongements dans le rationalisme cartésien" **Francis Bacon. Terminologia e fortuna nel XVII secolo**, ed. by M. Fattori (Roma 1984) 201-22.

1801 Powell, B. "Descartes' Machines" **AS** 71 (1970-71) 209-22.

1802* Pozzi, L. **Da Ramus a Kant. Il dibattito sulla sillogistica** (Milano 1981).

1803 Prenant, L. "Sur les références de Leibniz à Kepler contre Descartes" **AIHS** 13 (1960) 95-97.

1804 Prenant, L. "Sur la thèse d'Y. Belaval" Review of **Leibniz critique de Descartes,** by Y. Belaval [Paris 1960]. **Pens** 97 (1961) 57-82.

1805 Prendergast, T.L. "Descartes and the Relativity of Motion" **MS** 50 (1972-73) 64-72.

1806 Prendergast, T.L. "Motion, Action, and Tendency in Descartes' Physics" **JHP** 13 (1975) 453-62.

1807 Presas, M.A. "Historia e idea de la filosofía como ciencia en Husserl" **RLF** 7 (1981) 61-71.

1808 Prezioso, F.A. "La battaglia del 'cogito'" **Rassegna di Scienze Filosofiche** 20 (1967) 182-95.

1809 Priest, S. "Descartes, Kant, and Self-Consciousness" **PQ** 31 (1981) 348-51.
Dis. of: Wilkerson, T.E. **PQ** 30 (1980).

1810 Prior, A.N. "The Cogito of Descartes and the Concept of Self-Confirmation" **The Foundation of Statements and Decisions,** ed. by K. Ajdukiewicz (Berlin 1965) 47-53.
Repr. in **Papers in Logic and Ethics,** by A.N. Prior; ed. by P.T. Geach and A. Kenny (London 1976) 165-75.

1811 Prior, A.N. "Wittgenstein y el racionalismo de la modernidad" **Actas del Tercer Congreso Nacional de Filosofía** 1 (Buenos Aires 1982) 400-06.

1812* Proto, M. "Intorno alla psicologia di Cartesio" **Culture Française** 9 (1962) 101-04.

1813 Pruche, B. "Situation sartrienne de la conscience cartésienne d'après Regulae I à VII" **Science et Esprit** 31 (1979) 343-60.

1814 Prunier, F. **Pour un supplément au 'Discours de la méthode'** (Asnières [1970]).

1815 Pucelle, J. "La 'lumière naturelle' et le cartésianisme dans l'Esprit Géométrique et l'Art de Persuader" **Pascal. Textes du Tricentenaire,** ed. by J. Renoult and J. Gaudouin (Paris 1963) 50-61.

1816 Pucelle, J. "Le survol" **EP** 26 (1971) 427-39.

1817 Pucelle, J. "Malentendus sur 'Pascal et Descartes'. Pascal et les philosophes" **Chroniques de Port-Royal** 20-21 (1972) 96-103.

1818 Putman, D.A. "Doubting, Thinking, and Possible Worlds" **PRA** 9 (1983) 337-46.

1819* Quintás Alonso, G. "La presencia de Descartes en la ilustración" **Teorema** 4 (1974) 215-25.

1820 Quinton, A. "Matter and Space" **M** 73 (1964) 332-52.

1821 Rábade Romeo, S. "Dios y el problema del criterio en Descartes" **Miscelánea Comillas** 47-48 (1967) 369-88.

1822 Rábade Romeo, S. **Descartes y la gnoseología moderna** (Madrid 1971). Rev. by: Deregibus, A.   **GM** 28 (1973) 566-69.

1823 Radermacher, H. **Cartesianische Wissenschaftstheorie.** Beitr. 10 of **Philosophie als Beziehungswissenschaft. Festschrift für Julius Schaaf,** ed. by W.F. Niebel and D. Leisegang (Frankfurt 1971). Repr. in **Philosophie als Beziehungswissenschaft. Festschrift für Julius Schaaf,** ed. by W.F. Niebel and D. Leisegang (Frankfurt 1974).

1824 Radford, C. "Wittgenstein and Descartes: The Best of Both Worlds" **Wittgenstein und sein Einfluss auf die gegenwärtige Philosophie,** ed. by E. Leinfellner et al. (Wien 1978) 420-24.

1825 Radner, D. "Descartes' Notion of the Union of Mind and Body" **JHP** 9 (1971) 159-70.

1826 Radner, D. "Spinoza's Theory of Ideas" **PR** 80 (1971) 338-59.

1827 Radner, D. **Malebranche: A Study of a Cartesian System** (Assen 1978). Rev. by: Watson, R.A.   **RM** 32 (1978-79) 564-65.
               Dreyfus, G.   **SC** 1 (1979) 211-15.
               Mattern, R.   **PR** 89 (1980) 278-82.

1828 Radner, D. "Berkeley and Cartesianism" **CJP** Supp. 4 (1978) 165-76.

1829* Rahim, S.A. "The Cartesian Doubt" **PPC** 10 (1963) 250-58.

1830 Rahman, M. Lutfur. "Are Clear and Distinct Ideas True?" **PPC** 16 (1970) 150-61. Repr. in **PPJ** 10 (1971) No. 1, 100-11.

1831* Raju, P.T. **Spirit, Being and Self: Studies in Indian Philosophy** (New Delhi 1982).

1832 Rambach, J.-C. "A propos des passions: Ombres et lumières avant Descartes" **TLL** 15 (1977) 43-65.

1833 Randall, J.H., Jr. "Descartes and the Cartesian Revolution" Bk. III, chap. ii of **From the Middle Ages to the Enlightenment. The Career of Philosophy** 1 (New York 1962) 371-95.

1834 Randall, J.H., Jr. "The Triumph of Reason in France and Holland" Bk. III, chap. iii of **From the Middle Ages to the Enlightenment. The Career of Philosophy** 1 (New York 1962) 396-412.

1835 Randall, J.H., Jr. "Augustinian Interpretations of the Cartesian Philosophy: Scepticism and Rationalism" Bk. III, chap. iv of **From the Middle Ages to the Enlightenment. The Career of Philosophy** 1 (New York 1962) 413-33.

1836 Rapaport, W.J. "On Cogito Propositions" **PS** 29 (1976) 63-68.
      Dis. of: Nakhnikian, G.   **N** 3 (1969).

1837* Raskin, R. "Esquisse d'une critique du cogito" **(Pré)Publications** 15
      (1975) 40-46.

1838* Raskin, R. "On the Decolonization of the Mind in Descartes's
      Méditations métaphysiques" **(Pré)Publications** 15 (1975) 36-39.

1839 Rat, M. "Descartes contre Descartes" **Revue des Deux Mondes** 19 (1967)
      387-90.
      Dis. of: Chauvois, L.   **Descartes. Sa méthode et ses erreurs
                                    en physiologie** (Paris 1966).

1840 Rather, L.J. "Old and New Views of the Emotions and Bodily Changes:
      Wright and Harvey versus Descartes, James and Cannon" **Clio Medica** 1
      (1965-66) 1-25.

1841 Rathmann, B. "Descartes inventeur. Les principes méthodologiques dans
      les Regulae ad directionem ingenii" **PFSL** 7 (1980) 59-72.
      Dis. of: Hammacher, K.   **ZAW** 4 (1973) 203-23.

1842 Rathmann, B. "L'imagination et le doute. Essai sur la genèse de la
      pensée cartésienne" **PFSL** 8 (1981) 57-73.

1843 Rattansi, P.M. "Voltaire and the Enlightenment Image of Newton"
      History and Imagination: Essays in Honor of H.R. Trevor-Roper, ed. by
      H. Lloyd-Jones et al. (New York 1982) 218-31.

1844 Ratzsch, D. "I Think, Therefore I Am Not: A Reply" **ILR** 8 (1977) 92.
      Dis. of: Orenstein, A.   **ILR** 6 (1975).
      Dis. by: Cobb-Stevens, V.   **ILR** 11 (1980).

1845 Recht, R. "'The Foundations of an Admirable Science': Descartes's
      Dreams of 10 November 1619" **Humanities in Society** 4 (1981) 203-19.

1846 Redondi, P. "Gallilée aux prises avec les théories aristoteliennes de
      la lumière (1610-1640)" **DsS** 34 (1982) 267-83.

1847 Rée, J. **Descartes** (London 1974).
      Rev. by: McLaren, J.C.   **Thought** 51 (1976) 109-10.
               Hooker, M.   **PR** 86 (1977) 278-81.
               Rosenfield, L.C.   **JHP** 15 (1977) 468-71.

1848 Rée, J. "Descartes's Comedy" **PL** 8 (1984) 151-66.

1849 Reed, E.S. "Descartes' Corporeal Ideas Hypothesis and the Origin of
      Scientific Psychology" **RM** 35 (1981-82) 731-52.

1850* Reeder, H. "Cogito, ergo sum: Inference and Performance" **Eidos**
      [Canada] 1 (1978) 30-49.

1851 Régnault, F. "La pensée du prince (Descartes et Machiavel). Descartes et Elisabeth: Quatre lettres sur Machiavel" **Cahiers pour l'Analyse** 6 (1967) 21-66.

1852 Reif, P. "The Textbook Tradition in Natural Philosophy, 1600-1650" **JHI** 30 (1969) 17-32.

1853 Reijen, W.L. van. "Freiheit und Moral in der Philosophie Descartes'" **ZPF** 29 (1975) 125-37.

1854 Reinhardt, L.R. "Dualism and Categories" **AS** 66 (1965-66) 71-92.

1855 Reiss, T.J. "Poésie 'libertine' et pensée cartésienne: Etude de l'Elégie à une dame de Théophile de Viau" **Baroque** 6 (1973) 75-80.

1856 Reiss, T.J. "Cartesian Discourse and Classical Ideology" Review of **L'illusion chez Descartes,** by S. Romanowski [Paris 1974]. **Diacritics** 6 (1976) 19-27.

1857 Reiss, T.J. "The 'concevoir' Motif in Descartes" **La cohérence intérieure. Etudes sur la littérature française du XVIIe siècle présentées en hommage à Judd D. Hubert,** ed. by J. Van Baelen and D.L. Rubin (Paris 1977) 203-22.

1858 Reiss, T.J. **The Discourse of Modernism** (Ithaca NY 1982).

1859 Relyea, S.L. "Classical Seme and Classical Episteme" Chap. i of **Signs, Systems, and Meanings: A Contemporary Semiotic Reading of Four Molière Plays** (Middletown CT 1976) 12-35.

1860 Remnant, P. "Descartes: Body and Soul" **CJP** 9 (1979) 377-86.

1861 Renaud, M. "La 'Philosophie du corps' selon M. Claude Bruaire" **RPL** 67 (1969) 104-42.

1862 Rescher, N. "The Legitimacy of Doubt" **RM** 13 (1959-60) 226-34.

1863 Rescher, N. "The Illegitimacy of Cartesian Doubt" **Essays in Philosophical Analysis,** by N. Rescher (Pittsburgh PA 1969) 309-19.

1864 Rescher, N. **Scepticism: A Critical Reappraisal** (Oxford 1980).

1865 Rethy, R.A. "The Descartes Motto to the First Edition of Menschliches, Allzumenschliches" **Nietzsche Studien** 5 (1976) 289-97.

1866 Revel, J.-F. **Descartes inutile et incertain** (Paris 1976). Repr. in **Discours de la méthode,** by René Descartes; ed. by J.-M. Beyssade (Paris 1976) 7-86.
      Rev. by: George, F.   **Temps Modernes** 32 (1976-77) 1925-27.
               Gabaude, J.-M.   **Nouvelle Critique** 103 (1977) 77.
               M[arion], J.-L.   **BC** 7 (1978) 25.

1867 Rex, W.E. "Bayle, Jurieu, and the Politics of Philosophy: A Reply to
      Professor Popkin" **PC** (Kingston and Montréal 1982) 83-94.
      Dis. of: Popkin, R.H.   **PC** (Kingston and Montréal 1982).

1868 Ribeiro de Moura, C.A. "A cera e o abelhudo. Expressão e percepção em
      Merleau-Ponty" **RLF** 6 (1980) 235-53.

1869 Ribes Montané, P. "Las sensaciones orgánicas y su influjo gnoseológico
      en la doctrina de Descartes" **Analecta Sacra Tarraconensia** 43 (1970)
      209-37.

1870 Ricci, F. "Le bâton courbé" **Annales de la Faculté des Lettres et
      Sciences Humaines de Nice** 32 (1977) 117-29.

1871 Ricci, F. "Descartes et la personnalité classique" **Actes du groupe de
      recherches sur la conscience de soi. Annales de la Faculté des
      Lettres et Sciences Humaines de Nice** 18 (1980) 65-76.

1872 Richard, R. "Le contre-sujet" **Spirales** 11 (1982) 35-36.

1873 Richardson, R.C. "The 'Scandal' of Cartesian Interactionism" **M** 91
      (1982) 20-37.

1874 Ricken, U. "Zur erkenntnistheoretischen Wertung der Sinne in der
      französischen Sprachdiskussion bis Locke" **Beiträge zur französischen
      Aufklärung und zur spanischen Literatur. Festgabe für Werner Krauss zum
      70. Geburtstag**, ed. by W. Bahner (Berlin 1971) 337-61.

1875 Ricken, U. "Interpretationen der Sprache als Argument für und gegen den
      Dualismus. Descartes und seine sensualistischen Gegenspieler im 17.
      Jahrhundert" **Beiträge zur Romanischen Philologie** 20 (1981) 29-49.

1876 Rickman, H.P. "Descartes: The Quest for Certainty" Chap. iii of **The
      Adventure of Reason: The Uses of Philosophy in Sociology** (Westport CT
      1983) 47-70.

1877 Riese, W. "La thèse cartésienne" Chapter of **La théorie des passions à
      la lumière de la pensée médicale du XVIIe siècle** (Basel 1965) 1-18.

1878 Riese, W. "Descartes as a Psychotherapist. The Uses of Rational
      Philosophy in the Treatment of Discomfort and Disease; Its Limitations"
      Medical History 10 (1966) 237-44.

1879 Riese, W. "On Symbolic Thought in Cartesianism" **Science, Medicine and
      Society in the Renaissance: Essays to Honor Walter Pagel**, ed. by A.G.
      Debus. 2 (London 1972) 163-65.

1880 Riese, W., and Raynaud, D. "Connaissance et Moralité: Interprétation
      d'une Note de Gilson" **Episteme** [Italia] 6 (1972) 135-40.
      Dis. of: Gilson, E., ed.   **Discours de la méthode** (Paris 1925).

1881* Riet, G. van. "Le cogito cartésien" **Presença Filosofica** 8 (1982)
      79-82.

1882* Riggs, L.W. "Seventeenth-Century French Humanism: An Early Debate on the Curriculum of the Human" **Apollo Agonistes: The Humanities in a Computerized World,** ed. by M.E. Grenander (Albany NY 1979) 186-95.

1883 Riley, G. "Self-Knowledge: A Tale of the Tortoise which Supports an Elephant" **PF** 1 (1968-69) 274-92.

1884 Ring, M. "Descartes' Intentions" **CJP** 3 (1973-74) 27-49.
Dis. by: Schouls, P.A.   **CJP** 3 (1973-74).

1885 Risse, W. "Zur Vorgeschichte der cartesischen Methodenlehre" **AGP** 45 (1963) 269-91.

1886 Risse, W. "Die rationalistischen Systeme. Descartes" Chap. viii of **Die Logik der Neuzeit** 2 (Stuttgart 1970) 30-131.
Rev. by: A[rmogathe], J.-R.   **BC** 1 (1972) 287-90.

1887 Ritchie, A.M. "Can Animals See? A Cartesian Query" **AS** 64 (1963-64) 221-42.

1888 Rittmeister, J., and Storch, A. "Die mystische Krise des jungen Descartes. Mit einem Nachtrag zur heutigen Beurteilung Descartes" **Confinia Psychiatrica** 4 (1961) 65-98.
Repr. in **Zeitschrift für Psychosomatischen Medizin und Psychoanalyse** 15 (1969) 206-24.

1889* Riu Farré, F. "Introducción en la metafísica según Descartes" **Gaceta de Pedagogía** 14 (1966) 31-42.

1890 Robert, J.-D. "Descartes, créateur d'un nouveau style métaphysique. Réflexions sur l'introduction du primat de la subjectivité en philosophie première" **RPL** 60 (1962) 369-93.

1891 Roberts, G.W. "Some Questions in Epistemology" **AS** 70 (1969-70) 37-60.

1892 Robinet, A. "Cartésianisme et Leibnizianisme" Review of **Leibniz critique de Descartes,** by Y. Belaval [Paris 1960]. **RS** 82 (1961) 73-89.

1893 Robinet, A. "Descartes à l'ordinateur" **EP** 25 (1970) 219-23.
Dis. of: Morris, J.M.   **Computers and the Humanities** 3 (1968-69).

1894 Robinet, A. "La condition de l'automate (Descartes)" Pt. II, chap. ii of **Le défi cybernétique. L'automate et la pensée** (Paris 1973) 78-91.
Rev. by: Gochet, P.   **RIP** 27 (1973) 112-19.

1895 Robinet, A. "Descartes, Malebranche et Monsieur Alquié" Review of **Le cartésianisme de Malebranche,** by F. Alquié [Paris 1974]. **RIP** 28 (1974) 532-39.

1896 Robinet, A. "Dom Robert Desgabets: Le conflit philosophique avec Malebranche et l'oeuvre métaphysique" **RS** 95 (1974) 65-83.

1897   Robinet, A.   "La specificité du langage philosophique au XVIIe siècle"
       1CIL (Roma 1976) 65-80.

1898   Robinet, A.   "Premiers pas dans l'application de l'informatique a
       l'étude des textes philosophiques" 1CIL (Roma 1976) 139-47.

1899   Robinet, A.   "L'oubli cartésien du langage" Bk. III of Le langage à
       l'âge classique (Paris 1978) 79-103.
       Rev. by: Hottois, G.   RIP 33 (1979) 570-86.
                  Reix, A.   EP (1980) 498-99.
                  Watson, R.A.   JHP 20 (1982) 203-05.

1900   Robinet, A.   "La pensée pensant" Chap. i of La pensée à l'âge
       classique (Paris 1981) 3-52.

1901   Robinet, A.   "Malebranche et Leibniz: Vérité, Ordre et Raison face au
       'Cogito' cartésien" TKR (1981) 97-106.

1902   Robinson, G.   "Scepticism about Scepticism" AS Supp. 51 (1977) 237-53.

1903* Roche Ruiz, J.   Filósofos. Aristoteles, Descartes, Hume, Kant, Hegel,
       Marx, Nietzsche (Valencia 1980).

1904   Roche, M.   "Un homme: Monsieur Descartes" Humanisme Contemporain 2
       (1966) 71-98.

1905   Rochot, B.   "Infini mathématique et infini métaphysique chez Descartes"
       Review of Mathématiques et métaphysique chez Descartes, by J.
       Vuillemin [Paris 1960]. RS 82 (1961) 67-71.

1906   Rochot, B.   "La preuve ontologique interprétée par M. Gueroult. (Réponse
       aux 'Objections' de M. Jacques Brunschwig)" RP 86 (1961) 125-30.
       Dis. of: Brunschwig, J.   RP 85 (1960).
       Dis. by: Brunschwig, J.   RP 87 (1962).

1907   Rochot, B.   Review of La pensée métaphysique de Descartes, by H.
       Gouhier [Paris 1962]. RS 84 (1963) 491-501.

1908   Rochot, B.   "Le P. Mersenne et les relations intellectuelles dans
       l'Europe du XVIIe siècle" Cahiers d'Histoire Mondiale 10 (1966-67)
       55-73.

1909   Rochot, B.   "Descartes et la physique mathématique" Review of
       Descartes, premier théoricien de la physique mathématique, by E.
       Denissoff [Louvain 1970]. RS 92 (1971) 85-92.

1910   Rockmore, T.   "Vico, Marx, and Anti-Cartesian Theory of Knowledge"
       Vico and Marx: Affinities and Contrasts, ed. by G. Tagliacozzo
       (Atlantic Highlands NJ 1983) 178-91.

1911   Röd, W.   "Zum Problem des premier principe in Descartes' Metaphysik"
       KS 51 (1959-60) 176-95.

1912   Röd, W.   "Zur Problematik der Gotteserkenntnis bei Descartes ('Le cercle
       cartésien')"   **AGP** 43 (1961) 128-52.

1913   Röd, W.   "Gewissheit und Wahrheit bei Descartes"   **ZPF** 16 (1962) 342-62.

1914   Röd, W.   **Descartes. Die innere Genesis des cartesianischen Systems**
       (München 1964); 2nd ed. [**Descartes. Die Genese des cartesianischen
       Rationalismus**] (1982).
       Rev. by: Obertello, L.   **F** 17 (1966) 397-401.
                  Decloux, S.   **Eras** 19 (1967) 453-54.
                  Ley, H.   **Deutsche Literaturzeitung** 105
                                         (1984) 449-52.
                  M[arion], J.-L.   **BC** 13 (1984) 50-52.

1915   Röd, W.   "Objektivismus und Subjektivismus als Pole der Descartes-
       Interpretation"   Review of **The Metaphysics of Descartes**, by L.J. Beck
       [Oxford 1965]; and of **Aufklärung und Metaphysik**, by G. Schmidt
       [Tübingen 1965].   **PRu** 16 (1969) 28-39.

1916   Röd, W.   **Descartes' Erste Philosophie. Versuch eine Analyse mit
       besonderer Berücksichtigung der cartesianischen Methodologie.   KS**
       Ergänzungsh. 103 (Bonn 1971).
       Rev. by: Seidl, H.   **PLa** 25 (1972) 65-66.
                  M[arion], J.-L.   **BC** 2 (1973) 463-69.
                  Steinbeck, W.   **KS** 65 (1974) 201-02.
                  Baruzzi, A.   **PJ** 82 (1975) 210-13.
                  Vandenbulcke, J.   **TF** 37 (1975) 100-104.

1917   Röd, W.   "Richtungen der gegenwärtigen Descartes-Forschung"   Review of
       An Introduction to Philosophy, by G. Nahknikian [New York 1967]; of
       Descartes, by A. Kenny [New York 1967]; of **Der Aufbau des
       philosophischen Wissens nach René Descartes**, by D. Mahnke [München
       1967]; of **Descartes' Frage nach der Existenz der Welt**, by W. Halbfass
       [Meisenheim 1968]; of **Metaphysics and the Philosophy of Science**, by G.
       Buchdahl [Oxford 1969]; and of **Descartes, premier théoricien de la
       physique mathématique**, by E. Denissoff [Louvain 1970].   **PRu** 18 (1971)
       78-92.

1918   Röd, W.   "Descartes' Mythus oder Ryles Mythus? Uberlegungen zu Ryles
       Descartes-Kritik"   **AGP** 55 (1973) 310-33.
       Dis. by: Savigny, E. von   **AGP** 57 (1975).
                  A[rmogathe], J.-R.   **BC** 4 (1975).

1919* Röd, W.   "René Descartes"   **Enzyklopädie. Die Grossen der
       Weltgeschichte**, 5 (Zürich 1974) 708-21.

1920   Röd, W.   "Würzeln der dialektischen Methode in der vorsokratischen
       Philosophie"   Chap. i of **Dialektische Philosophie der Neuzeit. Von Kant
       bis Hegel** 1 (München 1974) 15-29.

1921   Röd, W.   "Erwiderung auf E. von Savignys Diskussionsbeitrag"   **AGP** 57
       (1975) 207-11.
       Dis. of: Savigny, E. von   **AGP** 57 (1975).

1922 Röd, W. "Die Beurteilung der analytischen Methode der klassischen Naturwissenschaft in der Philosophie des 17. und 18. Jahrhunderts" **SV** (Bonn 1976) 107-22.

1923 Röd, W. "L'argument du rêve dans la théorie cartésienne de l'expérience" **EP** (1976) 461-73.

1924* Röd, W. "René Descartes" Chapter of **Die Philosophie der Neuzeit 1: Von Francis Bacon bis Spinoza.** Vol. 7 of **Geschichte der Philosophie,** ed. by W. Röd (München 1977).

1925 Röd, W. "Einige Uberlegungen sur Debatte über das 'Cogito ergo sum' in der Philosophie des 20. Jahrhunderts" **SC** 1 (1979) 129-43.

1926 Röd, W. "Le cogito ergo sum dans la philosophie universitaire allemande au XVIIIe siècle" **PaRa** (Paris 1983) 305-22.

1927 Rodis-Lewis, G. **René Descartes, Français, philosophe** (Paris 1953); new ed. [**Descartes. Initiation à sa philosophie**] (1964). Rev. by: [Rizza, C.]   **SFr** 10 (1966) 141-42.

1928 Rodis-Lewis, G. **La morale de Descartes** (Paris 1957); 2nd ed. (1962); 3rd ed. (1970).

1929 Rodis-Lewis, G. "Le paradoxe cartésien" **L'âme et le corps. Recherches et Débats du Centre Catholique des Intellectuels Français** 35 (Paris 1961) 149-62.

1930 Rodis-Lewis, G. "Les philosophes du XVIIe siècle devant Dieu" **DsS** 54-55 (1962) 17-28.

1931 Rodis-Lewis, G. "Le domaine propre de l'homme chez les Cartésiens" **JHP** 2 (1964) 157-88.

1932 Rodis-Lewis, G. **Descartes et le rationalisme** (Paris 1966); 2nd ed. (1970); 3rd ed. (1977). Rev. by: Barjonet-Huraux, M.   **Pens** 132 (1967) 151-53. Malter, R.   **PLa** 22 (1969) 47-50.

1933 Rodis-Lewis, G. "Langage humain et signes naturels dans le cartésianisme" **Le langage. 13CS** 1 (1966) 132-36.

1934 Rodis-Lewis, G. "Il cartesianismo del Seicento. Introduzione" **Il pensiero moderno (Secoli XVII-XVIII),** ed. by M.F. Sciacca and M. Schiavone. **Grande antologia filosofica** 12 (Milano 1968) 498-544. Rev. by: Di Girolamo, N.   **Culture Française** 16 (1969) 69-71.

1935 Rodis-Lewis, G. "Descartes" **Contemporary Philosophy: A Survey,** ed. by R. Klibansky. 3 (Firenze 1969) 73-81.

1936 Rodis-Lewis, G. **L'oeuvre de Descartes.** 2 vols. (Paris 1971). Rev. by: Beaude, J.   **RS** 93 (1972) 301-04. Dufourt, H.   **RP** 97 (1972) 437-45. Etienne, J.   **RPL** 70 (1972) 661-63.

Clair, P.	**DsS** 98-99 (1973) 158-59.
C[ostabel], P., and	
A[rmogathe], J.-R.	**BC** 2 (1973) 469-74.
Marion, J.-L.	**EP** (1973) 263-65.
Spire, A.	**RMM** 80 (1975) 111-14.
Watson, R.A.	**JHP** 13 (1975) 406-07.
Marion, J.-L.	**DsS** 114-15 (1977) 120-21.

1937 Rodis-Lewis, G. "'Cartesius'" **RP** 96 (1971) 211-20.
Dis. by: C[ostabel], P. **BC** 2 (1973) 444-46.

1938 Rodis-Lewis, G. "Descartes aurait-il eu un professeur nominaliste?"
AP 34 (1971) 37-46.

1939 Rodis-Lewis, G. "Musique et passions au XVIIe siècle (Monteverdi et
Descartes)" **DsS** 92 (1971) 81-98.

1940 Rodis-Lewis, G. "Pascal devant le doute hyperbolique de Descartes"
Chroniques de Port-Royal 20-21 (1972) 104-15.

1941 Rodis-Lewis, G. "Descartes--Cartésiens et anticartésiens français" **De
la Renaissance à la révolution kantienne.** Vol. 2 of **Histoire de la
philosophie** ed. by Y. Belaval (Paris 1973) 364-403.

1942 Rodis-Lewis, G. "L'écrit de Desgabets. Sur la transfusion du sang et sa
place dans les polémiques contemporaines" **RS** 95 (1974) 31-64.

1943 Rodis-Lewis, G. "Descartes" Pt. II, chap. iii of **Histoire littéraire
de la France,** ed. by P. Abraham and R. Desné. 3 (Paris 1975) 131-47.

1944 Rodis-Lewis, G. "L'organisation de la recherche chez Leibniz: son
'Discours de la méthode'" **Le XVIIe siècle et la recherche. A la
mémoire de Raymond Picard,** ed. by R. Duchêne. **O6CM** (Marseille 1976)
133-44.

1945 Rodis-Lewis, G. Review of **Descartes's Conversation with Burman,** by
René Descartes; tr. by J.G. Cottingham [Oxford 1976]. **RP** 102 (1977)
366-70.

1946 Rodis-Lewis, G. "L'arrière-plan platonicienne du débat sur les idées.
De Descartes à Leibniz" **Permanence de la philosophie. Mélanges
offerts à Joseph Mo reau,** ed. by R. Escarpit (Neuchâtel 1977) 221-40.

1947 Rodis-Lewis, G. "Doute et certitude chez Descartes et Pascal" **Eur** 56
(1978) 5-14.

1948 Rodis-Lewis, G. "Le monde philosophique contemporain de Spinoza" **RS**
99 (1978) 7-18.

1949 Rodis-Lewis, G. "Limitations of the Mechanical Model in the Cartesian
Conception of the Organism" **DCIE** (Baltimore MD 1978) 152-70.

1950 Rodis-Lewis, G. "Liminaire I. L'apport d'Etienne Gilson et de Martial Gueroult aux études sur Descartes. Bibliographies correspondantes" **BC** 8 (1979) 1-21.

1951 Rodis-Lewis, G. "Liminaire II. Note sur le 'cercle' cartésien" **BC** 8 (1979) 22-26.

1952 Rodis-Lewis, G. "Quelques échos de la thèse de Desgabets sur l'indefectibilité des substances" **SC** 1 (1979) 121-28.

1953 Rodis-Lewis, G. "Quelques compléments sur la création des vérités éternelles" **Etienne Gilson et nous: La philosophie et son historie,** ed. by M. Couratier (Paris 1980) 73-77.

1954 Rodis-Lewis, G. "Les diverses éditions des discussions entre Desgabets et le cardinal de Retz (Corrections d'après un manuscrit inédit)" **SC** 2 (1981) 155-64.

1955 Rodis-Lewis, G. "Polémiques sur la création des possibles et sur l'impossible dans l'école cartésienne" **SC** 2 (1981) 105-23.

1956 Rodis-Lewis, G. "Création des vérités éternelles, doute suprême et limites de l'impossible chez Descartes" **Actes de New Orleans,** ed. by F.L. Lawrence. **PFSL** Supp. 5 (1982) 277-318.

1957 Rodis-Lewis, G. "Les essences éternelles et leur création: Le détournement d'un texte augustinien" **DsS** 34 (1982) 211-15.

1958 Rodis-Lewis, G. "Introduction" **Oeuvres philosophiques inédites,** by Robert Desgabets; ed. by J. Beaude and G. Rodis-Lewis. **Analecta Cartesiana 2. SC** Supp. (Amsterdam 1983) v-xxxviii.

1959 Rodis-Lewis, G. "Les limites initiales de cartésianisme de Malebranche" **PaRa** (Paris 1983) 231-53.

1960 Rodis-Lewis, G. "Quelques questions disputées sur la jeunesse de Descartes" **AP** 46 (1983) 613-19.

1961 Rodis-Lewis, G. **Descartes. Textes et débats** (Paris 1984).

1962 Rodis-Lewis, G. "Liminaire III. Une édition 'Malebranchiste' des Passions de <u>Descartes</u>" **BC** 13 (1984) 25-31.

1963 Rodis-Lewis, G., and Malbreil, G. "Notices, notes et variantes" **Oeuvres,** by Nicolas Malebranche; ed. by G. Rodis-Lewis and G. Malbreil. 1 (Paris 1979) 1321-1791.

1964 Roger, J. "Descartes" Pt. I, chap. iii, sect. 4 of **Les sciences de la vie dans la pensée française du XVIIIe siècle. La génération des animaux de Descartes à l'<u>Encyclopédie</u>** (Paris 1963) 140-54; 2nd ed. (1971). Rev. by: Roelens, M. **RSH** 29 (1964) 595-600.

1965 Roger, J. "La théorie de la terre au XVIIe siècle" **RHS** 26 (1973) 23-48.

1966   Roger, J.   "The Cartesian Model and Its Role in Eighteenth-Century
       'Theory of the Earth'"   **PC** (Kingston and Montréal 1982) 95-112.

1967   Rogers, G.A.J.   "Descartes and the Method of English Science"   **ASc** 29
       (1972) 237-55.

1968* Rohatyn, D.   "Precursores del romanticismo ontologico"   **Logos** [Italia]
       6 (1978) 59-72.

1969   Romanowski, S.   "Descartes: From Science to Discourse"   **YFS** 49 (1973)
       96-109.

1970   Romanowski, S.   **L'illusion chez Descartes. La structure du discours
       cartésien** (Paris 1974).
       Rev. by: Labrousse, E.   **Revue d'Histoire Littéraire de la
                                     France** 75 (1975) 834-35.
                Greef, J. de   **RPL** 74 (1976) 106-08.
                Keefe, T.   **Modern Language Review** 71 (1976)
                                     669-70.
                Reiss, T.J.   **Diacritics** 6 (1976) 19-27.
                Beyssade, J.-M.   **EP** (1979) 481-83.
                James, E.D.   **FS** 33 (1979) 341-42.

1971   Rombach, H.   "Die Bedeutung von Descartes und Leibniz für die Metaphysik
       der Gegenwart"   **PJ** 70 (1962-63) 67-97.

1972* Roncuzzi, A.   "Innatismo cartesiano"   **Osservatore Romano** (1964) 5.

1973   Rorty, A.O.   "From Passions to Emotions and Sentiments"   **P** 57 (1982)
       159-72.

1974   Rorty, A.O.   "Experiments in Philosophic Genre: Descartes' Meditations"
       Critical Inquiry 9 (1982-83) 545-64.

1975   Rorty, A.O.   "Formal Traces in Cartesian Functional Explanation"   **CJP**
       14 (1984) 545-60.

1976   Rorty, R.   "The Invention of the Mind"   Chap. i of **Philosophy and the
       Mirror of Nature** (Princeton NJ 1979) 17-69.

1977   Rorty, R.   "The Idea of a 'Theory of Knowledge'"   Chap. iii of
       Philosophy and the Mirror of Nature (Princeton NJ 1979) 131-64.

1978* Rose, D.   "A propos du malentendu entre philosophie et psychanalyse"
       Revue de l'Enseignement Philosophique 33 (1983) 26-32.

1979   Rose, L.E.   "The Cartesian Circle"   **PPR** 26 (1965-66) 80-89.
       Dis. by: Kretzmann, N.   **PPR** 26 (1965-66).

1980   Rose, L.E.   "Reply to Mr. Kretzmann"   **PPR** 26 (1965-66) 93.
       Dis. of: Kretzmann, N.   **PPR** 26 (1965-66).

1981   Rose, M.C.   "Descartes' Malevolent Demon"   **ACPA** 46 (1972) 157-66.

1982 Rosen, S. "A Central Ambiguity in Descartes" **CE** (The Hague 1969) 17-35.

1983 Rosen, S. "Hegel, Descartes and Spinoza" **Spinoza's Metaphysics: Essays in Critical Appreciation,** ed. by J.B. Wilbur (Assen 1976) 114-31.

1984 Rosen, S. "Commentary" **IJP** 4 (1983) 47-49.
      Dis. of: Lachterman, D.R.   **IJP** 4 (1983) 31-46.

1985 Rosenfield, L.C. **From Beast-Machine to Man-Machine: Animal Soul in French Letters from Descartes to La Mettrie** (New York 1941); new ed. (1968).
      Rev. by: Watson, R.A.   **JHP** 9 (1971) 95-98.

1986 Ross, S. "Painting the Passions: Charles Le Brun's Conférence sur l'Expression" **JHI** 45 (1984) 25-47.

1987 Rossi, P. "Studi sul Lullismo e sull'arte della memoria nel Rinascimento. La memoria artificiale come sezione della logica: Ramo, Bacone, Cartesio" **RCSF** 15 (1960) 22-62.

1988 Rossi, P. "Filosofia, tecnica e storia delle arti nel Seicento" Chap. iii of **I filosofi e le macchine (1400-1700)** (Milano 1962) 103-37; 2nd ed. (1971).

1989* Rossi, P.A. **Dalla conquista della naturalità dell'artificiale alla meccanizzazione delle funzioni organiche. Note sulla nascita della macchina biologica nel Seicento** (Bologna 1978).

1990 Rossi, P.A. "Il tema dell'animale macchina alle origini del meccanicismo moderno" **Miscellanea Filosofica** (1981) 9-49.

1991 Rosso, C. "L'honnête homme dans la tradition italienne et française" **Actes de New Orleans,** ed. by F.L. Lawrence. **PFSL** Supp. 5 (1982) 105-24.

1992* Rostand, J. "Descartes et les sciences de la vie" **PCa** 19 (1965) 59-61.
      Dis. by: Chauvois, L.   **PCa** 20 (1966).

1993 Roth, G. "Thomas d'Aquin et René Descartes. Leur rivalité anthropologique en psychiatrie" **Evolution Psychiatrique** 31 (1966) 537-44.

1994* Rothschuh, K.E. "René Descartes: 'Tractatus de homine'" **Neue Zeitschrift für Artzliche Fortbildung** 49 (1960) 232-33.

1995 Rothschuh, K.E. "René Descartes und die Theorie der Lebenserscheinungen" **SA** 50 (1966) 25-42.

1996 Rothschuh, K.E. "Zur Geschichte der physiologischen Reizmethodik im 17. und 18. Jahrhundert" **Gesnerus** 23 (1966) 147-60.

1997 Rothschuh, K.E. "Descartes, Stensen und der Discours sur l'anatomie du cerveau (1665)" **Steno and Brain Research in the Seventeenth Century,** ed. by G. Scherz (Oxford 1968) 49-57.

1998 Rothschuh, K.E. "Henricus Regius und Descartes. Neue Einblicke in die frühe Physiologie (1640-1641) des Regius" **AIHS** 21 (1968) 39-66.

1999 Rothschuh, K.E. "Descartes und die Zirbeldrüse" **Wissenschaft, Wirtschaft und Technik. Studien zur Geschichte. Wilhelm Treue zum 60. Geburtstag,** ed. by K.-H. Manegold (München 1969) 438-47.

2000 Rothschuh, K.E. "Technomorphes Lebensmodell contra Virtus-Modell. (Descartes gegen Fernel)" **SA** 54 (1970) 337-54.

2001 Rothschuh, K.E. "Descartes erklärt die Bildung des Foetus" **Circa tiliam: studia historiae medicinae Gerrit Arie Lindeboom, septuagenario oblata** (Leiden 1974) 278-91.

2002 Rothschuh, K.E. "Studien zu Friedrich Hoffmann (1660-1742). Zweiter Teil: Hoffmann, Descartes und Leibniz" **SA** 60 (1976) 235-70.

2003 Rothschuh, K.E., and Dechange, K. "La tradition et le progrès dans la Physiologia (1641) de Henricus Regius et ses relations avec les idées de Descartes" **12CI** 3B (Paris 1971) 109-12.

2004 Rotta, S. "Scienza e 'pubblica felicità' in Geminiano Montanari" **Miscellanea Seicento** 2 (Firenze 1971) 63-208.

2005* Roy, K. "Sartre and the Cartesian Cogito" **Mind, Language and Necessity,** ed. by K.K. Banerjee (Atlantic Highlands NJ 1982) 1-18.

2006 Rozsnyai, E. "Descartes et la philosophie moderne" **Etudes sur Descartes,** by E. Rozsnyai, D. Kalocsai and Z. Tordai (Budapest 1964) 5-63.

2007 Rozsnyai, E., Kalocsai, D., and Tordai, Z. **Etudes sur Descartes. Studia Philosophica Academiae Scientiarum Hungaricae** 6 (Budapest 1964). Rev. by: Ciger, J. **Otzky Marxistickej Filosofie** 20 (1965) 644-53.
Wroblewsky, G. von, and Wroblewsky, V. von **Deutsche Zeitschrift für Philosophie** 14 (1966) 1524-30.

2008 Rubin, R. "Descartes' Validation of Clear and Distinct Apprehension" **PR** 86 (1977) 197-208.
Dis. by: Smith, M.P. **PS** 36 (1979).

2009 Rucker, D. "Our Cartesian Heritage" **Western Humanities Review** 22 (1968) 285-96.

2010 Ruestow, E.G. **Physics at Seventeenth and Eighteenth-Century Leiden: Philosophy and the New Science in the University** (The Hague 1973).

2011   Ruiz, F. "Reflexiones en torno a Pascal: San Augustín - Pascal - Descartes" **Augustinus** 7 (1962) 411-20.

2012   Sabra, A.I. "Explanation of Optical Reflection and Refraction: Ibn-al-Haytham, Descartes, Newton" **10CI** 1 (Paris 1964) 551-54.

2013   Sabra, A.I. **Theories of Light: From Descartes to Newton** (London 1967); new ed. (Cambridge 1981).
     Rev. by: Westfall, R.   **HS** 6 (1967) 150-56.
             Steffans, H.   **BJPS** 22 (1971) 55-57.
             Eastwood, B.   **I** 63 (1972) 445-46.

2014* Sacchi, M. "'Discorso sul metodo' di Cartesio" **Per la Filosofia. Filosofia e Insegnamento** 2 (1984) 59-69.

2015   Sacy, S. de. "Les lettres de Descartes" Review of **Descartes. Correspondance,** ed. by C. Adam and G. Milhaud. 8 vols. [Paris 1936-63]. **Mercure de France** 349 (1963) 604-08.

2016   Sailor, D.B. "Cudworth and Descartes" **JHI** 23 (1962) 133-40. Dis. of: Saveson, J.E.   **JHI** 21 (1960).

2017   Saisselin, R.G. "Room at the Top of the Eighteenth Century: From Sin to Aesthetic Pleasure" **Journal of Aesthetics and Art Criticism** 26 (1967-68) 345-50.

2018   Saisselin, R.G. "Descartes" Pt. II of **The Rule of Reason and the Ruses of the Heart. A Philosophical Dictionary of Classical French Criticism, Critics, and Aesthetic Issues** (Cleveland OH 1970) 243-53.

2019   Sakellariadis, S. "Descartes' Experimental Proof of the Infinite Velocity of Light and Huygens' Rejoinder" **AHES** 26 (1982) 1-12.

2020   Sakellariadis, S. "Descartes's Use of Empirical Data to Test Hypotheses" **I** 73 (1982) 68-76.

2021   Salmon, E.G. "Mathematical Roots of Cartesian Metaphysics" **NS** 39 (1965) 158-69.

2022   Salmon, J.H.M. "Descartes and Pascal" **History Today** 21 (1971) 482-90.

2023* Sambarino, M. "La hipótesis cartesiana del genio maligno y el problema del valor de la evidencia" **Cuadernos Uruguayos de Filosofia** 2 (1963) 63-92.

2024* Sánchez Durá, N. "**A** priori, deducción y experiencia. La metodologia en la física cartesiana" **Cuadernos de Filosofía y Ciencia** 1 (1983) 173-83.

2025   Sánchez Durá, N., and Sanfélix Vidarte, V. "Matemáticas, intuición y Dios en Descartes. Un apunte sobre el 'círculo cartesiano'" **Pensamiento** 39 (1983) 437-48.

2026   Sandblad, H. "The Reception of the Copernican System in Sweden" **Colloquia Copernicana I,** ed. by J. Dobrzycki. **SCop** 5 (1972) 241-70.

2027* Sanhueza-G., G., and Salinas-J., R. "Descartes, lector de Maquiavelo" **Teoria** [Chile] No. 4 (1975) 83-103.

2028* Santinello, G. "Gli studi cartesiani di P. Carabellese" **Giornate di studi carabellesiani. Atti del Convegno tenuto presso l'Istituto di Filosofia dell'Università di Bologna nell'ottobre 1960** (Genova 1964) 293-305.

2029* Santos B., E. "El 'cogito' y su estructura empirica. Relaciones entre el sujeto cartesiano del conocimiento y el de Santo Tomás" **Franciscanum** [Colombia] 7 (1965) 5-62, 210-40.

2030* Sarti, S. **Io cogitante ed io problematica** (Brescia 1962).

2031 Sarti, S. "Considerazioni sul 'cogito' e sull'idea cartesiana di perfezione" **GM** 18 (1963) 71-88.

2032 Sassen, F. **Descartes** (Den Haag 1963).

2033 Sasso, R. "Fardella et la philosophie comme discours systématique" **RDS** 4 (1980) 115-25.

2034 Sauer, E.F. "Brief über Descartes" Chap. i of **Französische Philosophen. Von Descartes bis Sartre** (Bonn 1976) 9-43.

2035 Saveson, J.E. "Differing Reactions to Descartes Among the Cambridge Platonists" **JHI** 21 (1960) 560-67.
Dis. by: Sailor, D.B.   **JHI** 23 (1962).

2036 Savigny, E. von. "Röds Fehlinterpretation von Ryles Fehlinterpretation von Descartes" **AGP** 57 (1975) 54-59.
Dis. of: Röd, W.   **AGP** 55 (1973).
Dis. by: Röd, W.   **AGP** 57 (1975).

2037 Savile, A. "René Descartes: Grandeur et Misère" **CJP** Supp. 4 (1978) 13-36.

2038 Sayward, C. "Minds, Substances, and Capacities" **PPR** 44 (1983-84) 213-26.

2039 Scarrow, D.S. "Descartes on His Substance and His Essence" **APQ** 9 (1972) 18-28.

2040 Schacht, R. "Descartes" Chap. i of **Classical Modern Philosophers: Descartes to Kant** (London 1984) 5-39.

2041 Schaerer, R. "Points de repère et points de vue sur le cheminement philosophique" **Studia Philosophica** 30-31 (1970-71) 244-71.

2042 Schäfer, L. "Pascal und Descartes als methodologische Antipoden" **PJ** 81 (1974) 314-40.

2043 Schall, J.V. "Cartesianism and Political Theory" **Review of Politics** 24 (1962) 260-82.

2044 Schankula, H.A.S. "Locke, Descartes and the Science of Nature" JHI
41 (1980) 459-77.
Repr. in **John Locke. Symposium Wolfenbüttel 1979,** ed. by R. Brandt
(Berlin 1981) 163-80.

2045 Scharfstein, B.-A. "Descartes' Dreams" **PF** 1 (1968-69) 293-317.

2046 Scharfstein, B.-A. "Cogito Ergo Sum: Descartes, Augustine, and Sankara"
Pt. II, chap. v of **Philosophy East/Philosophy West: A Critical
Comparison of Indian, Chinese, Islamic, and European Philosophy,** by
B.-A. Scharfstein et al. (Oxford 1978) 199-217.

2047 Scharfstein, B.-A. "Descartes to Rousseau" Chap. vi of **The Philosophers: Their Lives and the Nature of their Thought** (Oxford 1980)
123-208.

2048 Schehr, L.R. "Le dialogue en contre-pied: Sur 'La recherche de la
vérité' de Descartes" **Romanic Review** 74 (1983) 293-305.

2049 Scheier, C.-A. "Die unmittelbare Idee: Descartes" Chap. i of **Die
Selbstentfaltung der methodischen Reflexion als Prinzip der neueren
Philosophie. Von Descartes zu Hegel** (Freiburg 1973) 13-30.

2050 Scheier, C.-A. "Descartes' genius malignus und die Wahrheit der
Gewissheit" **Theologie und Philosophie** 52 (1977) 321-40.

2051 Schiavo, M. **Il problema etico in Cartesio** (Roma 1965).

2052* Schiff, J. **A Word Index to Descartes' Discours de la méthode**
(University Park PA 1970).

2053 Schiffer, S. "Descartes on His Essence" **PR** 85 (1976) 21-43.

2054 Schiffman, Z.S. "Montaigne and the Rise of Skepticism in Early Modern
Europe: A Reappraisal" **JHI** 45 (1984) 499-516.

2055 Schifres, J. **'Discours de la méthode', Descartes: Analyse critique**
(Paris 1978).

2056 Schiller, J., and Théodoridès, J. "Stenon et les milieux scientifiques
parisiens" **Steno and Brain Research,** ed. by G. Scherz (Oxford 1968)
155-70.

2057 Schmidt, G. **Aufklärung und Metaphysik. Die Neubegründung des Wissens
durch Descartes** (Tübingen 1965).
Rev. by: Negri, A.   **RCSF** 22 (1967) 343-46.
         Röd, W.   **PLa** 20 (1967) 202-07.
         Röd, W.   **PRu** 16 (1969) 28-39.

2058 Schmidt, G. "Das ontologische Argument bei Descartes und Leibniz" **Die
Wirkungsgeschichte Anselms von Canterbury. Akten der ersten
Internationalen Anselm-Tagung. 1: Das ontologische Argument in der
Geschichte der Philosophie,** ed. by H. Kohlenberger. **Analecta
Anselmiana** 4 (1975) 221-30.

2059 Schmitt, C. "Lo stato come meccanismo in Hobbes e Cartesio" **Centauro** 10 (1984) 169-77.

2060 Schmitz, H. "'Cogito ergo sum'. Bemerkungen aus Anlass des gleichnämigen Buches von Hartmut Brands" **PJ** 91 (1984) 382-91.

2061 Schneider, I. "Descartes' Diskussion der Fermatschen Extremwertmethode - ein Stück Ideengeschichte der Mathematik" **AHES** 7 (1970-71) 354-74.

2062 Schneider, I. "Die Rolle des Formalen und des Individuums in der Mathematik bei Descartes und Leibniz" **SA** 58 (1974) 225-34.

2063 Schneier, C.K. "Descartes' Proofs for the Existence of God: Comparison and Contrast" **Di** 23 (1980-81) 22-26.

2064 Schoenborn, A. von. "The Cartesian Cogito and the Death of God" **God Knowable and Unknowable,** ed. by R.J. Roth (New York 1973) 73-84.

2065 Schouls, P.A. "Cartesian Certainty and the 'Natural Light'" **AJP** 48 (1970) 116-19.
Dis. of: Morris, J.M.   **AJP** 47 (1969).

2066 Schouls, P.A. "Descartes and the Autonomy of Reason" **JHP** 10 (1972) 307-22.

2067 Schouls, P.A. "Reason, Method, and Science in the Philosophy of Descartes" **AJP** 50 (1972) 30-39.

2068 Schouls, P.A. "The Extent of Doubt in Descartes' Meditations" **CJP** 3 (1973-74) 51-58.
Dis. of: Ring, M.   **CJP** 3 (1973-74).

2069 Schouls, P.A. "An Incapacitating Presupposition of Rationalism" **PRef** 40 (1975) 33-46.

2070 Schouls, P.A. "The Cartesian Method of Locke's Essay concerning Human Understanding" **CJP** 4 (1974-75) 579-601.
Dis. by: Duchesneau, F.   **CJP** 4 (1974-75).
          Yolton, J.W.   **CJP** 4 (1974-75).

2071 Schouls, P.A. "Comments on Professors Yolton and Duchesneau" **CJP** 4 (1974-75) 617-21.
Dis. of: Duchesneau, F.   **CJP** 4 (1974-75).
          Yolton. J.W.   **CJP** 4 (1974-75).

2072 Schouls, P.A. **The Imposition of Method: A Study of Descartes and Locke** (Oxford 1980).
Dis. by: Schouls, P.A.   **PRef** 46 (1981) 37-59.
Rev. by: Watson, R.A.   **ISP** 13 (1981) 115-16.
          M[arion], J.-L.   **BC** 11 (1982) 45-47.
          Schankula, H.A.S.   **M** 92 (1983) 601-04.

2073   Schouls, P.A.   "Descartes and Locke: Case Studies in Imposition of
        Method"   **PRef** 46 (1981) 37-59.
        Dis. of: Schouls, P.A.   **The Imposition of Method** (Oxford
                                        1980).

2074   Schouls, P.A.   "Peirce and Descartes: Doubt and the Logic of Discovery"
        Pragmatism and Purpose: Essays Presented to Thomas A. Goudge, ed. by
        L.W. Sumner, J.G. Slater and F. Wilson (Toronto 1981) 88-104.

2075   Schrader, G.   "The 'I' and the 'We': Reflections on the Kantian Cogito"
        RIP 35 (1981) 358-82.

2076   Schrynemakers, A. H.   "Descartes and the Weight-Driven Chain-Clock"   I
        60 (1969) 233-36.

2077   S[chuhl], P.-M.   "A Descartes, la patrie reconnaissante"   **RP** 93 (1968)
        123-24.

2078   Schuhl, P.-M.   "Encore le mádecin de soi-même"   Review of **Le médecin de
        soi-même,** by E. Aziza Shuster [Paris 1972].   **RP** 100 (1975) 147-52.

2079   Schulz, W.   "God of the Philosophers in Modern Metaphysics"   **MW** 6
        (1973) 353-71.

2080   Schuster, J.A.   "Descartes' Mathesis Universalis: 1619-28"   **DPMP**
        (Brighton 1980) 41-96.

2081   Scott, W.L.   "Development of a Controversial Idea"   Chap. i of **The
        Conflict between Atomism and Conservation Theory, 1644 to 1860** (London
        1970) 3-21.

2082   Scott, W.L.   "Continuity versus Discontinuity in the History of Physical
        Science"   **13CI** 1 (Moscow 1974) 19-24.

2083   Scriba, C.J.   "Zur Lösung des 2. Debeauneschen Problems durch Descartes"
        AHES 1 (1960-62) 406-19.

2084   Scribano, M.E.   "I cartesiani e il libero arbitrio: 1650-1710"   **Annali
        dell'Istituto di Filosofia** [Firenze] 5 (1983) 127-75.

2085   Scruton, R.   "Descartes"   Chap. iii of **From Descartes to Wittgenstein:
        A Short History of Modern Philosophy** (London 1981) 29-39.

2086   Scruton, R.   "The Cartesian Revolution"   Chap. iv of **From Descartes to
        Wittgenstein: A Short History of Modern Philosophy** (London 1981) 40-49.

2087   Seager, W.   "The Principle of Continuity and the Evaluation of Theories"
        D 20 (1981) 485-95.

2088   Sebba, G.   "Some Open Problems in Descartes Research"   **MLN** 75 (1960)
        222-29.

2089   Sebba, G. "Descartes" **The Seventeenth Century,** ed. by N. Edelman.
       Vol. 3 of **A Critical Bibliography of French Literature,** ed. by D.C.
       Cabeen and J. Brody (Syracuse NY 1961) 504-56.

2090   Sebba, G. "A 'New' Descartes Edition?" **JHP** 1 (1963-64) 231-36.
       Dis. by: Gouhier, H.   **JHP** 2 (1964).

2091   Sebba, G. **Bibliographia Cartesiana: A Critical Guide to the Descartes
       Literature 1800-1960** (The Hague 1964).
       Rev. by: Perkins, R.   **Papers of the Bibliographical Society
                                     of America** 58 (1964) 496-98.
               Wenin, C.   **RPL** 62 (1964) 507-09.
               Halbfass, W.   **Eras** 17 (1965) 72-75.
               Hall, H.G.   **SFr** 10 (1966) 348-49.
               Potter, J.A.   **JHP** 4 (1966) 257-60.

2092   Sebba, G. "What is 'History of Philosophy'?" **JHP** 8 (1970) 251-62.
       Dis. of: Watson, R.A.   **The Downfall of Cartesianism 1673-
                                     1712** (The Hague 1966).

2093   Sebba, G. "Time and the Modern Self: Descartes, Rousseau, Beckett"
       Studium Generale 24 (1971) 308-25.
       Repr. in **The Study of Time** [1] (1972) 452-69.

2094   Sebba, G. "Descartes and Pascal: A Retrospect" **MLN** 87 (1972) Spec.
       No., 96-120.

2095   Sebba, G. "Retroversion and the History of Ideas: J.-L. Marion's
       Translation of the Regulae of Descartes" Review of **Règles utiles et
       claires pour la direction de l'esprit en la recherche de la vérité,** by
       René Descartes; tr. by J.-L. Marion [The Hague 1977]. **SC** 1 (1979)
       145-65.

2096   Sebba, G. "Adrien Baillet and the Genesis of His Vie de M. Des-Cartes"
       PC (Kingston and Montréal 1982) 9-60.

2097   Seck, F. "Persönliche Bekanntschaft zwischen Kepler und Descartes?"
       SA 52 (1968) 162-65.

2098* Seguí, A. "Sobre la prueba ontológica cartesiana" **Sapientia** 30
       (1975) 255-60.

2099   Seidel, W. "Descartes' Bemerkungen zur musikalischen Zeit" **Archiv für
       Musikwissenschaft** 27 (1970) 287-303.

2100   Sell, A.P.F. "Locke and Descartes through Victorian Eyes" **PSt** 30
       (1984) 220-29.

2101   Sellars, W. "Berkeley and Descartes: Reflections on the Theory of
       Ideas" **Studies in Perception: Interrelations in the History of
       Philosophy and Science,** ed. by P.K. Machamer and R.G. Turnbull
       (Columbus OH 1978) 259-311.

2102   Sellars, W.   "Foundations for a Metaphysics of Pure Process. III. Is
       Consciousness Physical?"   **Mon** 64 (1981) 66-90.
       Dis. by: Dennett, D.   **Mon** 64 (1981) 102-08.

2103   Semerari, G.   "Intorno all'anticartesianesimo di Vico"   **Omaggio a
       Vico,** by A. Corsano et al. (Napoli 1968) 193-232.

2104* Semerari, G.   "Sulla metafisica de Vico"   **Annali della Facoltà di
       Lettere e Filosofia dell'Università di Bari** 13 (1968) 247-74.

2105* Sen, S.   "The Ontological Argument Revisited"   **Indian Philosophical
       Quarterly** 10 (1982-83) 219-42.

2106   Serres, M.   "Descartes et Leibniz dans les deux manières de penser le
       réel et la science"   Review of **Leibniz critique de Descartes,** by Y.
       Belaval [Paris 1960].   **Crit** 17 (1961) 50-75.

2107   Serres, M.   "Un modèle mathématique du cogito"   **RP** 90 (1965) 197-205.

2108   Serres, M.   "L'évidence, la vision et le tact"   **EP** 23 (1968) 191-95.

2109   Serres, M.   "Sur le cercle cartésien"   **RP** 97 (1972) 311-14.

2110   Sesonske, A., and Fleming, N., edd.   **Meta-Meditations: Studies in
       Descartes** (Belmont CA 1965).

2111   Sève, R.   "L'ontologie moderne et la loi"   **Archives de Philosophie du
       Droit** [France] 25 (1980) 191-209.

2112   Shaffer, J.   "Persons and Their Bodies"   **PR** 75 (1966) 59-77.

2113   Shapere, D.   "Descartes and Plato"   **JHI** 24 (1963) 572-76.
       Repr. in **10CI** 1 (Paris 1964).

2114   Shapiro, A.E.   "Kinematic Optics: A Study of the Wave Theory of Light in
       the Seventeenth Century"   **AHES** 11 (1973) 134-266.

2115   Shapiro, A.E.   "Light, Pressure, and Rectilinear Propagation: Descartes'
       Celestial Optics and Newton's Hydrostatics"   **SHPS** 5 (1974-75) 239-96.

2116   Shea, W.R.   "Descartes as Critic of Galileo"   **New Perspectives on
       Galileo,** ed. by R.E. Butts and J.C. Pitt (Dordrecht 1978) 139-59.

2117* Shea, W.R.   "Descartes and the Rosicrucians"   **Annali dell'Istituto e
       Museo di Storia della Scienza di Firenze** 4 (1979) 29-47.

2118* Shea, W.R.   "Descartes and the French Artisan Jean Ferrier"   **Annali
       dell'Istituto e Museo di Storia della Scienza di Firenze** 7 (1982)
       145-60.

2119   Shea, W.R., ed.   **Nature Mathematized: Historical and Philosophical Case
       Studies in Classical Modern Natural Philosophy,** ed. by W.R. Shea.
       **Papers Deriving from the Third International Conference on the History
       and Philosophy of Science** (Dordrecht 1983).

2120 Shea, W.R. "Descartes: Methodological Ideal and Actual Procedure"
      Philosophia Naturalis 21 (1984) 577-89.

2121 Shear, J. "The Experience of Pure Consciousness: A New Perspective for
      Theories of the Self" Met 14 (1983) 53-62.

2122 Sheikh, M. Saeed. "Al-Ghazali's Influence on the West" PPC 15 (1968)
      113-26.
      Repr. in PPJ 11 (1973) No. 2, 53-67.

2123 Sherman, K. "Descartes' Change of Mind" PF 5 (1973-74) 557-71.

2124 Shoemaker, S. "On an Argument for Dualism" Knowledge and Mind:
      Philosophical Essays, ed. by C. Ginet and S. Shoemaker (Oxford 1983)
      233-58.

2125 Shugg, W. "The Cartesian Beast-Machine in English Literature (1663-
      1750)" JHI 29 (1968) 279-92.

2126 Sibajiban. "Can Doubt be Doubted?" M 69 (1960) 84-87.

2127 Sibajiban. "Descartes' Doubt" PPR 24 (1963-64) 106-16.
      Dis. by: Neisser, H.   PPR 25 (1964-65).
                Kumar, D.   Visva-Bharati Journal of Philosophy
                                     3 (1966-67).

2128 Sichirollo, L. "Descartes nell'idealismo classico e la storiografia"
      Pt. II, chap. i of Per una storiografia filosofica. Platone Descartes
      Kant Hegel 1 (Urbino 1970) 71-108.

2129 Siciliano, I. "La ricerca dell'uomo: da Montaigne a Descartes" Pt. II,
      chap. iii of Saggi di letteratura francese (Firenze 1977) 163-69.

2130 Siciliano, I. "La ricerca dell'umano: da Descartes a Pascal" Pt. II,
      chap. iv of Saggi di letteratura francese (Firenze 1977) 170-79.

2131 Sicker, P. "Shades of Descartes: An Approach to Stephen's Dream in
      Ulysses" James Joyce Quarterly 22 (1984-85) 7-24.

2132 Siebers, T. "The Blindspot in Descartes' La Dioptrique" MLN 94
      (1979) 836-42.

2133 Siegler, F.A. "Descartes' Doubts" M 72 (1963) 245-53.

2134 Sievert, D. "Descartes's Self-Doubt" PR 84 (1975) 51-69.
      Dis. by: Humber, J.M.   PR 87 (1978).
                Hauptli, B.W.   PRA 6 (1980).

2135 Sievert, D. "Frankfurt on Descartes' View of Truth" NS 51 (1977)
      372-83.
      Dis. of: Frankfurt, H.G.   Demons, Dreamers, and Madmen
                                     (Indianapolis IN 1970).

2136 Sievert, D. "Descartes' Criteria of Truth: Conception and Perception" **MS** 56 (1978-79) 151-60.

2137 Sievert, D. "Does Descartes Doubt Everything?" **NS** 53 (1979) 107-17.

2138 Sievert, D. "The Importance of Descartes's Wax Example" **R** 21 (1979) 73-84.
      Dis. by: Thomas, J.   **R** 24 (1982).

2139 Sievert, D. "Sellars and Descartes on the Fundamental Form of the Mental" **PS** 37 (1980) 251-57.

2140 Sievert, D. "Descartes on Theological Knowledge" **PPR** 43 (1982-83) 201-19.

2141 Silveira, L.F. "A união substancial corpo-alma no âmbito da nova ciência cartesiana" **Trans/Form/Ação** 7 (1984) 25-36.

2142 Simon, G. "A propos de la théorie de la perception visuelle chez Kepler et Descartes: Réflexions sur le rôle du mécanisme dans la naissance de la science classique" **13CI** 6 (Moscow 1974) 237-45.

2143 Simon, G. "Descartes incertain, mais pas inutile" **Eur** 56 (1978) 138-47.

2144 Simon, G. "Les vérités éternelles de Descartes, évidences ontologiques" **SC** 2 (1981) 124-35.

2145 Simon, J. "Descartes' methodischer Wahrheitsbegriff" Pt. II, chap. ii of **Wahrheit als Freiheit. Zur Entwicklung der Wahrheitsfrage in der neueren Philosophie** (Berlin 1978) 121-49.

2146 Simon, J. "Das Problem der Begründung von Wahrheit im 'cogito'" Pt. II, chap. iii of **Wahrheit als Freiheit. Zur Entwicklung der Wahrheitsfrage in der neueren Philosophie** (Berlin 1978) 149-84.

2147 Simon, Y.R.M. **The Great Dialogue of Nature and Space,** ed. by G.J. Dalcourt (Albany NY 1970).

2148 Simpson, D. "Putting One's House in Order. The Career of the Self in Descartes' Method" **New Literary History** 9 (1977-78) 83-101.

2149* Simpson, P. "The Dream Argument and Descartes' First Meditation" **Auslegung** 9 (1982) 300-10.

2150* Sina, R. **Descartes and the Extension of the Theorem of Pythagoras** (Paris 1983).

2151 Slezak, P. "Descartes's Diagonal Deduction" **BJPS** 34 (1983) 13-36.

2152 Sloan, P.R. "Descartes, the Sceptics, and the Rejection of Vitalism in Seventeenth-Century Physiology" **SHPS** 8 (1977) 1-28.
      Dis. by: C[ostabel], P.   **BC** 8 (1979) 51-52.
                Garber, D.   **SC** 2 (1981) 224-25.

2153 Slote, M.A. "Empirical Certainty and the Theory of Important Criteria" **Inquiry** 10 (1967) 21-37.

2154 Smart, B. "How can Persons be Ascribed M-Predicates?" **M** 86 (1977) 49-66.

2155 Smith, A. "Descartes' Cogito" **Undergraduate Journal of Philosophy** 6 (1974) No. 2, 10-16.

2156 Smith, C.U.M. "Descartes" Chap. xv of **The Problem of Life: An Essay in the Origins of Biological Thought** (New York 1976) 159-76.

2157 Smith, F.J. "Music Theory and the History of Ideas" **Music and Man** 2 (1976-78) 125-49.

2158 Smith, M.P. "Rubin's Validation of Descartes" **PS** 36 (1979) 425-31. Dis. of: Rubin, R.   **PR** 86 (1977).

2159 Smithner, E.W. "Descartes and Auguste Comte" **FR** 41 (1967-68) 629-40.

2160 Snelders, H.A.M. "Christiaan Huygens and the Concept of Matter" **Studies on Christiaan Huygens,** ed. by H.J.M. Bos et al. (Lisse 1980) 104-25.

2161* Snelders, H.A.M. "Descartes et le Pays-Bas" **Septentrion** [Nederland] 11 (1982) 18-25.

2162 Snyder, P. "Holism and Pluralism as Philosophies of Nature" Chap. vi of **Toward One Science: The Convergence of Traditions** (New York 1978) 134-68.

2163 Soffer, W. "Descartes, Rationality and God" **Thomist** 42 (1978) 666-91.

2164 Soffer, W. "The Methodological Achievement of Cartesian Doubt" **SJP** 16 (1978) 661-74.

2165 Soffer, W. "Husserl's Neo-Cartesianism" **Research in Phenomenology** 11 (1981) 141-58.

2166 Soffer, W. "Descartes' Rejection of the Aristotelian Soul" **ISP** 16 (1984) 57-68.

2167* Solinas, G. **Il microscopio e le metafisiche. Epigenesi e preesistenza da Cartesio a Kant** (Milano 1967).

2168 Solomon, R.C. "Wittgenstein and Cartesian Privacy" **PTod** 16 (1972) 163-79.

2169 Solomon, R.C. "On Cartesian Privacy" **SJP** 12 (1974) 527-36. Dis. of: Kenny, A.   **Wittgenstein: The Philosophical In-vestigations** (Garden City NY 1966). Dis. by: Kenny, A.   **SJP** 12 (1974).

2170   Solotareff, J.   "'Dans son sommeil il vit d'abord quelques fantômes':
Descartes"   Pt. II, Rêve 27 of **Le symbolisme dans les rêves. La méthode
de traduction de Paul Diel** (Paris 1979) 347-57.

2171   Sommers, F.   "Predicability"   **Philosophy in America,** ed. by M. Black
(London 1965) 262-81.
Dis. by: Straaten, R. van.   **M** 80 (1971).

2172   Sommers, F.   "Dualism in Descartes: The Logical Ground"   **DCIE**
(Baltimore MD 1978) 223-33.
Dis. by: Cohen, E.   **PF** 14 (1982-83) 131-34.

2173   Somville, P.   "Hypotyposes Parménidiennes"   **TF** 32 (1970) 488-93.

2174* Somville, P.   "Descartes, notre contemporain"   **La Pensée et les Hommes**
26 (1982-83) 191-93.

2175   Sontag, F.   "The Secular Mystic: An East-West Dialogue"   **Japanese
Religions** 8 (1974-75) 62-67.

2176* Sorell, T.   **Descartes,** tr. by V. Raga (Valencia 1984).

2177   Sosa, E.   "Comment"   **FE** (Oxford 1969) 56-58.
Dis. of: Kenny, A.   **FE** (Oxford 1969).
Dis. by: Kenny, A.   **FE** (Oxford 1969).

2178   Sosa, E.   "Hasta dónde se puede llevar la duda?"   **RLF** 2 (1976) 71-73.
Dis. by: Pfeiffer, M.L.   **RLF** 4 (1978).

2179   Sosa, E.   "Más dudas. Respuesta a Pfeiffer"   **RLF** 4 (1978) 80-81.
Dis. of: Pfeiffer, M.L.   **RLF** 4 (1978).

2180   Souchon, H.   "Descartes et Le Brun. Etude comparée de la notion
cartésienne des 'signes extérieurs' et de la théorie de l'expression de
Charles Le Brun"   **EP** (1980) 427-58.

2181   Spaemann, R.   "Praktische Gewissheit. Descartes' provisorische Moral"
Epirrhosis. Festgabe für Carl Schmitt, ed. by H. Barion et al.   2
(Berlin 1968) 683-96.

2182   Spaemann, R.   "La morale provisoire de Descartes"   **AP** 35 (1972) 353-67.

2183   Spallanzani, M.F.   "Il cartesianesimo di Malebranche"   Review of **Le
cartésianisme de Malebranche,** by F. Alquié [Paris 1974].   **RF** 72
(1981) 321-27.

2184   Spallanzani, M.F.   "Sull'albero enciclopedico delle conoscenze: una
classificazione del sapere tra Bacone e Descartes"   **RCSF** 37 (1982)
307-24.

2185* Spallanzani, M.F.   "Notes sur le cartésianisme dans l'Encyclopédie"
Transactions of the 6th International Congress on the Enlightenment
(Oxford 1983) 326-28.

2186   Specht, R.   "Descartes und das Lehramt"   **Hochland** 52 (1959-60) 131-38.

2187   Specht, R.   "Uber Descartes' politische Ansichten"   **Staat** 3 (1964) 281-94.

2188   Specht, R.   **Commercium mentis et corporis. Uber Kausalvorstellungen im Cartesianismus** (Stuttgart 1966).
       Rev. by: Janke, W.   **PRu** 18 (1971) 92-105.
                  Tonelli, G.   **JHP** 10 (1972) 89-90.

2189   Specht, R.   **René Descartes in Selbstzeugnissen und Bilddokumenten** (Reinbek bei Hamburg 1966); new ed. (1980).

2190   Specht, R.   "Descartes. Un ejemplo de ciencia natural en los albores de la época moderna"   **Dian** 16 (1970) 20-41.

2191   Specht, R.   "Uber 'Occasio' und verwandte Begriffe vor Descartes" **Archiv für Begriffsgeschichte** 15 (1970-71) 215-55.

2192   Specht, R.   "Descartes: Veränderung der Physik"   Chap. iii of **Innovation und Folgelast. Beispiele aus der neueren Philosophie- und Wissenschaftsgeschichte** (Stuttgart 1972) 93-135.
       Rev. by: A[rmogathe], J.-R.   **BC** 3 (1974) 489-92.

2193   Specht, R.   "Uber 'Occasio' und verwandte Begriffe bei Zabarella und Descartes"   **Archiv für Begriffsgeschichte** 16 (1972) 1-27.

2194   Specht, R.   "Uber 'Occasio' und verwandte Begriffe im Cartesianismus" **Archiv für Begriffsgeschichte** 16 (1972) 198-226; 17 (1973) 36-65.

2195   Specht, R.   "René Descartes (1596-1650)"   **Von den Vorsokratikern bis David Hume,** ed. by O. Höffe.   **Klassiker der Philosophie** 1 (München 1981) 301-21.

2196   Specht, R.   "Pierre-Alain Cahné: Descartes, stilistisch"   Review of **Un autre Descartes,** by P.-A. Cahné [Paris 1980].   **ZPF** 37 (1983) 599-605.

2197   Spector, M.   "Leibniz vs. the Cartesians on Motion and Force"   **SL** 7 (1975) 135-44.

2198* Spillebout, G.   "De Rabelais à Descartes et de Descartes à Rabelais" **Bulletin de l'Association des Amis de Rabelais et de la Devinière** 3 (1977) 238-40.

2199   Spiller, M.R.G.   "The Idol of the Stove: The Background to Swift's Criticism of Descartes"   **Review of English Studies** 25 (1974) 15-24.

2200   Spiller, M.R.G.   "Descartes and the Decay of Learning"   Chap. iv of **"Concerning Natural Experimental Philosophie". Meric Casaubon and the Royal Society** (The Hague 1980) 60-79.
       Rev. by: Battail, J.-F.   **SC** 2 (1981) 213-18.

2201   Spink, J.S.   **French Free-Thought from Gassendi to Voltaire** (London 1960).

2202 Splett, J. "Vérité, certitude et historicité" **AP** 30 (1967) 163-86.

2203 Spoerri, T. "Das Ende der Bilder" **Schweizer Monatshefte** 40 (1960-61) 179-93.

2204 Springmeyer, H. "Eine neue kritische Textausgabe der Regulae ad directionem ingenii von René Descartes" **ZPF** 24 (1970) 101-25. Dis. by: M[arion], J.-L.   **BC** 1 (1972) 302-05.

2205 Squadrito, K. "Descartes, Locke and the Soul of Animals" **PRA** 6 (1980) No. 1378.

2206 Stainsby, H.V. "Descartes' Argument for God" **Soph** 6 (1967) No. 3, 11-16.

2207 Stallknecht, N.P. "The Cogito and Its World" **Per** 46 (1965) 52-64.

2208* Stefani, P. "Dio e le 'verità eterne' nelle filosofie di Descartes e Leibniz" **Renovatio** 13 (1978) 70-77.

2209 Steinbeck, W. "Descartes' Erste Philosophie. Zu Wolfgang Röds Descartesbuch" Review of **Descartes' Erste Philosophie**, by W. Röd [Bonn 1971]. **KS** 65 (1974) 201-02.

2210 Steiner, M. "Cartesian Scepticism and Epistemic Logic" **A** 39 (1978-79) 38-41. Dis. by: Gordon, D.   **A** 39 (1978-79).

2211 Stempel, D. "The Garden: Marvell's Cartesian Ecstasy" **JHI** 28 (1967) 99-114.

2212 Stern, A. "Nietzsche - El Descartes de la moral" **Dia** 4 (1967) No. 8-9, 93-105.

2213 Stern, K. "Descartes and Explainability" **PF** 7 (1975-76) 316-22. Dis. of: Wilson, M.D.   **CJP** 3 (1973-74).

2214 Stern, K. "A Defence of Cartesian Doubt" **D** 17 (1978) 480-89.

2215 Stevens, J. C. "Why Descartes' Belief That He Is Not Perfect Can't Be Wrong" **Per** 58 (1977) 134.

2216 Stevens, J.C. "Unknown Faculties and Descartes's First Proof of the Existence of God" **JHP** 16 (1978) 334-38. Dis. of: Norton, D.F.   **JHP** 6 (1968).
                Brewster, L.E.   **JHP** 12 (1974).
                Norton, D.F.   **JHP** 12 (1974).
Dis. by: Norton, D.F.   **JHP** 16 (1978).

2217 Stich, S.P. "Introduction: The Idea of Innateness" **Innate Ideas,** ed. by S.P. Stich (Berkeley CA 1975) 1-22.

2218   Stierle, K. "Gespräch und Diskurs. Ein Versuch im Blick auf Montaigne, Descartes und Pascal" **Das Gespräch**, ed. by K. Stierle and R. Warning (München 1984) 297-334.

2219   Stock, B. "Eriugena's 'Cogito': Intelligo me esse" **Jean Scot Erigène et l'histoire de la philosophie. Colloques internationaux du Centre National de la Recherche Scientifique** 561 (1977) 327-35.

2220   Stohrer, W.J. "Descartes and Ignatius Loyola: La Flèche and Manresa Revisited" **JHP** 17 (1979) 11-27.

2221   Stone, J. "Dreaming and Certainty" **PS** 45 (1984) 353-68.

2222   Stone, M.H. "Modern Concepts of Emotion as Prefigured in Descartes' 'Passions of the Soul'" **Journal of the American Academy of Psychoanalysis** 8 (1980) 473-95.

2223   Straaten, R. van. "Sommers on Strawson's and Descartes' Ontology" **M** 80 (1971) 148-49.
       Dis. of: Sommers, F.   **Philosophy in America** (London 1965).

2224   Strasser, J. "Lumen naturale - sens commun - common sense. Zur Prinzipienlehre Descartes', Buffiers und Reids" **ZPF** 23 (1969) 177-98.

2225   Strawson, P.F. "Comments and Replies" **Phi** 10 (1981) 315-28.
       Dis. of: Baier, A.C.   **Phi** 10 (1981).

2226* Strengholt, L. **Dromen is denken. Constantin Huygens over...en denken** (Amsterdam 1977).

2227   Strong, E.W. "Barrow and Newton" **JHP** 8 (1970) 155-72.

2228   Stroud, B. **The Significance of Philosophical Scepticism** (Oxford 1984).

2229   Stuart, J.D. "The Role of Dreaming in Descartes' Meditations" **SJP** 21 (1983) 97-108.

2230   Stubbs, A.C. "Bernard Williams and the Cartesian Circle" **A** 40 (1979-80) 103-08.
       Dis. of: Williams, B.   **Descartes: The Project of Pure Enquiry** (Harmondsworth 1978).

2231* Subirats, E. "Razón y subjetividad. Un comentario en torno a la 'primera meditación' de Descartes" **Enrahonar** 4 (1982) 81-85.

2232   Suchodolski, B. "La solitude de Descartes" **Mélanges de littérature comparée et de philologie offerts à Mieczyslaw Brahmer** (Warszawa 1967) 511-20.

2233   Sullivan, H.W. "Tam clara et evidens: 'Clear and Distinct Ideas' in Calderón, Descartes and Francisco Suárez S.J." **Perspectivas de la comedia, II: Ensayos sobre la comedia del Siglo de Oro español**, ed. by A.V. Ebersole (Valencia 1979) 127-36.

2234 Sullivan, J.L. "Noam Chomsky and Cartesian Linguistics" **Psychology of Language and Thought: Essays on the Theory and History of Psycholinguistics,** ed. by R.W. Rieber (New York 1980) 197-223. Dis. of: Chomsky, N.   **Cartesian Linguistics** (New York 1966).

2235 Suppes, P. "Aristotle's Concept of Matter and its Relation to Modern Concepts of Matter" **Synthese** 28 (1974) 27-50.

2236 Suter, R. "Sum is a Logical Consequence of Cogito" **PPR** 32 (1971-72) 235-40.

2237 Suter, R. "The Dream Argument" **APQ** 13 (1976) 185-94.

2238 Suter, R. "Disolviendo el argumento del sueño" **Dia** 13 (1978) 73-90.

2239* Szabo, I. "Der philosophische Streit um 'das wahre Kraftmass' im XVII. und XVIII. Jahrhundert" **Humanismus und Technik** 15 (1971) 17-53.

2240 Taliaferro, R.C. **The Concept of Matter in Descartes and Leibniz** (Notre Dame IN 1964).

2241 Talmor, E. **Descartes and Hume** (Oxford 1980). Rev. by: Noxon, J.   **JHP** 20 (1982) 436-38.

2242 Tanaka, H. "Où se situe le 'poêle' de Descartes?" **Etudes de Langue et Littérature Françaises** 34 (1979) 11-18.

2243 Taranto, D. "I filosofi e la storia tra Descartes e Locke" **Studi Storici** 25 (1984) 785-97.

2244 Targosz, K. "Autour du 'philosophe latent'. Les premières traces des connaissances de Descartes et de sa pensée en Pologne" [Résumé] **BC** 11 (1982) 34-36.

2245 Tatarkiewicz, W. "Ontological and Theological Perfection" **Dialectics and Humanism** 8 (1981) 187-92.

2246 Taylor, C. "Réponse à Jean-Marie Beyssade" **RIP** 37 (1983) 288-92. Dis. of: Beyssade, J.-M.   **RIP** 37 (1983).

2247* Tedeschi, F.A. "Ragione e fede in Socrate, Cartesio ed Hegel" **Educare** 12 (1961) 50-61.

2248* Texier, R. "La théorie cartésienne de l'action" **Impacts** (1971) 49-63.

2249* Texier, R. "Foi en l'homme et foi en Dieu ou de la condition humaine selon Descartes" **Impacts** (1975) 5-31.

2250* Thayer-M., W. "Descartes. La vigilancia del sueño" **Revista de Filosofía** [Chile] 23-24 (1984) 99-108.

2251 Theau, J. "Comment on est passé de l'idée cartésienne à l'idée berkeleyenne de la matière" **D** 11 (1972) 509-34.

2252 Theveau, P., and Charlot, P. "René Descartes (1596-1650)" Chapter of **XVIIe Siècle. 1re partie. La période baroque. 1600 environ à 1650.** Histoire de la pensée française 3 (Paris 1978) 111-29.

2253 Thiébaut, M. "Descartes masqué?" **Revue de Paris** 67 (1960) 136-52.

2254 Thomas, J. "Descartes' Trust of Clear and Distinct Perception" R 24 (1982) 83-86.
Dis. of: Sievert, D.   R 21 (1979).

2255 Thomas, J.-J. "Descartes: langue, signe et relecture chomskyenne" **Semiotica** 51 (1984) 197-210.

2256 Thompson, J. "Women and the High Priests of Reason" **Radical Philosophy** 34 (1983) 10-14.

2257 Thomson, A. "Ignace de Loyola et Descartes. L'influence des exercices spirituels sur les oeuvres philosophiques de Descartes" **AP** 35 (1972) 61-85.

2258 Thürnher, R. "Das Gottesbild bei René Descartes" **ZPF** 27 (1973) 190-204.

2259 Tibbetts, P. "An Historical Note on Descartes' Psychophysical Dualism" **Journal of the History of the Behavioral Sciences** 9 (1973) 162-65.

2260 Tichý, P. "Existence and God" **JP** 76 (1979) 403-20.

2261 Tilliette, X. "Problèmes de philosophie eucharistique" **Gregorianum** 64 (1983) 273-305.

2262 Tillman[n], A. Review of **Descartes ou le combat pour la vérité,** by P. Mesnard [Paris 1966]. **EP** 21 (1966) 391-94.

2263 Tillmann, A. "Descartes et la psycho-pédagogie de l'enfance" **12CI** 3B (Paris 1971) 161-65.

2264 Tillmann, A. **L'itinéraire du jeune Descartes** (Lille 1976).
Rev. by: Reix, A.   **RP** 101 (1976) 483-84.
         Namer, E.   **RMM** 84 (1979) 560-61.
         Reix, A.   **EP** (1981) 242-43.

2265 Timoner, K.I. "Descartes' Use of Some Historical Elements of the Demonstrations in the Meditations" **Di** 23 (1980-81) 14-21.

2266 Tlili, M. "La recherche du fondement chez Descartes, Hegel et Rousseau" **Cahiers de Tunisie** 27 (1979) 69-89.

2267 Tlumak, J. "Certainty and Cartesian Method" **DCIE** (Baltimore MD 1978) 40-73.

2268 Tlumak, J. "Squaring the Cartesian Circle" **SJP** 16 (1978) 247-57.

2269   Tlumak, J.   "Judgment and Understanding in Descartes's Philosophy"
       SJP 21 Supp. (1983) 89-99.
       Dis. by: Markie, P.J.   **SJP** 21 Supp. (1983).

2270   Tocanne, B.   **L'idée de nature en France dans la seconde moitié du XVIIe
       siècle. Contribution à l'histoire de la pensée classique** (Paris 1978).

2271   Todisco, O.   "L'influsso della scienza moderna sulla filosofia e la
       religione" **Miscellanea Francescana** 81 (1981) 317-88.

2272   Todisco, O.   "I motivi della condanna di Galileo e la riflessione
       filosofica di Cartesio" **Sapienza** 36 (1983) 5-19.

2273   Toellner, R.   "The Controversy Between Descartes and Harvey Regarding
       the Nature of Cardiac Motions" **Science, Medicine and Society in the
       Renaissance: Essays to Honor Walter Pagel**, ed. by A.G. Debus. 2
       (London 1972) 73-89.

2274   Toellner, R.   "Logical and Psychological Aspects of the Discovery of the
       Circulation of the Blood" **On Scientific Discovery: The Erice Lectures
       1977**, ed. by M.D. Grmek, R.S. Cohen and G. Cimino (Dordrecht 1981)
       239-59.

2275   Toffanin, G.   **Italia e Francia. Umanesimo e giansenismo, l'Arcadia e
       Cartesio** (Bologna 1960).

2276   Tokoro, T.   "Etat des études cartésiennes au Japon (1961-1971)" **BC** 2
       (1973) 431-38.

2277   Tomaselli, S.   "The First Person: Descartes, Locke and Mind-Body
       Dualism" **HSc** 22 (1984) 185-205.

2278   Tonelli, G.   Review of **The History of Scepticism from Erasmus to
       Descartes,** by R.H. Popkin [Assen 1960]. **F** 15 (1964) 327-32.
       Repr. as **Un libro sullo scetticismo da Erasmo a Descartes** (Torino
       1965).

2279   Tonnelat, M.-A.   "Quelques-unes des difficultés relatives à la vitesse
       de la lumière dans la physique cartésienne" **O9CI** (Paris 1960) 606-09.

2280   Tonnelat, M.-A.   "La relativité de Descartes à Newton" Pt. I, chap. iii
       of **Histoire du principe de relativité** (Paris 1971) 58-77.

2281   Tonnelat, M.-A.   "L'influence de Copernic sur l'évolution de la
       philosophie des sciences" **Eur** 51 (1973) 66-93.

2282   Tordai, Z.   "Esquisse de l'histoire du cartésianisme en Hongrie"
       Etudes sur Descartes, by E. Rozsnyai, D. Kalocsai and Z. Tordai
       (Budapest 1964) 135-68.

2283   Torretti, R.   "Finitud del hombre y límites del conocimiento en
       Descartes y Leibniz" **Anales de la Universidad de Chile** 121 (1963) No.
       128, 33-58.

2284   Torrini, M. "Il Cartesio di Giannone" **GCFI** 58 (1979) 131-43.

2285* Tortora, G. "Passione e libertà in Cartesio" **Discorsi** 2 (1982) 41-74.

2286   Totok, W. **Frühe Neuzeit: 17. Jahrhundert. Handbuch der Geschichte der Philosophie** 4 (Frankfurt 1981).

2287   Toulmin, S., and Goodfield, J. "The Debate Reopens" Chap. vii of **The Architecture of Matter** (New York 1962) 137-70.

2288   Toulmin, S., and Goodfield, J. "The Revival of Natural Philosophy" Chap. iv of **The Discovery of Time** (New York 1965) 74-102.

2289   Tournadre, G. **L'orientation de la science cartésienne** (Paris 1982).

2290* Tracy, T. "The Soul as Boatman of the Body: Presocratics to Descartes" **Diotima** 7 (1979) 195-99.

2291   Treder, H.-J. "Die Dynamik der Kreisbewegungen der Himmelskörper und des freien Falls bei Aristoteles, Copernicus, Kepler und Descartes" **Colloquia Copernicana IV**, ed. by M.H. Malewicz. SCop 14 (1975) 105-50.

2292   Treder, H.-J. "Descartes' Physik der Hypothesen, Newtons Physik der Prinzipien und Leibnizens Physik der Prinzipe" **SL** 14 (1982) 278-86.

2293   Trevisani, F. "Symbolisme et interprétation chez Descartes et Cardan" **RCSF** 30 (1975) 27-47.

2294   Trevisani, F. "La teoria corpuscolare in Cartesio dal 'Traité du monde' ai 'Principi'" **Ricerche sull'atomismo del Seicento**, by U. Baldini et al. **Atti del Convegno di Studio di Santa Margherita Ligure (1976)** (Firenze 1977) 179-223.

2295* Trevisani, F. "I Physico-mathematica di Cartesio" **Quaderni dell'Istituto Galvano della Volpe** 1 (1978) 257-89.

2296   Trevisani, F. **Inventio e demonstratio in Cartesio. Dalle 'scienze della natura' alla 'filosofia della natura'** (Messina 1979).

2297   Trevisani, F. "Johann Gottfried Berger (1659-1736). Cartesisches und Okkasionalistisches in seiner Neurophysiologie" **SA** 63 (1979) 45-70.

2298   Trevisani, F. "Un corrispondente di Cartesio: alcune note su Lazare Meyssonnier (1611/12-1673), medico e astrologo lionese e sulla sua Belle magie (1669)" **History and Philosophy of the Life Sciences** 1 (1979) 285-308.

2299   Trevisani, F. "Liminaire. Descartes et la Médecine. Essai de bibliographie" **BC** 9 (1981) 1-20.

2300   Trevisani, F. "J.J. Waldschmidt: Medicus Cartesianus" **Nouvelles de la République des Lettres** 1 (1981) 143-64.

2301 Trusted, J. "Descartes and a New Concept of Cause" Chap. iv of **Free Will and Responsibility** (Oxford 1984) 29-34.

2302 Turbayne, C.M. "Analysis and Synthesis" Chap. ii of **The Myth of Metaphor** (New Haven CT 1962); rev. ed. (Columbia SC 1970) 28-53.

2303 Turbayne, C.M. "New Metaphors for Old" Chap. iii of **The Myth of Metaphor** (New Haven CT 1962); rev. ed. (Columbia SC 1970) 54-70.

2304 Tweyman, S. "The Reliability of Reason" **CS** (Oxford 1972) 123-36.

2305 Tweyman, S. "Deus ex Cartesio" **SC** 1 (1979) 167-82.

2306 Tweyman, S. "Truth, No Doubt: Descartes' Proof that the Clear and Distinct Must be True" **SJP** 19 (1981) 237-58.

2307 Uitti, K.D. "Descartes and Port-Royal in Two Diverse Retrospects" Review of **Cartesian Linguistics,** by N. Chomsky [New York 1966]. **Romance Philology** 23 (1970) 75-85.

2308 Unger, P. "Our Knowledge of the External World" **APQ** Mon. 4 (Oxford 1970) 40-61.

2309* Valencia, R. "Claridad y distinción en la filosofía de Descartes" **Conflicto** 1 (1978) 21-26.

2310* Valéry, P. "Descartes" **Tableau de la Littérature Française** 1 (1962) 530-37.

2311 Van Cleve, J. "Foundationalism, Epistemic Principles, and the Cartesian Circle" **PR** 88 (1979) 55-91.

2312 Van Cleve, J. "Conceivability and the Cartesian Argument for Dualism" **PPQ** 64 (1983) 35-45.

2313 Van de Pitte, F.P. "Reservations on a Post-Wittgensteinian View of Descartes" **PPR** 35 (1974-75) 107-12.
Dis. of: Henze, D.F. **APQ** Mon. 6 (1972).

2314 Van de Pitte, F.P. "Descartes on Analogy and Other Minds" **ISP** 7 (1975) 89-110.

2315 Van de Pitte, F.P. "Descartes' Mathesis Universalis" **AGP** 61 (1979) 154-74.

2316 Van de Pitte, F.P. "Descartes' Role in the Faith-Reason Controversy" **PPR** 40 (1979-80) 344-53.
Dis. of: Caton, H.P. **JP** 72 (1975).

2317 Van de Pitte, F.P. "Descartes' Revision of the Renaissance Conception of Science" **Vivarium** 19 (1981) 70-80.

2318   Van den Abbeele, G.Y.   "Cartesian Coordinates: Metaphor, Topography and
       Presupposition in Descartes"   Voyages. Récits et imaginaire. Actes de
       Montréal, ed. by B. Beugnot.   PFSL Supp. 11 (1984) 3-14.
       Dis. by: Apostolidès, J.-M.   PFSL Supp. 11 (1984).

2319   van den Berg, J.H.   "Have You Seen the Pantheon?"   Journal of
       Phenomenological Psychology 6 (1975-76) 121-34.

2320   Vandenbulcke, J.   "Duitse Descartesliteratuur uit het begin van de
       zeventiger jaren"   Review of Descartes und die Moral, by A. Klemmt
       [Meisenheim 1971]; of Descartes' Erste Philosophie, by W. Röd [Bonn
       1971]; and of Descartes' Selbstkritik, by L. Gäbe [Hamburg 1972].
       TF 37 (1975) 95-111.

2321* Vanpaemel, G.   "Cartesiaanse en Newtoniaanse Natuurwetenschap aan de
       Leuvense Artesfakulteit"   Tijdschrift voor de Geschiedenis der
       Geneeskunde, Natuurwetenschappen, Wiskunde en Techniek 5 (1982) 39-49.

2322   Vanpaemel, G.   "Rohault's Traité de Physique and the Teaching of
       cartesian Physics"   Janus 71 (1984) 31-40.

2323* Varga von Kibed, A.   Die Philosophie der Neuzeit. Die grossen Denker
       Europas von Giordano Bruno bis Kant (München 1980).

2324   Vasale, C.   "Descartes fra neoilluminismo e filosofia della scienza"
       Review of Opere filosofiche di René Descartes, tr. by B. Widmar
       [Torino 1969]; and of Opere scientifici di René Descartes, 1, ed. by
       G. Micheli [Torino 1966].   Studium 68 (1972) 961-67.

2325   Vendler, Z.   "Descartes on Sensation"   CJP 1 (1971-72) 1-14.

2326   Vendler, Z.   "Descartes' Res Cogitans"   Chap. vii of Res Cogitans: An
       Essay in Rational Psychology (Ithaca NY 1972) 144-205.
       Rev. by: Watson, R.A.   JHP 14 (1976) 249-54.

2327   Verga, L.   Il pensiero filosofico e scientifico di Antoine Arnauld.
       2 vols. (Milano 1972).
       Rev. by: Tessiore, V.   Divus Thomas 78 (1975) 215-17.

2328   Verga, L.   L'etica di Cartesio (Milano 1974).
       Rev. by: Tessiore, V.   Divus Thomas 78 (1975) 213-15.

2329   Verga, L.   "Ragione ed esperienza nelle morali di Cartesio e dei
       Cartesiani"   RIP 29 (1975) 453-74.

2330   Verhaar, J.W.M.   "Philosophy and Linguistic Theory"   LS 14 (1971) 1-11.
       Dis. of: Chomsky, N.   Cartesian Linguistics (New York 1966).
                 Aarsleff, H.   Language 46 (1970).
       Dis. by: Aarsleff, H.   LS 17 (1971).

2331   Vernes, J.-R.   Critique de la raison aléatoire ou Descartes contre
       Kant (Paris 1982).
       Rev. by: Bernard, M.   RPL 81 (1983) 513-16.
                 C[ostabel], P.   BC 13 (1984) 54-57.

2332 Vernon, T.S. "Descartes' Three Substances" **SJP** 3 (1965) 122-26.
Dis. by: Cummins, P.D.   **SJP** 5 (1967).

2333 Verweyen, H. "Faith Seeking Understanding: An Aesthetic Interpretation"
NS 44 (1970) 372-95.

2334 Vesey, G. **Perception** (Garden City NY 1971).

2335 Vesey, G. "Foreword: A History of 'Ideas'" **Idealism Past and
Present**, ed. by G. Vesey. **Royal Institute of Philosophy Lectures** 13
(1982) 1-18.

2336 Vetter, T. "Louis de La Forge (1632-1667?). Angevin et fidèle adepte de
la physiologie cartésienne" **Comptes Rendus du 93e Congrès National
des Sociétés Savantes. Section des Sciences** 2 (1971) 31-50.

2337 Vial Larrain, J. de D. **La metafísica cartesiana** (Santiago de Chile
1971).

2338 Vial Larrain, J. de D. "Cogito, ergo sum" **Cuadernos de Filosofia** 16
(1976) 17-34.

2339* Vial Larrain, J. de D. **Tres ideas de la filosofía y una teoría**
(Santiago de Chile 1979).

2340 Vietta, S. "Selbsterfahrung bei Büchner und Descartes" **Deutsche
Vierteljahrsschrift für Literaturwissenschaft und Geistesgeschichte** 53
(1979) 417-28.

2341 Vietta, S. "Philosophische Begründung des Rationalismus: Descartes"
Chap. ii of **Neuzeitliche Rationalität und moderne literarische
Sprachkritik. Descartes, Georg Büchner, Arno Holz, Karl Kraus** (München
1981) 18-64.

2342* Vignoles, P.-H. "A propos de la première Méditation de Descartes"
Cahiers Philosophiques 8 (1981) 87-108.

2343 Villanueva, E. "Acerca de la tesis filosófica del pensamiento en
relación con la tesis del lenguaje de Renato Descartes" **Dian** 22
(1976) 17-26.

2344 Villanueva, E. "El dualismo sustancial de Renato Descartes" **Dian** 23
(1977) 74-87.

2345 Villanueva, E. "El principio de la certeza en Descartes" **Dian** 24
(1978) 66-79.

2346 Villard, F. "Le séjour à Chatellerault des enfants Descartes"
**Bulletin de la Société des Antiquaires de l'Ouest et des Musées de
Poitiers** 7 (1964) 465-66.

2347 Villoro, L. **La idea y el ente en la filosofía de Descartes** (México
1965).

2348 Vincenot, C. "Jeu, rêve et déduction dans le 'Discours de la méthode'" **RSH** 131 (1968) 355-62.

2349 Vinci, T. "Skepticism and Doxastic Conservatism" **PPQ** 64 (1983) 341-50.

2350 Viola, E. "Scolastica e cartesianesimo nel pensiero di J. Clauberg" **RFN** 67 (1975) 247-66.

2351 Virtanen, R. "Bernard's Relation to Philosophical Traditions" Chap. ii of **Claude Bernard and His Place in the History of Ideas** (Lincoln NE 1960) 27-48.

2352 Vision, G. "Cogito Per Cogitationem, Ergo Sum" **PF** 11 (1979-80) 340-62.

2353 Vleeschauwer, H.J. de. **More, seu ordine geometrico demonstratum** (Pretoria 1961).

2354 Vleeschauwer, H.J. de. **Le plan d'études de René Descartes** (Pretoria 1962).

2355 Vleeschauwer, H.J. de. "Le sens de la méthode dans le Discours de Descartes et la Critique de Kant" **Studien zu Kants philosophischer Entwicklung,** ed. by H. Heimsoeth, D. Henrich and G. Tonelli (Hildesheim 1967) 167-83.

2356 Vleeschauwer, H.J. de. "Les sources de la pensée d'Arnold Geulincx (1624-1669)" **KS** 69 (1978) 378-402.

2357 Voss, J. "Noam Chomsky et la linguistique cartésienne" **RPL** 71 (1973) 512-38.
      Dis. of: Chomsky, N.   **Cartesian Linguistics** (New York 1966).

2358 Voss, S.H. "How Spinoza Enumerated the Affects" **AGP** 63 (1981) 167-79.

2359 Voutsinas, D. "Maine de Biran critique des 'Méditations' cartésiennes" App. of **La psychologie de Maine de Biran (1766-1824)** (Paris 1975) 317-25.

2360 Vries, P. de. "Christiaan Huygens tussen Descartes en de Verlichting" **De Gids** 142 (1979) 293-305.

2361* Vries, P. de. "La reine Christine de Suède et la philosophie" **Wijsgerig Perspectief op Maatschappij en Wetenschap** 22 (1981-82) 74-82.

2362* Vries, R. de. "Ignoramus, ignorabimus. Het Geest-Lichaam Probleem tussen Ideologie en Objectiviteit" **Kennis en Methode** 4 (1980) 31-55.

2363 Vrooman, J.R. **René Descartes: A Biography** (New York 1970).

2364 Vuillemin, J. **Mathématiques et métaphysique chez Descartes** (Paris 1960).
      Rev. by: Clavelin, M.   **RP** 86 (1961) 509-19.
                Pflug, G.   **AGP** 43 (1961) 200-05.
                Rochot, B.   **RS** 82 (1961) 67-71.

2365 Vuillemin, J. "Sur la différence et l'identité des méthodes de la métaphysique et des mathématiques chez Descartes et Leibniz et sur la conception classique des principes de causalité et de correspondance" **AGP** 43 (1961) 267-302.

2366 Vuillemin, J. "Sur les propriétés formelles et matérielles de l'ordre cartésien des raisons" **Hommage à Martial Gueroult. L'histoire de la philosophie. Ses problèmes, ses méthodes** (Paris 1964) 43-58.

2367 Vuillemin, J. "Trois philosophes intuitionnistes: Epicure, Descartes et Kant" **Dialectica** 35 (1981) 21-41.

2368 Vullo, C. "La filosofia moderna e il cominciamento del filosofare" **Teoresi** 28 (1973) 325-30.

2369 Wade, I.O. "Descartes's Spirit" Pt. III, ch. vii of **The Intellectual Origins of the French Enlightenment** (Princeton NJ 1971) 230-67.

2370 Waelhens, A. de. "Descartes und das phänomenologische Denken" **Husserl,** ed. by H. Noack (Darmstadt 1973) 188-209.

2371 Wagner, H. "'Realitas objectiva' (Descartes-Kant)" **ZPF** 21 (1967) 325-40.

2372 Wagner, H., ed. **Sinnlichkeit und Verstand in der deutschen und französischen Philosophie von Descartes bis Hegel** (Bonn 1976).

2373 Wagner, J.-M. "Esquisse du cadre divinatoire des songes de Descartes" **Bar** 6 (1973) 81-95.

2374 Wagner, J.-M. "De la nécessaire distinction entre 'somnium'-songe et 'insomnium'-rêve" **Actes du 3me Congrès International d'Etudes Neo- latines,** ed. by J.-C. Margolin. 2 (Paris 1980) 709-20.

2375 Wagner, M. "Du bien-fondé de 'l'analyse hétéronomique' en histoire de la philosophie" **RDS** 2 (1978) 7-16.

2376 Wagner, S.J. "Descartes's Arguments for Mind-Body Distinctness" **PPR** 43 (1982-83) 499-517.

2377 Wagner, S.I. "Descartes' Cogito: A Generative View" **HPQ** 1 (1984) 167-80.

2378 Wahl, J. "Cartesius ille" **Episteme** [Venezuela] 3 (1959-60) 335-39.

2379 Walker, D.P. "Seventeenth-century Scientists' Views on Intonation and the Nature of Consonance" **AIHS** 27 (1977) 263-73.

2380 Wallace, W.A. "The Philosophers of Classical Science" Chap. i of **Causality and Scientific Explanation** 2 (Ann Arbor MI 1974) 3-75; repr. (Washington DC 1981).

2381 Walsh, W.H. "The Limits of Reason: Descartes and Cogito ergo sum" Chap. vi of **Metaphysics** (London 1963) 84-97.

2382 Walton, D. "Performative and Existential Self-Verifyingness" **D** 16 (1977) 128-38.
Dis. of: Hintikka, J.   **PR** 71 (1962).

2383 Wang, L.J. "A Controversial Biography: Baillet's La Vie de Monsieur Des-cartes" **Romanische Forschungen** 75 (1963) 316-31.

2384* Watanabe, H. "On the Divergence of the Concept of Motion in the Collaboration of Beeckman and Descartes" **14CI** 2 (Tokyo 1975) 338-40.

2385 Watling, J.L. "Descartes" Chap. x of **A Critical History of Western Philosophy,** ed. by D.J. O'Connor (New York 1964) 170-86.

2386 Watson, R.A. "Berkeley in a Cartesian Context" **RIP** 17 (1963) 381-94.

2387 Watson, R.A. "The Breakdown of Cartesian Metaphysics" **JHP** 1 (1963-64) 177-97.

2388 Watson, R.A. **The Downfall of Cartesianism 1673-1712: A Study of Epistemological Issues in Late 17th Century Cartesianism** (The Hague 1966).
Rev. by: Yolton, J.W.   **D** 5 (1966-67) 455-57.
          Rogers, G.A.J.   **M** 76 (1967) 611-12.
          Sebba, G.   **JHP** 8 (1970) 251-62.

2389 Watson, R.A. "Cartesianism" **Encyclopedia Britannica,** 15th ed. 3 (Chicago 1974) 968-70.

2390 Watson, R.A. "In Defiance of Demons, Dreamers, and Madmen" Review of **Demons, Dreamers, and Madmen,** by H.G. Frankfurt [Indianapolis IN 1970]. **JHP** 14 (1976) 342-53.

2391 Watson, R.A. "Cartesianism Compounded: Louis de la Forge" **SC** 2 (1981) 165-71.

2392 Watson, R.A. "What Moves the Mind: An Excursion in Cartesian Dualism" **APQ** 19 (1982) 73-81.

2393 Watson, R.A. "Transubstantiation among the Cartesians" **PC** (Kingston and Montréal 1982) 127-48.

2394 Watson, R.A. "Descartes Knows Nothing" **HPQ** 1 (1984) 399-411.

2395 Watson, R.I. "A Prescriptive Analysis of Descartes' Psychological Views" **Journal of the History of the Behavioral Sciences** 7 (1971) 223-48.

2396 Wear, A. "Aspects of Seventeenth-Century French Medicine" **Newsletter of the Society for Seventeenth-Century French Studies** 4 (1982) 118-32.

2397* Webb Elizondo, J. "A propósito de Renato Descartes" **Conflicto** 1 (1978) 27-32.

2398   Weber, H.   "Ficin, Pascal, Descartes et Saint Augustin"   **Mélanges sur
       la littérature de la Renaissance à la mémoire de V.-L. Saulnier**, ed.
       by P.-G. Castex (Genève 1984) 11-17.

2399   Weber, J.-G.   "Pascal and Music: World Harmony in Early Seventeenth-
       Century France"   **Symposium** 30 (1976) 75-91.

2400   Weber, J.-P.   "Commentaire des Règles VII et VIII des 'Regulae' de
       Descartes. Histoire du texte"   **RMM** 68 (1963) 180-212.

2401   Weber, J.-P.   **La constitution du texte des Regulae** (Paris 1964).
       Rev. by: Lauth, R.   **AP** 31 (1968) 648-56.

2402   Weber, J.-P.   "Sur la composition de la **Regula** IV de Descartes"   **RP** 89
       (1964) 1-20.

2403   Weber, J.-P.   "La méthode de Descartes d'après les **Regulae**"   **AP** 35
       (1972) 51-60.
       Dis. by: M[arion], J.-L.   **BC** 3 (1974) 487-89.

2404   Webster, C.   "Henry More and Descartes: Some New Sources"   **BJHS** 4
       (1968-69) 359-77.

2405   Wegelingh, W.   **Cartesiaanse uitzichten** (Lochem 1966).

2406   Weier, W.   "Zur Bedeutung des aristotelischen Daseinsbegriffs für die
       Weiterführung des durch Descartes begründeten Immanentismus"   **AGP** 48
       (1966) 277-305.

2407   Weier, W.   "Die introspektive Bewusstseinswahrnehmung beim hl. Augus-
       tinus und bei Descartes"   **Franziskanische Studien** 50 (1968) 239-50.

2408   Weier, W.   "Cartesianischer Aristotelismus im siebzehnten Jahrhundert"
       SbJP 14 (1970) 35-65.

2409   Weier, W.   "Der Okkasionalismus des Johannes Clauberg und sein
       Verhältnis zu Descartes, Geulincx, Malebranche"   **SC** 2 (1981) 43-62.

2410   Weil, S.   "Science et perception dans Descartes"   Chapter of **Sur la
       science** (Paris 1966) 9-99.

2411   Wein, H.   **Anticartesianische Meditationen: was war und ist Meditieren?
       ein Fragment** (Bonn 1983).

2412   Weinberg, F.M.   "The Idea of Soul in Descartes and Pascal"   **French
       Forum** 8 (1983) 5-19.

2413   Weinberg, J.R.   "**Cogito, Ergo Sum**: Some Reflections on Mr. Hintikka's
       Article"   **PR** 71 (1962) 483-91.
       Dis. of: Hintikka, J.   **PR** 71 (1962).
       Dis. by: Hintikka, J.   **PR** 72 (1963).

2414 Weinberg, J.R. "Descartes and the Distinction of Mind and Body" Chap. vi of **Ockham, Descartes, and Hume: Self-Knowledge, Substance, and Causality** (Madison WI 1977) 71-82.

2415 Weinberg, J.R. "The Sources and Nature of Descartes' Cogito" Chap. vii of **Ockham, Descartes, and Hume: Self-Knowledge, Substance, and Causality** (Madison WI 1977) 83-91.

2416 Weinberg, K. "Zum Wandel des Sinnbezirks von 'Herz' und 'Instinkt' unter dem Einfluss Descartes'" **Archiv für das Studium der Neueren Sprachen und Literaturen** 203 (1966) 1-31.

2417 Weinberg, K. "Les Fées" Chap. vii of **The Figure of Faust in Valéry and Goethe: An Exegesis of Mon Faust** (Princeton NJ 1976) 94-151.

2418 Weingartner, P. "The Ideal of the Mathematization of All Sciences and of 'More Geometrico' in Descartes and Leibniz" **NM** (Dordrecht 1983) 151-95.

2419 Weinrich, H. "Tempus-Ubergange" Chap. vii of **Tempus. Besprochene und erzählte Welt** (Stuttgart 1964); 2nd ed. (1971) 164-89.

2420 Weinrich, H. "Erzahlte Philosophie oder Geschichte des Geistes. Linguistische Bemerkungen zu Descartes und Rousseau" **Literatur für Leser. Essays und Aufsätze zur Literaturwissenschaft,** by H. Weinrich (Stuttgart 1971) 150-63.
Repr. in **Geschichte - Ereignis und Erzählung,** ed. by R. Koselleck and W.-D. Stempel (München 1973) 411-26.

2421 Weisgerber, J. "The Use of Quotations in Recent Literature" **Comparative Literature** 22 (1970) 36-45.

2422 Weiss, F.G. "Cartesian Doubt and Hegelian Negation" **Hegel and the History of Philosophy,** ed. by J.J. O'Malley, K.W. Algozin and F.G. Weiss (The Hague 1974) 83-94.

2423 Weitz, M. "Descartes's Theory of Concepts" **Contemporary Perspectives on the History of Philosophy. MSP** 8 (1983) 89-103.

2424 Welbourne, M. "Cartesian Madness" **A** 40 (1979-80) 48-50.
Dis. of: DeHaven, S.   **A** 38 (1977-78).
          Fahrnkopf, R.   **A** 39 (1978-79).
Dis. by: Fahrnkopf, R.   **A** 41 (1980-81).

2425 Welbourne, M. "My Body and I - A Reply to Fahrnkopf" **A** 42 (1981-82) 86-88.
Dis. of: Fahrnkopf, R.   **A** 41 (1980-81).

2426 Wells, N.J. "Descartes and the Scholastics Briefly Revisted" **NS** 35 (1961) 172-90.

2427 Wells, N.J. "Descartes and the Modal Distinction" **MS** 43 (1965-66) 1-22.

2428   Wells, N.J.   "Descartes on Distinction"   **The Quest for the Absolute,**
       ed. by F.J. Adelmann (The Hague 1966) 104-34.

2429   Wells, N.J.   "Objective Being: Descartes and His Sources"   **MS** 45
       (1967-68) 49-61.

2430   Wells, N.J.   "Old Bottles and New Wine: A Rejoinder to J.C. Doig"   **NS**
       53 (1979) 515-23.
       Dis. of: Doig, J.C.   **NS** 51 (1977).

2431   Wells, N.J.   "Descartes' Uncreated Eternal Truths"   **NS** 56 (1982) 185-99.

2432   Wells, N.J.   "Material Falsity in Descartes, Arnauld, and Suarez"   **JHP**
       22 (1984) 25-50.

2433   Wertz, S.K.   "Descartes and the Paradox of the Stone"   **Soph** 23 (1984)
       No. 1, 16-24.

2434   Westfall, R.S.   **The Construction of Modern Science: Mechanism and
       Mechanics** (New York 1971).

2435   Westfall, R.S.   "Circular Motion in Seventeenth-Century Mechanics"   **I**
       63 (1972) 184-89.

2436   Westman, R.S.   "Huygens and the Problem of Cartesianism"   **Studies on
       Christiaan Huygens,** ed. by H.J.M. Bos et al. (Lisse 1980) 83-103.

2437   White, C.J., and Gillespie, T.C.   "Markie on Dreams and Deceivers"   **PS**
       42 (1982) 287-95.
       Dis. of: Markie, P.J.   **PR** 90 (1981) 185-209.

2438   White, H.   "Rembrandt and the Human Condition"   **Interpretation** 4
       (1974-75) 17-37.

2439   Wiehl, R.   "L'anti-cartésianisme et les connexions psycho-physiques"
       Crit 37 (1981) 1076-90.

2440   Wilbur, J.B.   "The Cogito, An Ambiguous Performance"   **CE** (The Hague
       1969) 65-76.

2441   Wilkerson, T.E.   "Kant on Self-Consciousness"   **PQ** 30 (1980) 47-60.
       Dis. by: Priest, S.   **PQ** 31 (1981).

2442   Will, F.L.   **Induction and Justification: An Investigation of Cartesian
       Procedure in the Philosophy of Knowledge** (Ithaca NY 1974).

2443   Will, F.L.   "Reason, Social Practice, and Scientific Realism"
       Philosophy of Science 48 (1981) 1-18.

2444   Williams, B.   "Descartes"   **The Concise Encyclopedia Of Western
       Philosophy and Philosophers,** ed. by J.O. Urmson (New York 1960) 91-97.

2445 Williams, B. "The Certainty of the Cogito" **Cahiers de Royaumont** 4
      (1962) 40-57.
      Repr. in **DCCE** (Garden City NY 1967) 88-107.

2446 Williams, B. "René Descartes" **The Encyclopedia of Philosophy**, ed. by
      P. Edwards. 2 (New York 1967) 344-54.

2447 Williams, B. "Comment" **FE** (Oxford 1969) 55-56.
      Dis. of: Kenny, A.   **FE** (Oxford 1969).
      Dis. by: Kenny, A.   **FE** (Oxford 1969).

2448 Williams, B. **Descartes: The Project of Pure Inquiry** (Harmondsworth
      1978).
      Trans. as **Descartes. Das Vorhaben der reinen Philosophie**, by W. Dittel
      and A. Viviani (Königstein 1981).
      Rev. by: Jolley, N.   **SL** 11 (1979) 150-54.
                Schouls, P.A.   **PB** 20 (1979) 61-66.
                Wilson, M.D.   **JP** 76 (1979) 421-35.
                Ashworth, E.J.   **Queen's Quarterly** 86 (1979-80)
                                     653-56.
                Hooker, M.   **N** 14 (1980) 279-82.
                Rubin, R.   **BJPS** 31 (1980) 104-08.
                Stern, K.   **D** 19 (1980) 359-66.
                Caton, H.P.   **PF** 12 (1980-81) 273-94.
                Harrison, J.   **M** 90 (1981) 122-35.
                Lachterman, D.R.   **SC** 2 (1981) 195-201.
                Rogers, G.A.J.   **P** 57 (1982) 263-69.
      Dis. by: Stubbs, A.C.   **A** 40 (1979-80).

2449 Williams, B. "Descartes's Use of Skepticism" **The Skeptical
      Tradition**, ed. by M. Burnyeat (Berkeley CA 1983) 337-52.

2450 Williams, T.A., Jr. "Albert Camus and the Two Houses of Descartes"
      Romance Notes 5 (1963-64) 115-17.

2451 Wilson, C. "Sensation and Explanation: The Problem of Consciousness in
      Descartes" **Nature and System** 4 (1982) 151-65.

2452 Wilson, G.A. "Henry of Ghent and René Descartes on the Unity of Man"
      Franziskanische Studien 64 (1982) 97-110.

2453 Wilson, M.D. "Introduction" **The Essential Descartes,** by René
      Descartes; ed. by M.D. Wilson (New York 1969) vii-xxxii.

2454 Wilson, M.D. "Leibniz and Materialism" **CJP** 3 (1973-74) 495-513.
      Dis. by: Stern, K.   **PF** 7 (1975-76).

2455 Wilson, M.D. "Descartes: The Epistemological Argument for Mind-Body
      Distinctness" **N** 10 (1976) 3-15.
      Dis. by: Nakhnikian, G.   **N** 10 (1976).

2456 Wilson, M.D. "Leibniz: Self-Consciousness and Immortality in the Paris
      Notes and After" **AGP** 58 (1976) 335-52.

2457   Wilson, M.D.   "Confused Ideas"   **Rice University Studies** 63 (1977)
       123-37.

2458   Wilson, M.D.   **Descartes** (London 1978); 2nd ed. (1982).
       Rev. by: Jolley, N.   **SL** 11 (1979) 150-54.
                  McRae, R.   **SC** 1 (1979) 215-19.
                  Schouls, P.A.   **PB** 20 (1979) 61-66.
                  Bracken, H.M.   **BJPS** 31 (1980) 307-10.
                  Caton, H.P.   **PF** 12 (1980-81) 273-94.
                  Beyssade, J.-M.   **BC** 10 (1981) 22-26.
                  Lennon, T.M.   **JHP** 19 (1981) 250-53
                  Montague, R.   **M** 90 (1981) 304-06.
                  Rogers, G.A.J.   **P** 57 (1982) 263-69.
       Dis. by: Doney, W.   **PRA** 6 (1980) No. 1376.

2459   Wilson, M.D.   "Cartesian Dualism"   **DCIE** (Baltimore MD 1978) 197-211.

2460   Wilson, M.D.   "Body-Mind from a Cartesian Point of View"   **Body & Mind:
       Past, Present and Future,** ed. by R.W. Rieber (New York 1980) 35-56.

2461   Wilson, M.D.   "Objects, Ideas, and 'Minds': Comments on Spinoza's Theory
       of Mind"   **PBS** (Washington DC 1980) 103-20.

2462   Wilson, M.D.   "Skepticism Without Indubitability"   **JP** 81 (1984) 537-44.

2463   Wilson, N.   "Discourses on Method and Professions of Faith: Rousseau's
       Debt to Descartes"   **FS** 37 (1983) 157-67.

2464   Winch, P.   "Ceasing to Exist"   **Proceedings of the British Academy** 68
       (1982) 329-53.

2465   Winspur, S.   "Bonnefoy cartésien?"   **French Forum** 9 (1984) 236-50.

2466   Winters, B.   "Sceptical Counterpossibilities"   **PPQ** 62 (1981) 30-38.

2467   Winther, T.   "Classicisme et Cartésianisme: Le 'Traité de la Vraie
       Beauté' de Pierre Nicole"   **Orbis Litterarum** 33 (1978) 123-37.

2468* Witzenmann, H.   **Ein Dreigestirn am Horizont unserer Epoche: Descartes-
       Spinoza-Leibniz.**   2nd ed. (Dornach 1984).

2469   Wolfe, P.   "Commentaire sur la métaphore optique chez Descartes"   **Actes
       de New Orleans,** ed. by F.L. Lawrence.   **PFSL** Supp. 5 (1982) 337-42.
       Dis. of: Gaudiani, C.   **PFSL** Supp. 5 (1982).

2470   Wong, D.B.   "Cartesian Deduction"   **PRA** 8 (1982) 1-19.

2471   Wright, J.P.   "Hysteria and Mechanical Man"   **JHI** 41 (1980) 233-47.

2472   Wurtz, J.-P.   **Les problèmes de la méthode au XVIIe siècle** (Strasbourg
       [1974]).

2473   Xirau, J.   **Descartes, Leibniz, Rousseau** (México 1973).

TWENTY-FIVE YEARS OF DESCARTES SCHOLARSHIP

2474 Xirau, R. "Innatismo. De ideas y de no-ideas" Review of **Cartesian Linguistics,** by N. Chomsky [New York 1966]. **Dian** 18 (1972) 138-52.

2475 Xirau, R. "Apuntes de lectura. Una lectura de Descartes: primera parte de 'Discurso del Método'" **Dian** 29 (1983) 105-20.

2476 Yamada, H. "Ambivalence of Sense in Descartes" **Journal of the Faculty of Literature. Nagoya University** 87, Philosophy 29 (1983) 1-10.

2477 Yamazaki, E. "La physique de Descartes" **Japanese Studies in the History of Science** 7 (1968) 27-36.

2478 Yarvin, H. "Language and the Cogito" **Journal of Critical Analysis** 6 (1975-77) 109-18.

2479 Yolton, J.W. "Sense-Data and Cartesian Doubt" **PS** 11 (1960) 25-30.

2480 Yolton, J.W. "Philosophy of Science from Descartes to Kant" Review of **Metaphysics and the Philosophy of Science,** by G. Buchdahl [Oxford 1969]. **HSc** 10 (1971) 102-13.

2481 Yolton, J.W. "Comments on Professor Schouls' Paper" **CJP** 4 (1974-75) 611-15.
      Dis. of: Schouls, P.A.   **CJP** 4 (1974-75).
      Dis. by: Schouls, P.A.   **CJP** 4 (1974-75).

2482 Yolton, J.W. "Ideas and Knowledge in Seventeenth-Century Philosophy" **JHP** 13 (1975) 145-65.

2483 Yolton, J.W. "On Being Present to the Mind: A Sketch for the History of an Idea" **D** 14 (1975) 373-88.
      Dis. by: McRae, R.   **D** 14 (1975).
                Lennon, T.M.   **D** 19 (1980).

2484 Yolton, J.W. "Perceptual Cognition with Descartes" **SC** 2 (1981) 63-83.

2485 Yolton, J.W. **Thinking Matter: Materialism in Eighteenth-Century Britain** (Minneapolis MN 1983).
      Rev. by: Woolhouse, R.S.   **P** 59 (1984) 554-55.
                Berman, D.   **PB** 26 (1985) 85-87.
                Garber, D.   **JP** 82 (1985) 729-34.
                Watson, R.A.   **JHP** 23 (1985) 433-37.
                Jolley, N.   **PR** 95 (1986) 111-13.

2486 Yolton, J.W. **Perceptual Acquaintance from Descartes to Reid** (Minneapolis MN 1984).
      Rev. by: Michael, F.,
                and Michael, E.   **PB** 26 (1985) 214-17.
                Watson, R.W.   **JHP** 23 (1985) 433-37.
                Wilson, C.   **PR** 95 (1986) 105-11.

2487 Young, J.Z. "The Pineal Gland" **P** 48 (1973) 70-74.

2488   Young, R.M. **Mind, Brain and Adaptation in the Nineteenth Century:**
       Cerebral Localization and its Biological Context from Gall to Ferrier
       (Oxford 1970).

2489   Youschkevitch, A.P. "The Concept of Function up to the Middle of the
       19th Century" **AHES** 16 (1976-77) 37-85.

2490   Zaner, R.M. "La realidad radical del cuerpo humano" **Revista de**
       Occidente 8 (1970) Tom. 30, 290-310.

2491   Zaner, R.M. "The Other Descartes and Medicine" **Phenomenology and the**
       Understanding of Human Destiny, ed. by S. Skousgaard (Washington DC
       1981) 93-119.

2492   Zanoncelli, L. "I fondamenti della musica: Terreno di indagine alla
       ricerca del metodo" **Breviario di musica,** by René Descartes; tr. by
       L. Zanoncelli (Mestre 1979) 5-69.

2493   Zemplén, J. "The Cartesianism in the Physics of Hungary" **13CI** 4
       (Moscow 1974) 226-32.

2494   Ziggelaar, A. **Le physicien Ignace Gaston Pardies, S.J. (1636-1673)**
       (Odense 1971).
       Rev. by: Beaude, J.   **RHS** 29 (1976) 261-67.

2495* Zilah, E. de. "Letero de Kartezio pri lingvo internacia" **Simpozio** 1
       (1983) 11-16.

2496   Zimmermann, K. "Kants Descartes-Kritik und die 'Kopernikanische Wende'
       in der Philosophie" **12IC** 12 (Firenze 1961) 485-92.

2497   Ziomek, H. "Descartes as a Writer in the Discours de la Méthode" **USF**
       Language Quarterly 14 (1975) No. 1-2, 27-30.

2498   Zubimendi Martínez, J. "La teoría de las distinciones de Suárez y
       Descartes" **Pensamiento** 40 (1984) 179-202.

2499* Zúñiga López, J. "Locke entre Descartes y Hume" **ASM** 11 (1976) 141-58.

2500   ----------. **Studia Cartesiana** 1 (Amsterdam 1979).
       Rev. by: B[eyssade], J.-M.   **BC** 12 (1983) 34-36.

2501   ----------. **Nouvelles cartésiennes** 1. **SC** 1 Supp. (Amsterdam 1980).

2502   ----------. **Studia Cartesiana** 2 (Amsterdam 1981).
       Rev. by: B[eyssade], J.-M.   **BC** 13 (1984) 53-54.

APPENDIX

Editions and Translations of Descartes's Own Writings

Editions and translations are listed separately. Within each listing,
publications containing several different Cartesian works (or selections
therefrom) are distinguished from those devoted to a single work. Items in
the former category are ordered according to their date of publication.
Items in the latter category are first arranged in the order in which
Descartes composed the works concerned; different editions or translations of
the same work are then listed in the order of their publication in 1960-84.
Editions comprising several works are further divided into "Collections,"
containing all or most of Descartes's writings, and "Selections," in which
only a few works are included, whether as a whole or in part. Translations
are divided according to the language into which Descartes's original Latin or
French has been rendered: Dutch, English, French, German, Hebrew, Hungarian,
Italian, Japanese, Polish, Portuguese, Romanian, Spanish, or Turkish.

Editions: Collections

A001 **Oeuvres de Descartes,** ed. by C. Adam and P. Tannery. 11 vols. (Paris:
Cerf, 1897-1909); new ed., ed. by B. Rochot, J. Beaude, P. Costabel et
al. 11 vols. (Paris: Vrin, 1964-74).

Vol. 1: **Correspondance I** (1897); new ed., ed. by J. Beaude and P.
Costabel (1969).

Vol. 2: **Correspondance II** (1898); new ed., ed. by J. Beaude and P.
Costabel (1969).

Vol. 3: **Correspondance III** (1899); new ed., ed. by J. Beaude and P.
Costabel (1971).

Vol. 4: **Correspondance IV** (1901); new ed., ed. by J. Beaude and P. Costabel (1972).

Vol. 5: **Correspondance V** (1903); new ed., ed. by P. Costabel, J. Beaude and A. Gabbey (1974).

Vol. 6: **Discours de la méthode & Essais** (1902); new ed., ed. by B. Rochot (1965); new ed. (1982).

Vol. 7: **Meditationes de prima philosophia** (1904); new ed., ed. by B. Rochot (1964); new ed. (1983).

Vol. 8-1: **Principia philosophiae** (1905); new ed., ed. by B. Rochot (1964); new ed. (1982).

Vol. 8-2: **Epistola ad G. Voetium. Lettre apologetique. Notae in programma** (1905); new ed., ed. by B. Rochot (1965).

Vol. 9: **Méditations et Principes,** Traduction française (1904); new ed., ed. by B. Rochot, 2 pts. (1964); Pt. 1, new ed. (1982).

Vol. 10: **Physico-mathematica. Compendium musicae. Regulae ad directionem ingenii. Recherche de la vérité. Supplément à la Correspondance** (1908); new ed., ed. by B. Rochot and P. Costabel (1966).

Vol. 11: **Le monde. Description du corps humain. Passions de l'âme. Varia** (1909); new ed., ed. by J. Beaude (1967).

A002 **Oeuvres et lettres,** ed. by A. Bridoux (Paris: Nouvelle Revue Française, 1937); 2nd ed. (Gallimard, 1952); new ed. (1966). Bibliothèque de la Pléiade 40.

A003 **Oeuvres philosophiques,** ed. by F. Alquié. 3 vols. (Paris: Garnier, 1963-73). Classiques Garnier.

A004 **Oeuvres,** ed. by S.S. de Sacy. 2 vols. (Paris: Club Français du Livre, 1966). Les Portiques 82.

Editions: Selections

A005 **Discours de la méthode suivi des Méditations,** ed. by F. Mizrachi (Paris: UGE, 1963). Le Monde en 10/18 1.

A006 **Traité des passions suivi de la Correspondance avec la Princesse Elisabeth,** ed. by F. Mizrachi (Paris: UGE, 1965). Le Monde en 10/18 276-277.

A007 **Discours de la méthode suivi d'extraits de la Dioptrique, des Météores, de la Vie de Descartes par Baillet, du Monde, de l'Homme, et de Lettres,** ed. by G. Rodis-Lewis (Paris: Garnier-Flammarion, 1966). Garnier-Flammarion 109.

A008 **Discours de la méthode suivi des Méditations** (Lyon: Editions du Fleuve, 1966).

A009 **Textes de Descartes,** ed. by R. Lefèvre (Paris: Bordas, 1967). Sélection Philosophique Bordas.

A010 **Le discours de la méthode. La naissance de la paix. Lettres,** ed. by R. Campbell (Paris: Mazenod, 1967). Les Ecrivains Célèbres 55. Les Classiques.

A011 **Discours de la méthode suivi des Méditations,** ed. by C. Mauriac (Paris: Tallandier, 1973). Trésor des Lettres Françaises.

A012 **Discours de la méthode suivi des Méditations,** ed. by J.-P. Sartre (Verviers: Marabout, 1974). Marabout Université 256.

A013 **Descartes,** ed. by G. Rodis-Lewis (Paris: LGF, 1984). Textes et Débats. Le Livre de Poche 5003.

Editions: Single Works

A014 **Regulae ad directionem ingenii,** Texte critique...avec la version hollandaise du xviième siècle, ed. by G. Crapulli (The Hague: Nijhoff, 1966). Archives Internationale d'Histoire des Idées 12.

A015 **Regulae ad directionem ingenii,** ed. by H. Springmeyer and H.G. Zekl (Hamburg: Meiner, 1973). Philosophische Bibliothek 262c.

A016 **Discours de la méthode,** ed. by J.-M. Fataud (Paris: Bordas, 1965). Petits Classiques Bordas.

A017 **Discours de la méthode,** ed. by A. Robinet (Paris: Larousse, 1969). Nouveaux Classiques Larousse.

A018 **Discours de la méthode,** ed. by S.S. de Sacy; introductions by Alain and P. Valery (Paris: LGF, 1970). Le Livre de Poche 2593.

A019 **Discours de la méthode,** ed. by F. Farago (Paris: Didier, 1971). Classiques de la Civilisation Française.

A020 **Discours de la méthode,** ed. by J.-M. Beyssade; introduction by Alain (Paris: LGF, 1973). Le Livre de Poche 2593.

A021 **Discours de la méthode,** ed. by J.-M. Beyssade; preceded by "Descartes inutile et incertain" by J.-F. Revel (Paris: LGF, 1976). Le Livre de Poche 2593.

A022 **Discours de la méthode. Descartes. Analyse critique,** ed. by J. Schifres (Paris: Hatier, 1978). Profil d'une Oeuvre 60.

A023 **Discours de la méthode,** ed. by D. Huisman (Paris: Nathan, 1981). Les Intégrales de Philo 1.

A024 **Discours de la méthode,** ed. by S. Mazauric (Paris: Messidor/Editions Sociales, 1983). Essentiel 19.

A025 **"Cogito 75". René Descartes. Méditations métaphysiques,** [French text with computerized indexes] ed. by A. Robinet (Paris: Vrin, 1976). Philosophie et Informatique 4.
Rev. by: M[arion], J.-L.   **BC** 7 (1978) 18-20.

A026 **Méditations métaphysiques. Objections et réponses suivies de quatre lettres,** [Latin and French texts] ed. by J.-M. Beyssade and M. Beyssade (Paris: Garnier-Flammarion, 1979). Garnier-Flammarion 328.

A027 **Méditations métaphysiques,** ed. by J.-P. Marty (Paris: Hachette, 1981). Oeuvres et Opuscules Philosophiques.

A028 **Méditations métaphysiques,** ed. by A. Vergez (Paris: Nathan, 1983). Les Intégrales de Philo 12.

A029 **Les passions de l'âme,** ed. by S.S. de Sacy (Paris: Gallimard, 1969). Idées 203.

A030 **Correspondance,** ed. by C. Adam and G. Milhaud. 8 vols. (Paris: Alcan, 1936-39; PUF, 1941-63).
Rev. by: Sacy, S. de   **MF** 349 (1963) 604-08.

Translations: Dutch: Single Works

A031 **Over de methode. Inleiding over de methode: hoe men zijn verstand goed kan gebruiken en de waarheid achterhalen in de wetenschappen,** tr. by T. Verbeek (Meppel: Boom, 1977). Boom Klassiek 1.

Translations: English: Collections and Selections

A032 **Discourse on Method and Other Writings,** tr. by A. Wollaston (Harmondsworth: Penguin, 1960). Penguin Classics L97.

A033 **Essential Works of Descartes,** tr. by L. Bair (New York: Bantam, 1961). Bantam Classics HC110.

A034 **Philosophical Essays: Discourse on Method, Meditations, Rules for the Direction of the Mind,** tr. by L.J. Lafleur (Indianapolis IN: Bobbs-Merrill, 1964). Library of Liberal Arts 99.

A035 **A Discourse on Method and Other Works,** ed. by J. Epstein; tr. by E.S. Haldane and G.R.T. Ross (New York: Washington Square, 1965). Washington Square Press Classics W525.

A036 **Discourse on Method, Optics, Geometry, and Meteorology,** tr. by P.J. Olscamp (Indianapolis IN: Bobbs-Merrill, 1965). Library of Liberal Arts 211.

A037 **Discourse on Method and the Meditations,** tr. by F.E. Sutcliffe (Harmondsworth: Penguin, 1968). Penguin Classics L206.

A038 **The Essential Descartes,** ed. by M.D. Wilson; tr. by E.S. Haldane and G.R.T. Ross (New York: NAL, 1969). Mentor Books MY954.

A039 **The Essential Writings,** tr. by J.J. Blom (New York: Harper & Row, 1977). Harper Torchbooks TB1909.

A040 **Descartes: His Moral Philosophy and Psychology,** tr. by J.J. Blom (New York: New York University Press, 1978).

A041 **The Philosophical Writings of Descartes,** tr. by J. Cottingham, R. Stoothoff and D. Murdoch. 2 vols. (Cambridge: CUP, 1985).

Translations: English: Single Works

A042 **Compendium of Music,** tr. by W. Robert (Roma: American Institute of Musicology, 1961). Musicological Studies and Documents 8.

A043 **Descartes on Polyhedra. A Study of the De solidorum elementis,** tr. by P.J. Federico (Berlin: Springer, 1982).

A044 **Rules for the Direction of the Mind,** tr. by L.J. Lafleur (Indianapolis IN: Bobbs-Merrill, 1961). Library of Liberal Arts 129.

A045 **Le Monde, ou Traité de la lumière,** [French text] ed. and tr. by M.S. Mahoney (New York: Abaris, 1979). Janus Library 2.
    Rev. by: Gaukroger, S.   **SC** 2 (1981) 208-11.
            Love, R.   **SC** 2 (1981) 211-13.

A046 **Treatise of Man,** French Text, ed. and tr. by T.S. Hall (Cambridge MA: Harvard University Press, 1972). Harvard Monographs in the History of Science.
    Rev. by: Keefe, T.   **FS** 29 (1975) 456-57.

A047 **Discourse on the Method of Rightly Conducting One's Reason and of Seeking Truth in the Sciences,** tr. by D.A. Cress (Indianapolis IN: Hackett, 1980).
    Rev. by: Cottingham, J.   **SC** 2 (1981) 201-02.

A048 **Meditations on First Philosophy,** tr. by D.A. Cress (Indianapolis IN: Hackett, 1979); 2nd ed. (1979).
Rev. by: Cottingham, J.   SC 2 (1981) 201-02.

A049 **Meditations on First Philosophy,** tr. by R. Rubin (Claremont CA: Arete, 1984).

A050 **Principles of Philosophy,** tr. by R.P. Miller and V.R. Miller (Dordrecht: Reidel, 1983). Synthese Historical Library 24.
Rev. by: Osler, M.J.   I 75 (1984) 418-19.

A051 **Philosophical Letters,** ed. and tr. by A. Kenny (Oxford: Clarendon, 1970); repr. (Minneapolis MN: University of Minnesota Press, 1981).

A052 **Descartes' Conversation with Burman,** tr. by J. Cottingham (Oxford: Clarendon, 1976).
Rev. by: Rodis-Lewis, G.   RP 102 (1977) 366-70.
        M[arion], J.-L.   BC 7 (1978) 16-18.
        Ariew, R.   SC 1 (1979) 183-87.
        Beyssade, J.-M.   EP (1980) 370-71.

Translations: French: Single Works

A053 **Règles utiles et claires pour la direction de l'esprit en la recherche de la vérité,** tr. by J.-L. Marion (The Hague: Nijhoff, 1977). Archives Internationales d'Historie des Idées 88.
Rev. by: Deschepper, J.-P.   RPL 76 (1978) 391-92.
        Lachenschmid, R.   Eras 30 (1978) 513-14.
        Robinet, A.   RIP 32 (1978) 416-17.
        Brunschwig, J.   BC 8 (1979) 27-34.
        Sebba, G.   SC 1 (1979) 145-65.
        Giard, L.   RHS 33 (1980) 168-70.

A054 **L'entretien avec Burman,** [Latin text] ed. and tr. by J.-M. Beyssade (Paris: PUF, 1981). Epiméthée.
Rev. by: B[uzon], F. de   BC 12 (1983) 21-26.

Translations: German: Collections and Selections

A055 **René Descartes,** ed. by I. Frenzel; tr. by K. Fischer, A. Buchenau and F. Baumgart (Frankfurt am Main: Fischer, 1960). Bücher des Wissens 357.

A056 **Ausgewählte Schriften,** ed. by G. Irrlitz; tr. by A. Buchenau and F. Baumgart (Leipzig: Reclam, 1980). Universal-Bibliothek.

Translations: German: Single Works

A057 **Leitfaden der Musik. Compendium musicae,** [Latin text] ed. and tr. by
J. Brockt (Darmstadt: Wissenschaftliche Buchgesellschaft, 1978). Texte
zur Forschung.

A058 **Regeln zur Ausrichtung der Erkenntniskraft,** tr. by L. Gäbe (Hamburg:
Meiner, 1972). Philosophische Bibliothek 262b.
Rev. by: M[arion], J.-L. **BC** 3 (1974) 460-62.

A059 **Uber den Menschen (1632) sowie Beschreibung des menschlichen Körpers
(1648),** tr. by K.E. Rothschuh (Heidelberg: Schneider, 1969).

A060 **Discours de la méthode,** [French text] ed. and tr. by L. Gäbe (Hamburg:
Meiner, 1960). Philosophische Bibliothek 261.

A061 **Abhandlung über die Methode,** ed. by H. Glockner; tr. by K. Fischer
(Stuttgart: Reclam, 1961). Universal-Bibliothek 3767.

A062 **Abhandlung über die Methode,** tr. by L. Fischer (Leipzig: Reclam,
1962). Universal-Bibliothek.

A063 **Meditationen uber die erste Philosophie,** tr. by G. Schmidt (Stuttgart:
Reclam, 1971). Universal-Bibliothek 2887-2888.
Rev. by: M[arion], J.-L. **BC** 2 (1973) 441-43.

A064 **Die Leidenschaften der Seele,** [French text] ed. and tr. by K.
Hammacher (Hamburg: Meiner, 1983). Philosophische Bibliothek 345.

A065 **Gespräch mit Burman,** [Latin text] ed. and tr. by H.W. Arndt (Hamburg:
Meiner, 1982). Philosophische Bibliothek 325.

Translations: Hebrew: Single Works

A066 **‹Principles of Philosophy›** and **‹Critical Remarks on the General Part
of Descartes' Principles of Philosophy›** [in Hebrew], ed. by M. Dascal;
tr. by S. Yaretzki and S. Karniel (Tel-Aviv: University Publication
Projects, 1979).

Translations: Hungarian: Collections and Selections

A067 **Válogatott filozófiai müvek,** tr. by S. Szemere (Budapest: Akadémiai
Kaidó, 1961). Filozófiai Irók Tára, Uj Folyam 20.

Translations: Italian: Collections and Selections

A068   **Il pensiero scientifico di Descartes,** tr. by F.E. Marciano (Torino: SEI, 1962). Classici della Filosofia e della Pedagogia. Rev. by: Micheli, G.   **RCSF** 21 (1966) 344-45.

A069   **La biologia,** ed. by G. Micheli. **Opere Scientifiche di René Descartes** 1 (Torino: UTET, 1966). Classici della Scienza.

A070   **Opere,** tr. by E. Garin, G. Galli, A. Carlini, A. Tilgher and M. Garin. 2 vols. (Bari: Laterza, 1967). Classici della Filosofia Moderna.

A071   **Antologia dalle opere,** tr. by B. Brunello (Firenze: Le Monnier, 1968). Collana di Testi di Filosofia e Pedagogia ad Uso delle Scuole.

A072   **Opere scelte,** tr. by P. Semama (Milano: Principato, 1969). Collana Filosofica.

A073   **Opere filosofiche di René Descartes,** tr. by B. Widmar (Torino: UTET, 1969). Classici della Filosofia 6.

A074   **Il pensiero di René Descartes. Una antologia dagli scritti,** tr. by G. Crapulli (Torino: Loescher, 1970). Classici della Filosofia.

A075   **La ricostruzione del mondo,** tr. by S. Escobar (Milano: Bietti, 1974). Classici della Filosofia.

A076   **Discorso sul metodo, La diottrica, Le meteore, La geometria,** ed. by E. Lojacono. **Opere Scientifiche di René Descartes** 2 (Torino: UTET, 1983). Classici della Scienza 6.

Translations: Italian: Single Works

A077   **Breviario di musica,** tr. by L. Zanoncelli (Mestre: Corbo e Fiori, 1979).

A078   **Regole per la direzione dello spirito,** tr. by S. Arcoleo (Padova: R.A.D.A.R., 1971). Classici della Filosofia.

A079   **Il mondo, trattato della luce. L'uomo,** tr. by M. Garin (Bari: Laterza, 1969). Piccola Biblioteca Filosofica Laterza 48.

A080   **Il mondo ovvero Trattato della luce e L'uomo,** ed. by M. Mamiani; tr. by A.L. Merlani (Roma: Theoria, 1983). I Segni 13.

A081   **Il mondo, ovvero Trattato della luce,** tr. by G. Cantelli (Torino: Boringhieri, 1959). Enciclopedia di Autori Classici 28.

A082   **L'uomo,** tr. by G. Cantelli (Torino: Boringhieri, 1960). Enciclopedia di Autori Classici 43. Rev. by: Micheli, G.   **RCSF** 16 (1961) 315-20.

A083   **Discorso sul metodo,** tr. by V.G. Galati (Roma: Paoline, 1960).
Philosophica. Testi 15.

A084   **Discorso sul metodo,** tr. by R. Mondolfo and E. Garin (Firenze:
Sansoni, 1963). Collana Scolastica di Testi Filosofici.

A085   **Discorso sul metodo,** tr. by A. Pozzolini (Milano: Rizzoli, 1968).
Biblioteca Universale Rizzoli 2465-2466.

A086   **Discorso sul metodo,** tr. by G. Brianda (Cagliari: Fossataro, 1973).
Biblioteca Italiana Cultura e Scuola 5.

A087   **Discorso sul metodo,** tr. by I. Cubeddu (Roma: Riuniti, 1978).
Universale 75.

A088   **Discorso sul metodo,** tr. by S. Arcoleo (Torino: SEI, 1978). Libri dei
Filosofi.

A089   **Meditazioni metafisiche,** tr. by M. Malaguti (Bologna: Patron, 1969).
Paideia 5.

A090   **Meditazioni metafisiche. Con estratti dalle Obbiezioni e riposte,** tr.
by A. Deregibus (Brescia: La Scuola, 1974). Il Pensiero 5683.

A091   **Meditazioni metafisiche,** ed. by G. Cantelli; tr. by A. Tilgher
(Firenze: La Nuova Italia, 1982). Pensatori Antichi e Moderni 112.

A092   **I principi della filosofia,** tr. by P. Cristofolini (Torino:
Boringhieri, 1967). Enciclopedia di Autori Classici.

A093   **Le passioni dell'anima,** tr. by A. Di Maio (Napoli: Il Tripode, 1968).

Translations: Japanese: Collections and Selections

A094   **⟨Descartes⟩** [in Japanese], tr. by M. Yamamoto, T. Obase, K. Masuda and
T. Ibuki (Tokyo: Kawade, 1965).

A095   **⟨Descartes⟩** [in Japanese], ed. by M. Noda; tr. by M. Noda, S. Inoue,
K. Kamino, K. Mizuno and A. Mori (Tokyo: Chuokoronsha, 1967).

A096   **Dekaruto chosakushu,** ed. by N. Miyake and T. Tokoro; tr. by N. Miyake,
T. Tokoro, S. Akagi et al. 4 vols. (Tokyo: Hakusuisha, 1973).

A097   **⟨Discourse on the Method and Passions of the Soul⟩** [in Japanese], tr.
by M. Noda (Tokyo: Chuokoronsha, 1974).

Translations: Japanese: Single Works

A098 <**Discourse on the Method**> [in Japanese], tr. by N. Miyake and H. Komatsu (Tokyo: Tozaigogatsusha, 1961).

A099 **Tetsugaku genri**, tr. by J. Katsura (Tokyo: Iwanami-shoten, 1964).

Translations: Polish: Single Works

A100 **Rozprawa o metodzie**, tr. by W. Wojciechowska (Warszawa: Państwowe Wydawnictwo Naukowe, 1970). Biblioteka Klasyków Filozofii.

A101 **Rozprawa o metodzie**, tr. by T. Boy-Zelenski (Warszawa: Państwowy Instytut Wydawniczy, 1980).

A102 **Zasady filozofii**, tr. by I. Dambska (Warszawa: Państwowe Wydawnictwo Naukowe, 1960). Biblioteka Klasyków Filozofii.

Translations: Portuguese: Collections and Selections

A103 **Obra escolhida**, tr. by J. Guinsburg and B. Prado Junior (São Paulo: Difusão Européia do Livro, 1962).

Translations: Portuguese: Single Works

A104 **Discurso do método**, tr. by J. Cruz Costa (Rio de Janeiro: Olympio, 1960); new ed. (Ouro, 1968). Clássicos de Ouro Franceses.

A105 **Discurso sobre o método**, tr. by T. Guimaraes (São Paulo: Exposição do Livro, 1964); new ed. (Hemus, 1975).

A106 **Carta de Descartes a Elisabeth**, tr. by C.A.R. do Nascimento **Trans/Form/ Ação** 7 (1984) 61-68.

Translations: Romanian: Single Works

A107 **A módszerrol**, tr. by T.G. Miklós (Bucureşti: Kriterion, 1977).

Translations: Spanish: Collections and Selections

A108 **Museo de filósofos. Sala del cartesianismo,** ed. by J. Gaos (México: Universidad Nacional Autónoma de México, 1960). Ediciones Filosofía y Letras 49.

A109 **Tratado de las pasiones y Discurso sobre el método,** tr. by J. Nuñez Prado (Barcelona: Iberia, 1963). Obras Maestras.

A110 **Discurso del método. Otros tratados,** tr. by A. Gual Mir (Madrid: EDAF, 1964). Biblioteca EDAF 22.

A111 **Obras escogidas,** tr. by M. Machado (Buenos Aires: Shapiro, 1965). Colección Tauro.

A112 **Descartes,** ed. by R. Frondisi (Buenos Aires: Centro Editor de América Latina, 1967). Enciclopedia del Pensamiento Esencial 1.

A113 **Obras escogidas,** tr. by E. de Olaso and T. Zwanck (Buenos Aires: Sudamericana, 1967); new ed. (Charcas, 1978). Biblioteca de Filosofía.

A114 **Obras de Renato Descartes,** ed. by H. García (La Habana: Instituto Cubano del Libro, 1971). Editorial de Ciencias Sociales: Filosofía.

A115 **Discurso del método. Meditaciones metafísicas. Reglas para la dirección del espíritu. Principios de la filosofía,** ed. by F. Larroyo; tr. by M. Machado (México: Porrúa, 1971). Sepan Cuantos 177.

A116 **Discurso del método, la dióptrica, los meteoros y la geometría,** tr. by G. Quintás Alonso (Madrid: Alfaguara, 1981). Clásicos Alfaguara. Rev. by: Alvarez Gómez, A. **Contextos** 1 (1983) 155-62.

A117 **Discurso del método. Reglas para la dirección de la mente,** tr. by A. Rodriguez Huescar and F.P. de Samaranch (Esplugas de Llobregat: Orbis, 1983). Historia del Pensamiento.

A118 **Discurso del método. Tratado de las pasiones del alma,** tr. by E. Frutos (Barcelona: Planeta, 1984). Clásicos Universales Planeta.

Translations: Spanish: Single Works

A119 **Reglas para la dirección de la mente,** tr. by F. de P. Samaranch (Buenos Aires: Aguilar, 1966). Biblioteca de Iniciación Filosófica 105.

A120 **Reglas para la dirección de la mente,** tr. by J. Soriano Gamazo (Maracaibo: Universidad del Zulia, 1968). Biblioteca de Textos Filosóficos.

A121 **Reglas para la dirección del entendimiento,** tr. by C. Aníbal Leal (Buenos Aires: Juarez, 1969). Colección Paideuma.

A122 **Reglas para la dirección del espíritu,** tr. by J. Manuel Navarro
(Madrid: Alianza, 1984).

A123 **Tratado del hombre,** tr. by G. Quintás Alonso (Madrid: Nacional
Editora, 1980). Clásicos para una Biblioteca Contemporánea.

A124 **Discurso del método,** tr. by C. Láscaris Comneno (San José de Costa
Rica: Ciudad Universitaria, 1961). Publicaciones de la Universidad de
Costa Rica. Serie Filosofía 21.

A125 **Discurso del método,** tr. by A. Espina (Madrid: Mediterráneo, 1966).

A126 **Discurso del método,** tr. by J.C. García Borrón (Barcelona: Bruguera,
1968). Libro Clásico 44.

A127 **Discurso del método** (Barcelona: Vosgos, 1972). Compendios Vosgos 11.

A128 **El discurso del método,** tr. by M. Armiño (Madrid: Akal, 1982).
Colección Bolsillo.

A129 **Discurso del método,** tr. by H. Arnau Gras (Barcelona: Humanitas,
1983). Material Didactico.

A130 **Meditaciones metafísicas,** tr. by J. Soriano Gamazo (Maracaibo:
Universidad del Zulia, 1967). Biblioteca de Textos Filosóficas.

A131 **Meditaciones metafísicas,** ed. by J. de D. Vial Larrain (Santiago de
Chile: Editorial Universitaria, 1974).

A132 **Meditaciones metafísicas con objeciones y respuestas,** tr. by V. Peña
Garcia (Madrid: Alfaguara, 1977). Clasicos Alfaguara.

A133 **Las pasiones del alma,** tr. by C. Berges (Buenos Aires: Aguilar, 1963).
Biblioteca de Iniciación Filosófica 86.

A134 **Las pasiones del alma,** tr. by F. Fernández Buey (Barcelona: Península,
1972). Ediciones de Bolsillo 218.

A135 **Observaciones sobre el programa de Regius,** tr. by G. Quintás Alonso
(Buenos Aires: Aguilar, 1978). Biblioteca de Iniciación Filosófica.

A136 **Observaciones sobre la explicación de la mente humana,** tr. by G.
Quintás Alonso (Valencia: Revista Teorema, 1981). Cuadernos Teorema.

Translations: Turkish: Single Works

A137 **Felsefenin Ilkeleri,** tr. by Mesut Akin (Istanbul: Say Kitap Pazarlama,
1983).

References are grouped under six major headings: BIBLIOGRAPHIES, INDEXES, OTHER RESEARCH TOOLS; BIOGRAPHICAL STUDIES; LITERARY AND TEXTUAL STUDIES; STUDIES OF PARTICULAR WORKS OF DESCARTES; TOPICAL STUDIES ACCORDING TO FIELD; and WORKS ON PARTICULAR TOPICS. References in the last three of these groups are further divided under several subheadings.

BIBLIOGRAPHIES, INDEXES, OTHER RESEARCH TOOLS

0074, 0105, 0336, 0353, 0375, 0488, 0500, 0501, 0502, 0537, 0554, 0632, 0638, 0658, 0662, 0713, 0714, 0715, 0716, 0717, 0718, 0719, 0720, 0722, 0723, 0724, 0725, 0726, 0727, 0836, 0960, 0985, 1112, 1115, 1446, 1451, 1469, 1506, 1546, 1585, 1618, 1695, 1725, 1893, 1935, 1950, 2052, 2088, 2089, 2091, 2276, 2286, 2299, 2501.

BIOGRAPHICAL STUDIES

0077, 0108, 0117, 0130, 0162, 0173, 0251, 0302, 0333, 0438, 0467, 0498, 0576, 0638, 0639, 0640, 0642, 0691, 0763, 0768, 0769, 0813, 0850, 0921, 0949, 0983, 1142, 1146, 1147, 1169, 1237, 1255, 1313, 1314, 1347, 1364, 1386, 1451, 1455, 1534, 1543, 1554, 1628, 1686, 1755, 1757, 1758, 1759, 1796, 1845, 1888, 1938, 1960, 2034, 2045, 2097, 2118, 2161, 2170, 2232, 2242, 2264, 2346, 2363, 2373, 2383.

LITERARY AND TEXTUAL STUDIES

0023, 0055, 0113, 0120, 0137, 0138, 0142, 0145, 0149, 0159, 0245, 0282, 0285, 0308, 0309, 0337, 0340, 0362, 0379, 0393, 0457, 0463, 0485, 0499, 0511, 0516, 0518, 0519, 0520, 0522, 0534, 0617, 0633, 0702, 0703, 0704, 0705, 0721, 0758, 0780, 0781, 0782, 0845, 0867, 0888, 0903, 0926, 0933, 1071, 1085, 1106, 1109, 1158, 1174, 1175, 1178, 1200, 1227, 1258, 1298, 1334, 1345, 1388, 1395, 1427, 1445, 1510, 1555, 1578, 1581, 1591, 1606, 1665, 1724, 1754, 1780, 1848, 1856, 1857, 1897, 1898, 1937, 1954, 1962, 1969, 1970, 2015, 2090, 2096, 2131, 2148, 2196, 2204, 2218, 2318, 2374, 2401, 2417, 2419, 2420, 2421, 2465, 2469, 2497.

STUDIES OF PARTICULAR WORKS OF DESCARTES

Regulae ad directionem ingenii

0074, 0246, 0282, 0313, 0318, 0474, 0475, 0479, 0487, 0489, 0495, 0516, 0518, 0840, 0902, 1016, 1251, 1298, 1443, 1444, 1448, 1449, 1450, 1473, 1560, 1610, 1630, 1632, 1675, 1746, 1750, 1752, 1813, 1841, 1872, 2095, 2204, 2264, 2400, 2401, 2402, 2403.

Le Monde (Traité de la lumière, L'homme)

0846, 1011, 1012, 1065, 1356, 1389, 1394, 1409, 1544, 1634, 1727, 1969, 1994, 2264, 2294.

Discours de la méthode

0068, 0096, 0120, 0192, 0308, 0309, 0336, 0355, 0373, 0389, 0393, 0399, 0453, 0548, 0608, 0610, 0772, 0795, 0796, 0802, 0841, 0845, 0848, 0920, 0933, 1061, 1124, 1158, 1175, 1247, 1273, 1282, 1321, 1370, 1396, 1427, 1442, 1560, 1566, 1604, 1606, 1629, 1631, 1632, 1659, 1661, 1704, 1707, 1780, 1814, 1848, 2014, 2052, 2055, 2203, 2348, 2355, 2419, 2420, 2475, 2497.

Essais (La dioptrique, Les météores, La géométrie)

0178, 0247, 0313, 0408, 0479, 0495, 0496, 0698, 0803, 0812, 0849, 1332, 1389, 1527, 1704, 1743, 1764, 1846, 2132.

Meditationes de prima philosophia

0002, 0054, 0143, 0145, 0146, 0159, 0171, 0193, 0194, 0249, 0289, 0294, 0304, 0343, 0360, 0370, 0380, 0381, 0407, 0416, 0469, 0508, 0518, 0519, 0520, 0522, 0530, 0561, 0592, 0664, 0668, 0671, 0675, 0702, 0703, 0704, 0705, 0712, 0728, 0737, 0742, 0743, 0746, 0793, 0797, 0798, 0799, 0809, 0848, 0871, 0888, 0944, 0947, 0961, 0963, 0969, 0987, 0994, 1039, 1064, 1076, 1104, 1168, 1227, 1229, 1258, 1274, 1347, 1375, 1395, 1422, 1461, 1465, 1472, 1510, 1565, 1580, 1658, 1662, 1670, 1728, 1762, 1787, 1818, 1838, 1848, 1884, 1974, 2068, 2136, 2229, 2231, 2265, 2306, 2337, 2342, 2359, 2375, 2411, 2424, 2437.

Principia philosophiae

0041, 0144, 0152, 0195, 0205, 0427, 0428, 0518, 0831, 0857, 1394, 1476, 1477, 1555, 1700, 2087, 2294.

Les passions de l'âme

0113, 0201, 0381, 0518, 0599, 0641, 0910, 1019, 1182, 1282, 1341, 1368, 1424, 1962, 2211, 2222, 2246, 2467.

Correspondence

0127, 0138, 0142, 0251, 0485, 0618, 0633, 0731, 0827, 0829, 0830, 1049, 1052, 1177, 1693, 2015.

Ethics, Politics, Social Theory

0014, 0050, 0052, 0079, 0160, 0165, 0188, 0218, 0224, 0244, 0253, 0307,
0322, 0347, 0351, 0387, 0390, 0392, 0404, 0448, 0452, 0454, 0471, 0531,
0532, 0573, 0590, 0602, 0611, 0614, 0616, 0628, 0696, 0709, 0710, 0762,
0765, 0767, 0796, 0814, 0824, 0843, 0874, 0899, 0920, 0936, 0937, 0941,
0965, 0967, 0986, 1017, 1048, 1053, 1060, 1093, 1097, 1145, 1154, 1165,
1170, 1181, 1182, 1183, 1184, 1194, 1195, 1201, 1220, 1230, 1243, 1250,
1255, 1270, 1301, 1337, 1340, 1341, 1361, 1362, 1374, 1432, 1435, 1441,
1486, 1505, 1509, 1533, 1556, 1577, 1640, 1648, 1661, 1666, 1697, 1741,
1788, 1790, 1799, 1832, 1851, 1853, 1870, 1880, 1900, 1928, 1931, 1991,
2027, 2035, 2043, 2051, 2059, 2111, 2181, 2182, 2187, 2212, 2241, 2249,
2256, 2320, 2328, 2329.

Fine Arts (including Literature, Music, Painting, Theatre, etc.)

0088, 0148, 0149, 0233, 0330, 0331, 0389, 0414, 0543, 0616, 0757, 0868,
1019, 1060, 1149, 1219, 1221, 1258, 1288, 1289, 1290, 1378, 1387, 1533,
1542, 1629, 1631, 1777, 1819, 1855, 1859, 1939, 1974, 1986, 2017, 2018,
2099, 2157, 2180, 2203, 2226, 2233, 2270, 2333, 2379, 2399, 2438, 2467,
2492.

Mathematics

0022, 0173, 0184, 0247, 0256, 0439, 0477, 0481, 0482, 0489, 0494, 0495,
0498, 0512, 0513, 0515, 0584, 0694, 0752, 0775, 0789, 0812, 0840, 0849,
0869, 0891, 0962, 1075, 1080, 1083, 1143, 1144, 1163, 1234, 1235, 1277,
1296, 1320, 1332, 1407, 1408, 1502, 1508, 1564, 1607, 1653, 1704, 1709,
1743, 1892, 1905, 1909, 2021, 2061, 2062, 2083, 2150, 2173, 2364, 2365,
2489.

Metaphysics

0025, 0030, 0035, 0058, 0071, 0073, 0081, 0093, 0125, 0145, 0146, 0166,
0167, 0179, 0196, 0198, 0207, 0210, 0217, 0221, 0228, 0259, 0262, 0274,
0284, 0293, 0300, 0317, 0321, 0322, 0348, 0363, 0368, 0369, 0373, 0414,
0416, 0417, 0427, 0428, 0442, 0452, 0455, 0458, 0468, 0469, 0491, 0503,
0514, 0528, 0529, 0544, 0545, 0546, 0559, 0561, 0572, 0574, 0588, 0615,
0644, 0645, 0651, 0652, 0664, 0665, 0670, 0674, 0676, 0679, 0684, 0687,
0721, 0738, 0739, 0749, 0751, 0760, 0764, 0766, 0777, 0778, 0788, 0794,
0801, 0810, 0815, 0817, 0823, 0851, 0858, 0886, 0899, 0916, 0920, 0923,
0943, 0966, 0970, 0972, 0978, 0981, 0990, 0992, 0995, 1003, 1023, 1025,
1028, 1029, 1039, 1046, 1047, 1051, 1063, 1066, 1069, 1082, 1083, 1086,
1094, 1098, 1104, 1120, 1132, 1139, 1141, 1145, 1155, 1164, 1185, 1186,
1205, 1226, 1236, 1280, 1287, 1296, 1299, 1302, 1303, 1311, 1315, 1322,
1325, 1327, 1328, 1339, 1349, 1363, 1367, 1369, 1371, 1372, 1376, 1390,
1391, 1392, 1398, 1399, 1417, 1444, 1445, 1447, 1452, 1453, 1454, 1456,
1457, 1472, 1473, 1479, 1481, 1511, 1514, 1515, 1559, 1565, 1588, 1592,
1605, 1609, 1613, 1630, 1632, 1636, 1638, 1642, 1647, 1675, 1681, 1687,
1689, 1692, 1694, 1702, 1708, 1714, 1726, 1727, 1735, 1749, 1750, 1764,
1766, 1768, 1769, 1771, 1776, 1789, 1790, 1817, 1828, 1866, 1872, 1889,

Philosophy - General

Physics (including Astronomy, Geology, Meteorology, Optics, etc.)

Religion, Theology

Science - General

WORKS ON PARTICULAR TOPICS

The Cartesian Circle

The Cogito

Doubt, Reasons for Doubting (Dreaming, the Evil Genius, etc.)

2164, 2165, 2178, 2179, 2210, 2214, 2221, 2228, 2229, 2231, 2237, 2238, 2241, 2266, 2283, 2304, 2308, 2342, 2349, 2394, 2422, 2424, 2425, 2437, 2449, 2462, 2466, 2479.

Eternal Truths

0197, 0544, 0545, 0559, 0760, 0810, 0817, 0998, 1213, 1280, 1287, 1453, 1953, 1955, 1956, 1957, 2144, 2208, 2431.

Freedom, the Will

0125, 0188, 0217, 0218, 0322, 0529, 0645, 0735, 0764, 0767, 0823, 0939, 0943, 0981, 0986, 0992, 1215, 1282, 1327, 1367, 1642, 1673, 1689, 1697, 1762, 1799, 1853, 2084, 2285, 2301.

God, Arguments for the Existence of God

0005, 0039, 0061, 0112, 0235, 0280, 0281, 0310, 0311, 0343, 0357, 0435, 0437, 0456, 0525, 0526, 0536, 0544, 0559, 0577, 0598, 0603, 0607, 0648, 0661, 0663, 0664, 0667, 0668, 0707, 0712, 0773, 0786, 0787, 0790, 0791, 0792, 0797, 0817, 0851, 0860, 0873, 0899, 0912, 0918, 0919, 0938, 0947, 0975, 1055, 1081, 1082, 1083, 1103, 1110, 1114, 1116, 1133, 1134, 1140, 1166, 1211, 1212, 1269, 1280, 1297, 1327, 1328, 1404, 1413, 1423, 1429, 1454, 1461, 1500, 1546, 1586, 1592, 1620, 1645, 1646, 1654, 1655, 1656, 1671, 1683, 1690, 1691, 1708, 1714, 1735, 1742, 1767, 1781, 1784, 1789, 1821, 1906, 1940, 1953, 1955, 2031, 2058, 2063, 2079, 2098, 2105, 2140, 2177, 2206, 2208, 2216, 2258, 2260, 2271, 2305, 2433, 2447.

Language

0003, 0004, 0027, 0104, 0242, 0248, 0261, 0271, 0272, 0273, 0276, 0277, 0287, 0319, 0413, 0575, 0623, 0672, 0988, 1167, 1238, 1279, 1524, 1545, 1744, 1785, 1858, 1874, 1875, 1899, 1933, 2234, 2255, 2307, 2330, 2343, 2357, 2478, 2495.

Man, Human Nature

0025, 0028, 0095, 0116, 0186, 0187, 0268, 0335, 0366, 0469, 0549, 0615, 0675, 0822, 1018, 1037, 1226, 1236, 1240, 1244, 1307, 1539, 1688, 1766, 1790, 1882, 1931, 1985, 1993, 2129, 2130, 2249, 2283, 2438, 2452, 2471, 2490.

Matter, Nature, Space

0151, 0177, 0209, 0210, 0223, 0315, 0451, 0553, 0654, 0749, 0751, 0794, 0855, 0934, 0942, 0959, 1007, 1026, 1037, 1039, 1040, 1067, 1127, 1284, 1299, 1308, 1324, 1325, 1375, 1389, 1394, 1419, 1420, 1441, 1495, 1508, 1514, 1522, 1537, 1547, 1682, 1718, 1764, 1820, 1861, 2113, 2119, 2147, 2160, 2235, 2240, 2251, 2287, 2288, 2294, 2454, 2485.

INDEX

Method

0043, 0053, 0060, 0075, 0078, 0086, 0089, 0099, 0101, 0102, 0114, 0160,
0170, 0171, 0173, 0183, 0211, 0212, 0219, 0227, 0233, 0244, 0249, 0256,
0316, 0344, 0345, 0366, 0369, 0386, 0399, 0425, 0429, 0430, 0431, 0439,
0473, 0475, 0517, 0539, 0584, 0585, 0587, 0609, 0630, 0669, 0685, 0689,
0696, 0698, 0738, 0778, 0804, 0847, 0852, 0857, 0876, 0935, 0972, 0998,
1000, 1003, 1016, 1021, 1027, 1079, 1091, 1097, 1103, 1110, 1124, 1153,
1160, 1191, 1193, 1207, 1224, 1231, 1232, 1235, 1240, 1241, 1247, 1251,
1294, 1295, 1316, 1320, 1324, 1330, 1332, 1398, 1438, 1442, 1450, 1468,
1507, 1513, 1560, 1561, 1562, 1566, 1590, 1610, 1612, 1637, 1694, 1699,
1704, 1717, 1721, 1741, 1749, 1786, 1800, 1802, 1807, 1813, 1841, 1866,
1876, 1885, 1886, 1892, 1916, 1920, 1922, 1944, 1967, 1974, 1987, 2020,
2024, 2033, 2042, 2044, 2049, 2067, 2070, 2071, 2072, 2073, 2074, 2080,
2113, 2119, 2120, 2145, 2148, 2164, 2267, 2281, 2288, 2296, 2302, 2305,
2315, 2353, 2354, 2356, 2365, 2403, 2411, 2418, 2472, 2481.

Mind, Mental Faculties and Operations, Mind and Body

0013, 0018, 0028, 0032, 0051, 0052, 0056, 0057, 0067, 0090, 0092, 0095,
0102, 0122, 0168, 0177, 0186, 0187, 0190, 0201, 0229, 0234, 0271, 0273,
0276, 0277, 0286, 0290, 0296, 0299, 0312, 0334, 0339, 0360, 0365, 0366,
0367, 0395, 0396, 0398, 0400, 0439, 0440, 0443, 0444, 0449, 0458, 0506,
0507, 0512, 0524, 0549, 0551, 0575, 0578, 0580, 0583, 0594, 0599, 0612,
0614, 0626, 0627, 0655, 0656, 0677, 0697, 0701, 0744, 0747, 0774, 0785,
0820, 0822, 0855, 0856, 0861, 0871, 0889, 0896, 0898, 0906, 0910, 0945,
0973, 0988, 1015, 1018, 1019, 1035, 1036, 1037, 1041, 1045, 1049, 1058,
1062, 1074, 1099, 1101, 1102, 1108, 1119, 1125, 1126, 1150, 1152, 1155,
1159, 1173, 1199, 1203, 1208, 1215, 1216, 1217, 1223, 1244, 1274, 1277,
1286, 1301, 1308, 1316, 1341, 1343, 1375, 1380, 1384, 1402, 1410, 1412,
1414, 1415, 1416, 1417, 1418, 1424, 1471, 1488, 1490, 1491, 1492, 1493,
1499, 1512, 1518, 1539, 1541, 1548, 1550, 1570, 1576, 1583, 1596, 1625,
1639, 1649, 1677, 1679, 1681, 1688, 1698, 1729, 1747, 1760, 1762, 1779,
1801, 1809, 1812, 1816, 1825, 1828, 1838, 1849, 1854, 1860, 1873, 1875,
1877, 1887, 1894, 1918, 1921, 1929, 1933, 1976, 1978, 1983, 1985, 1993,
2005, 2030, 2035, 2036, 2038, 2039, 2053, 2093, 2102, 2112, 2121, 2123,
2124, 2125, 2139, 2141, 2142, 2154, 2165, 2166, 2168, 2169, 2172, 2188,
2205, 2213, 2222, 2225, 2246, 2248, 2249, 2259, 2263, 2270, 2277, 2290,
2312, 2314, 2316, 2319, 2326, 2332, 2340, 2344, 2358, 2359, 2362, 2374,
2376, 2387, 2391, 2392, 2395, 2409, 2412, 2414, 2425, 2439, 2441, 2451,
2454, 2455, 2456, 2459, 2460, 2461, 2471, 2485, 2487, 2488, 2490, 2491.

The Passions

0092, 0201, 0531, 0532, 0578, 0588, 0599, 0627, 0910, 1017, 1106, 1316,
1486, 1747, 1760, 1832, 1840, 1877, 1878, 1939, 1973, 1986, 2222, 2285,
2358, 2416.

Perception, Ideas (Clear and Distinct, Innate, etc.)

Substance, Essence, Modes and Attributes

Titles in this Series

12. A. Boyce Gibson, *The Philosophy of Descartes*, New York, 1967

13. O. Hamelin, *Le Système de Descartes*, Paris, 1911

14. Anthony Kenny, *Descartes: A Study of His Philosophy*, New York, 1968

15. Alexandre Koyré, *Essai sur L'idée de Dieu et les Preuves de son Existence Chez Descartes*, Paris, 1922

16. Gaston Milhaud, *Descartes Savant*, Paris, 1921

17. Nicolas-Joseph Poisson, *Commentaire ou Remarques sur la Méthode de René Descartes*, Vendôme, 1670

18. Jacques Rohault, *Rohault's System of Natural Philosophy Illustrated with Dr. Samuel Clarke's Notes Taken Mostly out of Sir Isaac Newton's Philosophy with Additions* (trans. by John Clarke), London, 1728

19. J.F. Scott, *The Scientific Work of René Descartes, 1596–1650*, London, 1952

20. J. Sirven, *Les Années D'apprentissage de Descartes, 1596–1628*, Paris, 1930

21. Norman [Kemp] Smith, *Studies in the Cartesian Philosophy*, New York, 1902

22. Norman Kemp Smith, *New Studies in the Philosophy of Descartes: Descartes as Pioneer*, London, 1952